D1062872

Confessions of
SON OF SAM

New York Mills Public Library
New York Mills, N.Y. 13417

ALSO BY DAVID ABRAHAMSEN

Jeger Jøde (I am a Jew) (in Norwegian)

Crime and the Human Mind

Men, Mind and Power

The Mind and Death of a Genius

Report on a Study of 102 Sex Offenders at Sing Sing Prison as Submitted to Governor Thomas E. Dewey

Who are the Guilty? A Study of Education and Crime

The Road to Emotional Maturity

The Psychology of Crime

The Emotional Care of Your Child

Our Violent Society

The Murdering Mind

Nixon vs. Nixon: An Emotional Tragedy

The Mind of the Accused: A Psychiatrist in the Courtroom

CONFESSIONS OF
SON OF SAM

David Abrahamsen M.D.

New York Mills Public Library
New York Mills, N.Y. 13417

Columbia University Press
NEW YORK
1985

Book design by Ken Venezio

Library of Congress Cataloging in Publication Data

Abrahamsen, David, 1903–
  Confessions of Son of Sam

  Includes bibliographical references and index.
  1. Berkowitz, David Richard, 1953–
2. Crime and criminals—New York (N.Y.)—Biography.
3. Murder—New York (N.Y.) I. Title.
HV6248.B483A27   1985   364.1′523′0924 [B]   84–21487
ISBN 0-231-05760-1

Columbia University Press
New York
Copyright © 1985 by David Abrahamsen
All rights reserved

Printed in the United States of America

Clothbound editions of Columbia University Press Books are Smyth-sewn
and printed on permanent and durable acid-free paper

CONTENTS

Preface   vii

Acknowledgments   xiii

1   Encountering a Killer   1

2   The Terrorized Mind   27

3   Always Alone   44

4   Prologue to Murder: Search for Mother   67

5   Stalking the Victims   88

6   Madman or Malingerer?   107

7   The Battle of the Psychiatrists   125

8   Sex as a Force for Murder   162

9   David Berkowitz vs. Son of Sam   184

10   His Own Executioner   200

Afterword   216

Letters Quoted in This Work   226

Notes   229

Index   239

PREFACE

In the year 1976 the country was shocked and fascinated by a bizarre series of murders in New York City. The killer stalked his victims after dark, and chose as his prey young women — usually sitting with their dates in parked cars. The murders had all the characteristics of a romance, but the currency was death not love. For one long panic-filled year, millions of New Yorkers became hostages to the night.

The situation quickly became a major media event. Newspapers and television shrieked endlessly of the ".44 caliber killer," so named for the weapon used in the attacks. The killer himself added to the drama by leaving his calling card. He offered the public a name by which he could be known: "Son of Sam." Now the mystery deepened, became more baffling. Who was *Sam*? Who was *SON* of Sam?

The suspense ended suddenly with the arrest , on August 10, 1977, of someone named David Berkowitz for the "Son of Sam murders." America anxiously awaited the appearance of this vicious killer who had so frightened and fascinated us. Would his face, his person, match the horror of his crimes? Finally, thirteen months after he had begun his attacks, we were permitted a glimpse of the now-legendary murderer. Stunned by the soft, feminine, quizzical face we saw in the papers and on television, most of us were confused and in some way disappointed. He looked like a nice Jewish boy from the Bronx — like the boy next door! His sweet, seductive smile, his passive manner hardly fitted our image of a mass murderer.

But his story satisfied our wildest fantasies. He had killed, he declared, at the behest of his "voices." The "demons in Sam Carr's dogs" had "made him do it." He was helpless to resist their demonical commands.

Five days after Berkowitz's arrest, I was engaged by the prosecution to determine if he was mentally fit to stand trial. Three psychiatrists, two court appointed, had found him psychotic and not mentally competent to proceed to trial for murder. I was the fourth psychiatrist, and mine was the dissenting opinion: I concluded that he was mentally able to stand trial. Two New York justices concurred with my decision. My many years as a forensic psychiatrist had enabled me to see through Berkowitz's dubious "demon" stories. That he had faked insanity was the critical factor in the resolution of the case. Having been judged mentally fit for trial, he decided to plead guilty, and in June 1978 was sentenced to several hundred years in prison. He was incarcerated at Attica Prison.

Ordinarily the case would have ended for me there. But in February 1979 Berkowitz announced at a press conference at Attica that he had invented the story about the demons. A month later I received a letter from him. He confessed: "Sam Carr and the demons . . . was all a hoax, well planned and thought out. I just never thought this demon story would carry out so much."[1] He wrote, "I did know why I pulled the trigger. . . . It would be a good idea if we talked.[2] Berkowitz and I began to correspond.

In the spring of 1979, I made the first of several trips to Attica to meet with Son of Sam. In my first visit he said he wanted to have a book written that could deal not just with his crimes, but with his emotions, motivations, and psychology as well — in short, with his entire life. From that time, as far as it was possible, I alone have received the personal confidence of him. As he put it, *"Not my real mother, not my half-sister, no one. There is no one who could give you first-hand information. Only I know it."* Having already told me that "there is no fee or royalty to be paid," he later wrote me:

"After thinking it over for a long period of time, I am convinced that you are the only serious minded person capable of writing a biography about my life.

"I have read your book 'Nixon vs. Nixon, and the Murdering Mind,' and I truly see that you are a genuine psychoanalyst. Your writings and your high standing in the mental health field, acknowledge and pay tribute to your professional capabilities.

... "I believe that you and you alone is the only one capable.

"I give you, and you alone, express permission to author the book. You may write what you feel and believe to be the causative and motivating factors. I also trust that your opinion will be based on evidence which will be meticulously analyzed by you, resulting in your professional conclusions.

"Lastly, I feel that by helping you it will also be helping society. I want no financial rewards for my cooperation."[3]

Ironically, David Berkowitz chose as sole confessor me, the psychiatrist who pronounced him fit to stand trial and ultimately confess his guilt.

Berkowitz had come to trust me, perhaps because he realized that he couldn't fool me. He agreed to cooperate with me in every way. He traced his life history from the time he was given up for adoption as an infant born out of wedlock, to the moment he pulled the trigger of his .44 caliber pistol for the last time. I made it clear that he would have to level with me. I also warned him that the facts and feelings I would be dredging up from his past would surely cause him a great deal of pain. In spite of the mental suffering the process had caused him, he has lived up to his word. Later, I also told him that I would donate 25 percent of any royalities to the victims of his crimes. He agreed.

When David Berkowitz's murders in 1976–77 had become a media story and a heated debate was raging about his mental condition, his adoptive father Nathan was appointed by the New York State Supreme Court of Kings County (Brooklyn) as a Conservator to protect David's interests. But since the father had moved to Florida and it apparently was difficult for him to take care of his son's situation, Justice Dominic Laudato of the Supreme Court, Kings County, appointed, through the lawyer Seth Rubinstein, Doris Johnson to be Conservator of the estate of David Berkowitz. On February 14, 1984, the Conservator and Justice Laudato signed an agreement with me, extending to me "to make full and exclusive use of any and all written and oral communications received by him [Dr. A.] from David Berkowitz, and in fact, affirmatively authorizes and consents to such use. . . ."

"David Berkowitz shall not have any interest of any kind in any such literary work or works (including motion picture or other uses based thereon)."

The agreement further stated that (as I had previously volunteered to pay) "on any literary and/or scholarly work or works that is wholly or substantially based upon or that makes substantial use of communications he has received from or interviews he has had with David Berkowitz, he shall pay to the Conservator of the Estate of David Berkowitz a sum equal to 25 percent of all monies actually received . . . , after deduction of all expenses incurred by David Abrahamsen M.D. in connection with the creation, sale, or marketing of such work or works."

My findings are based upon material that I have accumulated during fifty hours of personal interviews with David Berkowitz at the prison ward of Kings County Hospital, Brooklyn (when he was first arrested), and at Attica Prison, New York; the many interviews I conducted with his family, friends, former teachers, co-workers, and others involved in his life; his school, army, court records; interrogations by the district attorneys in Queens, Bronx, and Brooklyn, and tape recordings; considerable psychological tests Berkowitz took, and his extensive correspondence with me (which now contains over 400 typed or handwritten pages of letters and notes never before in their totality revealed to the public). The psychoanalysis of a mass murderer with his cooperation, and the unique relationship I have developed with Berkowitz over a four-year period, may be considered a first in the annals of psychiatry.

My study is based primarily on the lengthy confessions and troubled emotions of the man himself, and on my interpretations of this material. Unlike the biography of any other mass killer, it is based on his voluntary confessions to a psychiatrist. His cooperation — be it frank, aggressive, reluctant, defensive, or hostile — in revealing the emotional secrets of his hidden self, giving rise to transference and countertransference reactions, affords us deep insight into the development of a man with a murdering mind. The reader can trace the evolution of a double nature, where tenderness fought rage, love battled hate, defiance pitted itself against compliance, brutal instinctiveness countered a marked, conscious intelligence; and where reality and fantasy lived side by side in a sometimes barely delineated coexistence. These polarities, simultaneously present in a single mind, created in Berkowitz the boy next door by day, the Son of Sam by night.

In this investigation, my concern has not been to put David Berkowitz in a specific diagnostic category, but rather to present a case study of a complex man. My intention has been to illuminate his early psychodynamic and hereditary development in order to pinpoint the conflicts that came to dominate him. I shall throw light on the unexplored phenomenon of multiple personality, which always has exerted a magnetic appeal (how thrilling to be someone other than you appear to be!), and has led people to believe that Berkowitz was another Dr. Jekyll and Mr. Hyde. Not so, as we shall see.

In part this is a narrative account of the life and emotional development of the Son of Sam. It is the story of a life steeped in trouble and guile; the story of a seemingly unfeeling man who undertakes a desperate search for the mother he has never known, and the horrifying consequences of finding her. In many ways the progress of this study resembles that of a detective story, in that a psychiatrist must unravel ambiguous and sometimes wrong or inadequate information in his efforts to evaluate personality and motivation. By combining the factual material about Berkowitz with my own reflections, I offer what I hope will be a comprehensive view of the inner man. In what ways was he different from others? In other words: how did he come to be Son of Sam? Finally, it is an attempt to cut through the specifics of Berkowitz's life and deeds, to go beyond them, to answer the nagging question: Why did he do it?

This book, however, goes beyond the specific case of David Berkowitz. For is he not in some way typical of the ever-increasing number of violent criminals who have come to dominate the American scene? We discover here his unending disappointments, and we discover also that they are different only in degree from those of other criminals — or, for that matter, from those of ordinary, law-abiding people. Most of these frustrations are (as we shall later see) rooted largely in the unreality and seductiveness of the American Dream, just one of whose myths is the misbegotten search for the "manly" man. It is precisely this virility that the criminal lacks.

To understand the psychological makeup of a Berkowitz is a challenge to any psychoanalyst, to any writer. His relevance to us is that he was not a mindless, psychotic killer, but rather a human being inexorably driven to destroy himself and others. The circumstances of his upbringing remind us of how much we are a product of our formative years. When we bring a new generation into the world, we transmit to it both our constructive and our destructive characteristics. In that sense, we are all victims of victims.

Berkowitz fought a tough battle between his unconscious drives and desires, and his conscious restraints — a conflict familiar, in some degree, to all of us. When David Berkowitz lost the battle to Son of Sam, he turned into a twisted being and an enemy of society.

David Abrahamsen

November 30, 1984

ACKNOWLEDGMENTS

This book, having been in the making for six years, owes its origination to David Berkowitz — Son of Sam, the young man who in 1976–1977 shot to death 5 young women and one man and crippled two others.

Eugene Gold, former District Attorney of Kings Court, Brooklyn and Sheldon Greenberg, former First Assistant District Attorney, now Judge of the Supreme Court, Brooklyn, have been very helpful in securing essential information about the murderer from the time he was arrested when he was was first interrogated by the District Attorney in Brooklyn, August 11, 1977 at 3:28 A.M., and followed up with interrogation in the Bronx at 4:07 A.M. and in Queens at 4:38 A.M.

I was also given all police reports about Berkowitz's shootings and his behavior. I am grateful to the Board of Education, New York City, which in August 1977 furnished me the school records of Berkowitz; the U.S. Post Office in New York City, where Berkowitz had been working as on operations clerk operator prior to his arrest; and from the U.S. Army, where he served from August 1971 to June 1974 in Korea.

I extend warm thanks to Kenneth A. Lohf, Librarian for Rare Books and Manuscripts at Nicholas Murray Butler Library, Columbia University, where all the letters from David Berkowitz have been donated for preservation, and to Michael Sovern, President of Columbia University.

I like to thank Susan Koscielniak, Executive Editor, and Leslie

Bialler, Manuscript Editor, Columbia University Press, for excellent editorial suggestions, and my former Secretary, Louise Kragelund, for her many retypings of the manuscript.

My grateful thanks to Don Congdon, my literary agent, who with his good advice has been with this book since its inception; and to Dr. Fred Brown, Professor Emeritus of Psychology at Mount Sinai Hospital, for assisting me in evaluating the psychological tests of David Berkowitz made at Kings County Hospital.

Last but not least, I wish to thank David Berkowitz who in his cooperation with me furnished me with details of his life which only he knew, and which provided the foundation for this book. By doing so, he has done society a great service by expanding our knowledge of the workings of his peculiar mind.

In closing, my warmest thanks go to my wife, Lova, who with her heart and mind participated in bringing this book to fruition.

D.A.

Confessions of
SON OF SAM

1

ENCOUNTERING

A KILLER

For a long and agonizing year the night had belonged to him. He had been a one-man nocturnal plague on a great city. Faceless and nameless — except for his own strange and inscrutable sobriquet—"Son of Sam" had held seven million people hostage to his seemingly endless bloodlust.

Now, in August 1977, it was finally over. He had been caught. The people of New York City would once again have to contend only with the more predictable and mundane demons that haunt a large urban area after dark.

On a miserably hot and uncomfortable day shortly after the arrest, I took the elevator to the prison ward on the sixth floor of the weatherbeaten Kings County Hospital in Brooklyn. After carefully inspecting my court order to examine the prisoner, a corrections officer showed me to a dirty yellow cubicle, not more than six by ten feet, to wait for David Berkowitz.

My thoughts were interrupted by the corrections officer, who bluntly informed me there would be a postponement because the corridors from the prisoner's cell to my "office" had to be cleared. Since the killer had been put in complete isolation, he was prohibited from seeing any other inmate. His isolation was so extreme that he was allowed to look at television only at certain times of day. He was not to be privy to any media accounts of his own behavior. Likewise, all newspapers and magazines were withheld. In my many years as a forensic psychiatrist, I never had witnessed anything like this degree of security. I began to sense the threat this prisoner manifested.

As I sat in that cramped room at a small desk, worn from years of use, I had a foreboding of spending many long hours in this cubicle. The air was heavy. After a few moments I got up to turn on the air-conditioner, but it offered more noise than comfort so I shut it off again. Suddenly I felt a presence. I turned around; a man had entered silently. He stood there wearing the prison's faded blue pajama-like uniform. The door was a little ajar. Outside sat the young guard, his chair in direct view of the prisoner, throwing curious glances our way. A smile of some secret satisfaction played on the prisoner's lips. Coming face to face with him gave me an eerie feeling.

As I got up to introduce myself, he interrupted me, and still smiling announced in a determined tone:

"I know who you are, you're Dr. Abrahamsen. I read your book *The Murdering Mind*. He stopped, dramatically. Silence. Then: "The book was good." It was the beginning of the confessions.

Approximately 2000 people are murdered every year in New York City. That statistic is not unusual for a city of its size; it is not even the worst in the country. Only 65 percent of the murders result in an arrest. About one out of every three killers goes uncaught, unpunished, and free to strike again.[1]

On July 29, 1976, at about 1 A.M., a person unknown shot to death 18-year-old Donna Lauria as she was sitting in a car parked on Buhre Avenue in the Bronx. Jody Valente, who was with her, was also shot, but survived. I still recall seeing the newspaper photo of the car's splintered window, and thinking the circumstances peculiar. Shooting through the window of a parked car is usually a gangland technique, used in "rubouts."[2] No facts in this case pointed to that conclusion. The killing had taken place at night, in darkness. Had the murderer even been able to see his quarry? I wondered. Did he know his victim?

The police suspected a jilted lover in New Mexico, but an investigation quickly proved this theory wrong. The brutal shooting might have remained just another unsolved homicide, but on October 23, in Flushing, Queens, Rosemary Keenan, daughter of Detective Redmond Keenan of the New York City Police Department, and her companion Carl DeNaro were shot under similar circumstances. The woman escaped serious injury, but DeNaro was shot in the back of the head and required surgery. At the scene the police picked up three .44 caliber shell casings.

On the evening of November 27, Donna DiMasi and Joanne Lomino were sitting on the Lomino family porch in Bellrose, a quiet residential section of Queens. They were both shot without provocation. The unidentified assailant disappeared into the darkness, leaving 18-year old Joanne Lomino paralyzed from the waist down.

Parents began to warn their daughters about staying out late. Stirrings of interest were becoming evident in the media, awakening anew the fear among Americans about lawlessness and wanton crime.

On January 30, 1977, the killer struck again. Christine Freund and John Diehl had parked on a Forest Hills side street. Brutally shot, she died within hours. And on March 8, in the same middle-class neighborhood, just half a block away, at 7:30 P.M., Virginia Voskerichian was shot to death while walking down the street.

The murders had a pattern — the victims were young girls, and the crimes, with one exception, took place at night. People had now become thoroughly frightened and were beginning to panic — they sensed that a mass murderer was on the loose. They were right.

On March 10, Mayor Abraham Beame and Police Commissioner Michael J. Codd held a press conference, at which they revealed that the same .44 caliber gun had been used for all the crimes. Now the papers relayed appeals for information under headlines that referred to the ".44 caliber killer." Though fear was not at a fever pitch, the public was at the same time fascinated by the grotesque drama. This fascination, this preoccupation with the brutal murders began early and lasted long after we learned who the ".44 caliber killer" actually was.

The apparently random selection of victims and the lack of clear motive led the media to depict him as a mindless beast, a demented creature totally out of touch with reality — a portrait that the public was ready to accept. I wasn't so sure. For an insane person, he appeared to be covering his tracks very consciously and very carefully. We often do not understand that not every killer is insane. There are those who murder because they are overcome by hateful, malicious, evil feelings, which in themselves are not evidence of insanity. As a matter of fact, most murders are committed by people who are sane.

When Berkowitz killed Valentina Sauriani and Alexander Esau in the Bronx on April 17, the .44 caliber killer left a note for the police: "Come and get me." He signed the note "Son of Sam."[3] What was this lunacy? The killer had started a dialogue with his public, initiated a cat-and-mouse game with the police, created a bizarre tie with the world. The victimizer wanted to talk with his victim, wanted to make sure they were "hooked." The overtones of his *nom de guerre*, "Son of Sam," made him perversely seductive, titillating the fascination and fears of the public, challenging authority, and cleverly manipulating the news media. No doubt about it: the killer was calling the shots.

On April 19 a special Homicide Task Force, headed by Inspector Timothy J. Dowd, was set up to coordinate the search for the killer. Three hundred men — 75 detectives and 225 uniformed policemen — were recruited from precincts in the five boroughs. Tips flooded precinct switchboards at a furious rate, at times averaging four calls per minute. Every one of them was checked, but they led nowhere. After several months of intensive and elaborate investigation by some of the finest policemen the city had to offer, they knew only that Son of Sam was using the same Charter Arms Bulldog .44 caliber revolver in each shooting, and that, except for one murder, all his victims had been shot in parked cars. This latter circumstance, I felt, was of psychological importance and must have had some meaning for the perpetrator. The police could infer that they were dealing with a lonely, secretive man, much preoccupied with women. Because of his repeated murders and his obvious rage against women, one could safely predict more killings if he were not caught soon.

On June 26, Judy Placido and Salvatore Lupo were shot in Bayside, Queens, near a disco. As the manhunt widened, detectives in unmarked cars and on foot were steadily patrolling what they thought were the killer's hunting grounds. Decoy teams were spread throughout the Bronx and Queens. Life-sized dummies were placed in cars at popular trysting places in hopes that the killer could be lured into a trap. It was rumored that alleged Mafia boss Carmine Galante had offered the services of his organization to bring the murderer to justice. The killer was being absorbed into American popular culture. Vendors appeared in Central Park with the inevitable tee shirts: "Son of Sam — Get him before he gets you."

The police continued their dogged investigation. All current and former mental patients in New York State were being checked. The 400 holders of permits for .44 caliber revolvers were being traced. Toward the end of July 1977, as the anniversary of Son of Sam's first murder approached, fear and fascination mounted. There were those who even admired him, in particular because he had been able to avoid detection by the largest manhunt ever mobilized by the New York Police.

When he struck again, on July 31, it was in Brooklyn. He shot to death 20-year-old Stacy Moskowitz and partially blinded her companion, Robert Violante. This time, however, the long hours of undramatic and grueling detail work produced a break. Cecilia Davis, a middle-aged woman who lived near the murder site, was out walking her dog at about 2 A.M. when she saw a car being ticketed for parking too close to a hydrant. Right after the police left, the woman was accosted by a young man holding a dark object. For a moment he looked at her carefully, then walked on. Frightened, she ran back to her house. She had barely gotten inside when she heard the sound of gunshots. It took her four days to take her story to the police, who now began to check every car that had been ticketed in the area of the Moskowitz killing.

David Berkowitz was the owner of one of the automobiles, a 1970 four-door yellow Ford Galaxie. He lived at 35 Pine Street, Yonkers, just north of New York City. In the spring and summer of 1977, some strange things had been happening in and near the building in which he lived.

On April 11, 1977, a man named Sam Carr, who lived at 316 Warburton Avenue, a house that could be seen from 35 Pine Street, had received some letters bitterly complaining about his black labrador retriever, Harvey. The letter writer said he had been tormented by the dog, could get no satisfaction from his complaints, and was prepared to eliminate the dog's owner. When his dog actually was shot, Carr reported the whole thing to the local police. On April 20, Wheat Carr, his daughter, received another anonymous letter complaining about the dogs, and signed "H. H., Yonkers," with the return address of a business in New York. Inquiries in New York City failed to reveal the identity of the sender. Who was this H. H.?

In June of that year, the Cassara family of New Rochelle received a get-well card (photo) from a Sam Carr. Nobody in the family was sick, and nobody had ever heard of a Sam Carr. When they contacted Carr to get to the bottom of the mystery, they discovered that the handwriting on the card matched that of the threatening letters Carr had received. The Cassaras then remembered that they briefly had a tenant, David Berkowitz, who disliked dogs. All this they reported to the Yonkers police. When Stacy Moskowitz was killed, Mrs. Cassara called again to suggest that Berkowitz might be the Son of Sam, but the officer she spoke to did not think her call was important.[4]

Meanwhile, the patrolmen who had originally responded to Sam Carr's complaints were beginning to take seriously the notion that Berkowitz might be the Son of Sam. On August 5, they passed this suspicion on to the intelligence division of the New York City Police Department, which began to consider it, along with the thousands of other tips and suggestions that they had received.

At 35 Pine Street, Craig Glassman, an investigator for the Westchester County Sheriff's office, was having problems. Having recently moved into the building, he began in June to receive crazy, threatening notes that alluded to "Satan" and "demons." Early on the morning of August 6, Glassman was awakened by a fire that had been set outside his door.[5] The Yonkers police, investigating the situation, also examined the letters Glassman had received. They concluded that the handwriting matched that on the letters to Carr and the note to the Cassaras. David Berkowitz was now under suspicion, but as yet no one had ventured to confront him.

Matters finally came to a head on August 9 when New York City Detective James Justus, who had been detailed to check into the Brooklyn parking tickets, called the Yonkers police to ask them to have a Mr. David Berkowitz get in touch with him. As chance would have it, the person who answered the phone at the Yonkers police station was Wheat Carr, daughter of Sam, and a civilian employee of the Department. She told Detective Justus of her suspicions about Berkowitz, and by the end of the phone call, plans for a stakeout of 35 Pine Street were already being made.

On August 10, with police from New York City and Yonkers already surrounding the building, one last bizarre twist remained to be played out. Craig Glassman, quite independently, was becoming convinced that his upstairs neighbor, David Berkowitz, was the author of the menacing letters he had received: He decided to go downstairs to search Berkowitz's car.

The police waiting downstairs had never laid eyes on Berkowitz. What happened next is related by Detective Charles Higgins of the Brooklyn 10th Homicide Zone:

On August 10, 1977, at approximately 18:30 hours [6:30 P.M.] I was in Department auto #329 with Detective John Falotico of the 10th Homicide Zone. We were parked on Pine Street, two car lengths behind the suspect's auto, a 1970 Ford, yellow and black, registration #591 XLB, which was parked at the curb. We observed a male, white, exit the building 35 Pine Street and proceed to this auto. This male was white, wearing short pants, mustache. When he came abreast of the car he looked into it and then started walking back towards the entrance of 35 Pine Street. At this time, Detective John Falotico and myself were right behind him with our guns drawn but pointed downward. At this time, Inspector McRann, Captain Coleman, Sargeant Gardella, with Detectives Longo and Zigo also converged on the entrance from a vehicle they had been in. This male was then walking back towards our parked autos. He then identified himself as Craig Glassman and that he was an investigator with the Westchester Sheriff's Office. He resided at 35 Pine Street, Apartment 6E. Further stated he suspected David Berkowitz of Apartment 7E, who lived directly above his apartment, of sending him threatening letters in the past and also being the one responsible for setting a fire outside his apartment door this past Saturday night. He said he had reported these incidents to the Yonkers Police Department. At this time, Glassman stated that Berkowitz was not in his own apartment as he could hear his footsteps above his apartment. He also mentioned that Berkowitz had blankets over his windows to hide out the light in his apartment.

Det. Longo and myself were then directed to take up a position on the roof of 35 Pine Street and observe Berkowitz's apartment, as he lived on the 7th floor (top floor) and had access to the fire escape from his window. Det. Longo and myself had the subject's windows in view and could see no lights from within his apartment. We also kept an eye on the entrance (front) of 35 Pine Street. We were in contact with Sgt. Gardella and Det. Falotico, who were in a Department auto, two lengths behind the suspect's auto. They also had Craig Glassman in their auto.[6]

The end followed quickly, almost anticlimactically.

At 9:45 P.M. a man carrying a paper bag came out of 35 Pine Street and got into the yellow sedan. Glassman, followed by Det. Falotico and Sgt. Gardella, quickly approached the car. Glassman said: "I put my gun through the open window while the man was starting the car. I told him: 'Freeze, you're under arrest.' He didn't offer any resistance." Det. Falotico identified himself as a police officer. Berkowitz said nothing at all. He was calm, responsive.

Det. Falotico said to him, "Now I have you, who do I have?"

and Berkowitz responded, "You know."[7] After a pause, Berkowitz added: "Well, you got me. How come it took you such a long time?"[8]

Much later, in the course of our correspondence, he wrote me the following:

"Of course I knew that the police would eventually come around. I've always known that it was standard procedure for the police to check for traffic violations given out in the neighborhood of a crime scene. Also, license plate numbers of all cars parked within a large radius of a crime are also noted and eventually checked. This is usually done within several hours after a crime. Uniform policemen go up and down nearby streets recording the plate numbers and the model of all cars in the vicinity. So I knew that they would be coming. It was just a matter of time. But it did surprise me that it took almost two weeks."[9]

"Do you want to make a statement?" Glassman asked.

"No," he answered sharply, staring at them with icy eyes.

Detective Higgins had watched the arrest from the roof:

At approximately 22:00 hours Detective Longo and myself, while on the roof, heard voices from the street below. "Police! Freeze!" We went to the ledge with our guns down and directly below, we saw Sgt. Gardella, Det. Falotico and Craig Glassman with their guns out and pointing into the subject's auto. Det. Longo and myself trained our guns down towards the auto. The car door opened and a male, white, stocky build, came out of the auto and was handcuffed in the rear by Det. Falotico. We yelled down to Sgt. Gardella and he replied "We have him." Det. Longo and myself then went downstairs and outside to the auto.

Sgt. Gardella directed me to sit in the rear seat where Berkowitz had been put. . . . Det. Falotico went behind the wheel and Craig Glassman sat in the front passenger seat. We were told to go to the Yonkers Police Department. . . . As soon as we pulled away from the curb . . . Berkowitz looked at me and stated, "How did you find me?" At this time I gave him his "rights"; he answered yes to all my words, in that he understood what I was saying. At this time I felt a lump in his left front pants pocket and asked him, "Are these bullets?" He nodded yes. I asked him if they were .45's. He nodded no. I then asked him, "Are they .44's?" He smiled and nodded yes. I then reached into his pocket and removed a small plastic bag [with] eight .44 caliber bullets, some with ammo. . . . As we were parking, Det. Falotico saw Inspector Dowd. . . . Det. Falotico . . . told him we had Berkowitz in the auto and about the .44 caliber ammo. Insp. Dowd asked to speak to Berkowitz. We took Berkowitz out of the auto and stood him by a wall. Insp. Dowd approached Berkowitz. At this time I asked Berkowitz if he knew who this man was. He looked at Insp. Dowd and smiled and said, "You're Insp. Dowd."

Chief Keenan looked at Berkowitz and asked, "What is your name?" Berkowitz looked around at all the faces and smiling said, "I'M SON OF SAM." No one said anything and at this time I asked Berkowitz did he know who he was speaking to. He looked and smiled and said, "you're Det. Keenan" at which time Insp. Dowd said, "It's Chief Keenan." . . .

From the auto a .44 caliber handgun was found in the front and a .45 caliber machine gun with clips of .45 caliber ammo was found in the rear. . . . Two (2) rifles and ammo were taken [from the apartment] back to the station house. . . .[10]

Throughout the entire time of Berkowitz's arrest, his demeanor was calm, almost stoic. It is important to note that he smilingly identified himself as "Son of Sam," as if he didn't know his real name. In contrast to this misidentification, he was able to recognize Detective Keenan, whom he had never seen.

In the Yonkers Police Station, "Detective Shilensky of the New York Police Department Legal Bureau re-read Berkowitz his rights and he responded after being asked if he understood each one. . . . Inspector Dowd questioned Berkowitz for approximately 45 minutes, who was calm, collected, and responsive to all questions. His answers were spontaneous and intelligent. If there was a factual error in the question, he corrected Inspector Dowd. When offered food or the use of a bathroom, the defendant declined."[11]

Then Detective Falotico interviewed the defendant about the Moskowitz homicide. Berkowitz maintained the same calm demeanor. This interview lasted for approximately five minutes. Berkowitz was then charged formally with homicide. He made no response.

"Det. Falotico [stayed] with Berkowitz until leaving the Yonkers Police Department to go to Police Headquarters in New York. . . . From Police Headquarters he was brought to the 84th Precinct. . . . The only conversation here . . . was when Falotico asked him if he wanted to make a phone call. Berkowitz placed the call to his sister himself but she wasn't home."[12]

"At the 84th Precinct, during the booking process the defendant was asked pedigree questions which he answered spontaneously. He was then fingerprinted. When he was about to wipe his hands from the grease he used an old newspaper which contained Son of Sam stories. The defendant looked at the papers when he wiped his hands, and turned to Det. Fox and said, 'Isn't it ironic.' Additional routine paperwork followed."[13]

During this period the defendant went to the bathroom several times, and washed his hands frequently. He was then taken from the 84th Precinct to 120 Schermerhorn Street and placed in a pen. The conversation related generally about whether he was tired and other small talk."

Throughout all the pretrial services interviews, during which the defendant answered every question and corrected the pretrial representative,[14] all the detectives noticed that Berkowitz was well oriented, knew where he was, and was logical in his thinking. He was so controlled and so eager to find out the latest news about himself that he even asked Detective Fox if he would be getting the day's newspapers. The answer was an emphatic no.

At that time Philip Peltz, a lawyer, appeared. Berkowitz wanted to know who had hired him.

"The defendant agreed to speak with Peltz who gave him his card, which he saved. After Peltz left, Det. Fox explained to the defendant what was going to happen at the arraignment. . . ."

"The arraignment was held and the defendant was turned over to the Department of Corrections at 12:15 A.M.

". . . the defendant was under no medication. [He] was alert and calm during the entire process except at the arraignment when his hands appeared to be shaking."[15]

At about 1 A.M., Mayor Beame was called to police headquarters to see the defendant personally. He entered the small cell-like room where Berkowitz was. Beame looked at him, but said nothing. Berkowitz said nothing to the Mayor. But, as he later told me, he was very impressed that the Mayor of New York City would come to see him.

Feelings against Berkowitz were running high, and Mayor Beame was to express bitter outrage when the Criminal Justice Agency, Inc., a public service corporation set up to make recommendations on bail, had suggested that David Berkowitz should be released on his own recognizance, because he had a permanent residence and a steady job! The crowd that had massed outside the Criminal Court in Brooklyn when Berkowitz was taken for arraignment knew what *they* wanted. They shouted, "Kill! Kill!"

Why had he killed? Berkowitz told police he had killed on command: Sam, a 6000-year-old man, had passed on instructions to kill through his dog. This "confession," along with the letters the police had received from Son of Sam, plus the ones to Carr and Glassman, conjured up a bizarre and grotesque portrait of a man obsessed with dogs, demons, and hatred — a sadist who apparently long ago had lost touch with the real world.

People, at first stunned by the newspaper photographs, doubted their own eyes. Could this be the mass murderer of so many young and innocent women? The face was so soft, so round, almost feminine; the smile so sweet, nearly seductive, his manner so mild and gentle. He looked like the boy next door, a nice Jewish boy from the Bronx. Surely there must be a mistake. But there was none.

The murderer's crimes, as a matter of fact, had been reported on the front page of the Vatican's *L'Osservatore Romano*, the Hebrew newspaper *Maariv*, and the Soviet *Izvestia*. His year-long murders of young women, in itself a historical event, were ended in a strange finale for the most publicized manhunt in recent history.

It was the middle of August, and I was enjoying the serenity of late summer at my country place when I received an imperative call from Brooklyn District Attorney Eugene Gold. Passing quickly over the usual pleasantries, he got right to the point: he wanted me to examine Berkowitz to see if he was sane and could stand trial. He also wanted me to determine what his mental condition had been at the time of the last murder.

In order to forestall any preconceived notion he might have of Berkowitz 's mental condition, I warned him that my professional evaluation would be my objective analysis as a psychoanalyst.

"I know," he answered in a determined voice. "Whatever you find, I'll accept. I would like you to come to my office at Borough Hall in Brooklyn."

Although I could not know it at the time, this was the beginning of something that was to be much, much more than a pretrial psychiatric examination, A forensic psychiatrist's job is usually finished when the verdict is returned. In this case however, the defendant was to continue his dialogue with the psychiatrist long after justice had been rendered.* For the first time, a mass murderer would cooperate in revealing his full story, his fantasies, fears, and secret history, to a psychoanalyst. The stark outline of the story—all that could be obtained in the adversarial atmosphere of a pretrial examination — he was later to fill in with rich detail, leisurely supplied from his cell at Attica Prison, over a period of three years.

Six days after the arrest Berkowitz's lawyers, Mark Heller, Ira Jultak, and Leon Stern, had filed a motion in State Supreme Court indicating that at the trial they would show evidence of mental disease or defect which would exclude Berkowitz's criminal responsibility.† A month before the arrest, a psychiatrist had described the Son of Sam as "neurotic, schizophrenic, and paranoid . . . preoccupied with religious and demonic ideas." And

---

* This was not the first time I would be dealing with a notorious killer. I had interviewed Nathan Leopold, the Chicago "thrill killer" of 1924, and was eventually instrumental in getting him paroled. I examined George Metesky, the "Mad Bomber" of the 1950's. I had been a consultant in the case of Lee Harvey Oswald, and had participated in numerous cases involving multiple killings.
† I was thoroughly familiar with the criminal insanity law in New York state, since I had played a role in writing it.

the general public had already made up its mind: Berkowitz was crazy. Case closed. But I had my doubts.

I quickly recovered from my momentary surprise at Berkowitz's sudden appearance in the interview room at Kings County Hospital. That he had read *The Murdering Mind* intrigued me. I have examined hundreds of murderers, and none has ever told me they read anything about murder from the psychiatric-psychological point of view. Had Berkowitz read it in order to understand his own motivations? Was it possible that he felt guilty?

We shook hands. His handshake was firm, and a half-smile appeared around his mouth. It was almost a look of superiority.

I didn't know whether he remembered my face from newspaper photos or from the photo on the book jacket, but he certainly recognized me. Whatever else might be true, his memory was clear.

Where had he found my book?

"At the Yonkers Public Library." He then volunteered that he had also read other less academic books about murderers, among them Nathan Leopold and the notorious mass murderer Richard Speck.

"I like to read about murders and murderers — it's a recent interest of mine — a little over two years." Such absorption, such concentrated interest hardly suggested the inner confusion usually present in an insane man. Quite the contrary; his observations showed that he was highly intelligent, alert, and perceptive. His eagerness to read and explore the subject of homicide indicated his need to reach an intellectual understanding of his own behavior. His manner was in sharp contrast to all that had been written about him. I had anticipated the possibility of meeting a madman, but he was far from mad.

Berkowitz looked at me with a look of triumph, as if he had totally astounded me with this revelation. He knew he had surprised me — as he had surprised so many others when he had been caught and turned out to be the Son of Sam. He certainly had stunned his adoptive father, Nathan Berkowitz, the elderly man we remember so vividly weeping in front of the television cameras and asking for forgiveness for the murders his son had committed.

His words, "Murder is a recent interest of mine," echoed in my mind. This death interest betrayed his concern about death, that for reasons then unknown to me, his mind had been more preoccupied with death and dying than one could have suspected from his quiet behavior at the prison ward. This preoccupation revealed his strong death wishes.

As the interview started Berkowitz, a master at hiding his real feelings, became, little by little, agitated. Following my initial questions, he angrily burst out:

"You work for Gold! Gold is my enemy!"

His words were sharp, heated, as if he had to get back at me for his compliment about my book. This uncalled-for rebuke betrayed his awareness that the law finally had caught up with him, that he had been charged with murder, and that the court had started its action against him. His manner and behavior seemed highly perceptive, and a far cry from insane (the legal term) or psychotic (the medical term).

Berkowitz's angry flareup had clearly been an attempt to undermine my psychiatric authority. Quietly I pointed out to him that the Court had ordered me to examine him, but that as a psychiatrist I was neutral. My sole purpose was to determine his mental condition on July 31, 1977, the date of his last murder, and his fitness to now stand trial. I would reach an independent conclusion.

Berkowitz only nodded and mumbled words which I gathered to mean, "I understand."

It was hardly surprising that he was defensive and aggressive. His hostile tone indicated that he was afraid of what I might be able to reveal about him and his crimes. Because there was no privileged confidential doctor-patient relationship between us — on the contrary, I was to report my findings to both judge and district attorney — he was certainly aware that whatever he told me could be used against him when his case came to trial. But he also knew that he didn't *have* to tell me anything.

He knew the score all right. But his behavior had already divulged to me his inclination to show off — his propensity for histrionics. I doubted that this interview would end in silence. I was right.

I asked him what the date was.

"August 31, 1977."

Hardly had he said it before his eyes had found a calendar on the far wall. Berkowitz was observant, and yes, it was August 31.

He said he was 24 years old. Born June 1, 1953.

"What is your first memory from childhood?"

"Playing," he answered spontaneously. The way he pronounced "playing" seemed to come deep from within, from a well of feeling he did not know or realize.

"What kind of playing?"

"Playing army games, cowboys and Indians."

First childhood memories are significant since they reflect basic early feelings which may color a person's later behavior. Playing, of course, means enjoyment, imagination, pleasure and egocentricity. If carried to an extreme it may also lead to turning away from reality.

As a child and adolescent he lived with his adoptive mother and father, Pearl and Nathan Berkowitz, at 1105 Stratford Avenue in the Bronx. [Nathan later told me that they had been married in 1942, and since they could not have children of their own, they were happy when they adopted David in 1953, when he was only a few days old. Nathan was then 43 and Pearl was 37.]

"David, was it a good home?"

"Yes."

"In what way?"

"Parents were good to me. I had a lot of friends."

As I was moving around in my chair, it squeaked and crackled, making a great deal of noise. Berkowitz laughed freely. I laughed with him, and for the moment he enjoyed himself.

Then, suddenly, he said he hadn't known he had a sister. They had not met until 1975.

"I found out I had a sister and I looked out for her."

"Who told you you had a sister?" [She was actually a half-sister.]

"My dad. I was maybe 21 when I found out my name was different, Richard Falco."

"And you mother?"

"Betty Falco. I was adopted at birth. My natural mother and father I never met at that time."

Admitting that he was adopted came out in an almost natural voice, but its tone was a mixture of bravado and defiance.

"Did you meet your mother and half-sister later on?"

"Yes."

"When?"

"About three [actually two] years ago (1975)."

Asked how he met them, he said he looked them up.

"How?"

"I joined the ALMA club [Adoptee's Liberty Movement Association]. I checked old telephone books."

He had worked feverishly, he said, for half a year to locate his mother, and was finally successful.

"Did you ever look for your real father?"

"I didn't know where to begin."

He felt very happy, he told me, about meeting his mother and half-sister. "It was a very warm, nice experience."

"Did you see her often?"

"Once every three months. . . . After a while, I got to know her well."

I wondered, why so long a time between visits? He had solved the mystery of his natural mother's whereabouts, but his feelings toward her seemed another mystery. Only later did he express his real feelings about her, which gave me to understand that his meeting her had been crucial to him.

Realizing he didn't want to say any more about her I asked him: "What work did your adoptive father do?"

"He was in the hardware business."

"Did he have his own store?"

"Yes."

"Did you visit him there?"

Yes, he said, it was a 20-minute ride from where he lived.

"How did you get along with your father?"

"We didn't get along that good, but we didn't get along that bad." Again his ambivalent feelings were piercing his defensive posture. "My dad and I played games with each other."

"Who won?"

"He did." He laughed.

He didn't remember that his mother or his father were ever strict with him.

How old was he when he learned that he was adopted?

"I was six or seven years old when both my parents told me." He was also told that his natural mother had died when he was born. [Nathan said to me, however, that they had told David much earlier, "when he was three years old. We passed the Courthouse where he had been legally adopted in November 1954 (when David was 18 months old), and I pointed out the building to him. The reason why we told David so early was to protect him from the other children, if they should say to him he was adopted without his knowing it. He accepted it."[16]

David's acceptance seemed, however, dubious.

"How did you feel about being adopted?"

"Surprised, confused," he answered quickly, without hesitation. Why surprised and confused? I wondered. Was it that he didn't understand what it meant to be adopted, or that he didn't want to accept it? Why didn't he want to talk about it? He already had shown himself to be intelligent.

"Didn't you talk any more about it?"

"They didn't want to talk about it," he answered hurriedly.

I had touched a sore spot, and noticing his impatience, I asked him to tell me more about his adoptive parents.

David told me that his adoptive mother, Pearl, had died from breast cancer in 1967 when he was 14 years old. He visited her in the hospital but was not told how ill she was until she was dying. [His father, Nathan, later informed me that David cried copiously at the funeral.]

"How did you feel about your mother's death?"

His reply was blunt and to the point. "I was both happy and sad."

"How so?"

"It was freedom. She was a pest sometimes. She was nagging."

"In what way?"

"In everything," he replied promptly.

His words had erupted, not casually, but with a great deal of thought. His being happy and sad about his mother's death reflected his ambivalent feelings, similar to how he felt about his father. His answer (about his mother's death and freedom it gave him) impressed me. He was clearly determined to control himself and those around him. Berkowitz had a strong desire to be free from restrictions so he could do as he pleased. This yearning to be free, the aversion to being hemmed in, emerged in his behavior at school.

"I graduated from high school," he said, "when I was 18." But he didn't like school.

"Why?"

"I didn't have the patience for it."

"Did you feel hemmed in?"

"Yes. Some classes I liked a lot—biology, history, some types of English. I didn't like shop."

"What kind?"

"Wood-working, auto shops. I played hooky. . . . During this period I was in tenth grade. I played hooky often."

Noting his frankness, I asked, "What did you do when you played hooky?"

"I stayed home."

Didn't his father notice he wasn't going to school?

"No, Dad went to his hardware store and I stayed home."

"What did you do?"

"Looked at TV."

"Didn't your father discover that you weren't in school?"

"No."

"Did he ever find out?"

"The school sent a letter home, and then they came from school to see what happened. Dad had to go there."

His marks had fallen.

It was necessary to get more information about his childhood experiences.

As a child he was chubby, liked to go to go to the movies, liked sports, played all sorts of ball. He had fights with boys, but "I didn't want to fight. I just go into them." He went to the stores with the other boys to shoplift — for fun. Sometimes he went by himself, and pilfered things from the counter, only to throw them away later on. He prided himself that he was never caught.

Was he ever sick as a child?

His reply, as if my question had offended him, was a resounding "No. Never."

"How about childhood diseases — measles, for instance?"

"Oh, yeah! That stuff. Everyone has that," he answered in a cocksure tone, as if I didn't know better.

What about accidents? Once he was hit by a car, another time he ran into a wall. "I was always cut and bleeding. My whole head was torn open, one time. I was hit in the head with a pipe when I was 7 or 8 . . . gave me tetanus. I took a long time before the bleeding stopped. All the ladies turned to help me. They didn't know what to do. They didn't call the ambulance; they didn't know what to do. My head burned. I remember my head, the front was open, four inches.

"Were you scared?"

"I was covered with blood. All the kids ran away from me. I couldn't see, my eyes were covered with blood. The whole neighborhood was out there."

"Were you glad they were trying to help you?"

"Who knows? I don't know," again arrogantly.

As he told his story he became more and more dramatic, facinated by the recounting of the excitement he had created during that accident. Here I saw the growing progression of his exhibitionistic behavior; the desire to be the center of attention and, through heroics, draw everyone's eyes to himself.

Berkowitz's last remark — that he didn't know whether he was glad to get help for his bleeding head — is worth noting. He himself wanted to be the hero, apparently not wanting to share the limelight with anyone, nor wanting help from anyone. He was independent.

As a youngster he was hyperactive, self-assertive, restless.

What kind of childhood did you have?

"A lot of things troubled me in connection with my parents."

"What were they?"

"Death troubled me," he said quietly and with self-absorption. Was he at that time afraid that they might die—as he was taught to believe his natural mother had done?

"Were you afraid *you* might die?"

"No. We were friends."

His answer surprised me. Never had anyone before given me such an answer. What did it mean that death and he were friends?

"Did you yourself want to die?" I asked.

"Yes," he nodded; and went on that he thought of death once in a while.

I noticed he looked preoccupied. His words had come from far way. The smile had left his face. He seemed fixed in his thoughts. His seriousness gave me an inkling that he had been thinking of death more than "once in a while."

Did he know how he came to be thinking of death?

"I don't know what happened."

He was quiet, sat there looking through the window, his clear blue eyes clearer than before.

It came as quite a surprise to me when later his adoptive father, in contrast to Berkowitz's description of his troubled childhood, depicted David as a normal child. "He was a lovable child, pleasant, smiling. We never had trouble. He had friends in the same building. he was affectionate when he was seven, eight, maybe ten years old. He kissed his mother, he used to come to sit close to me, lean his head on my shoulder." David was bottle-fed, toilet training normal, never a thumbsucker or a nailbiter.

There was apparently a great deal Nathan Berkowitz didn't know about his son. David was very secretive. He had carefully kept his thoughts and his escapades from his parents, as he was also to do later when he carried out his murderous activities.

As I watched him stare out the window it occurred to me that his face looked like that of a cat. Although it appeared rectangular, a closer look showed that it was in fact rounded, and that on the side of his skull, close to his black hairline, his ears appeared, not as a natural appendage to his head, but as if they had been planted there. Attached high on his skull, they gave Berkowitz's face a feline look. And, like a cat, he was self-possessed, secretive.

While sometimes these random first impressions can be wrong, my experience is that they often have turned out to be meaningful. It is this intuitive perception that the psychiatrist either verifies or nullifies in the ensuing examinations. Such intuitive understanding must always, finally, be corroborated by fundamental psychoanalytic concepts, formulated through experience, and based on a body of scientific knowledge.

David told me he was 5′ 10″, his weight 200 pounds; but since his arrest he had lost about 10 pounds. He resented being locked up, couldn't move around, felt hemmed in, constantly watched. While previously he had roamed the streets, drive around, now he was penned in.

Yet, despite his overweight and the prison guards who always accompanied him wherever he went, it was surprising how quickly he could move to and from his cell to my office when the passage was clear, as if he were a free man. Given his heavy torso, his hairy, muscular arms, his swift and silent stride seemed to originate more from his feelings, temper, and mood than his bodily corpulence.

"How do you spend your time here? Do you read?"

"Yes, but there are no books here." He clarified his remark: "Here they only have books about cowboys and Indians. In this country it is very selective; you cannot read what you want to read." He was pointedly scornful.

"Do you like poetry?"

"Yes, but only certain subjects," he answered.

"Anything specific in mind?"

"Death."

He also liked poetry of wildlife and the outdoors, and animals.

"I like animals." His voice had a challenging tone.

"Any animals in particular?"

"I like cats."

Of all the animals he could have named, he singled out cats. He identified himself to some extent with them, apparently because their behavior reminded him of his own. I was to learn that he also had an affinity, a peculiar attraction, to dogs.

"Were you as a child ever angry at yourself?" I asked.

"Yes," his answer was curt.

I put an obvious question: "How do you like it here?"

"I feel like a rat here," he replied, in an emotion-filled tone. "I always feel dirty here. I didn't feel dirty before. It is bad here."

"What do you think of yourself, David? Are you sensitive?"

"Yes, I'm a very sensitive person, " he answered eagerly. "As a kid I used to cry a lot, when I heard music or heard that someone had died."

"Did you feel sorry for yourself?"

"I suppose so." I had the impresion that despite the apparent good care given him as a child, he felt neglected.

Berkowitz had let it be known several times that the two court-appointed psychiatrists had asked him about the murders and the demons. I had told him I would get to it when it was time, meaning when we had developed a certain rapport between us. I was aware that he wanted to bring up the demons, which apparently had played such a large role in the rationalization of his killings.

Following up on his remark that he used to cry a great deal when he heard music, I asked if he was musical.

"I used to be musical," he said, "until the attack."

I didn't understand. What attack? He explained, "That was the demons. I lost my soul, it was removed from me. I thought all my possessions were taken from me."

"Who did it?"

"SAM."

"Did you feel your possessions were taken away from you while you were in the Army?" [He had volunteered in 1971]

His answer was simply "No."

He became mute, seemingly lost in thought. When I asked him about his work, he said he began the job in the Post Office in April of 1977, but then corrected himself: "I think I started earlier [on March 12, 1977]. I worked there until I was arrested. Worked eight hours a day, afternoons and evening."

He remembered his murders vividly — when and under what circumstances they occurred.

"Did you run away from the murder scenes in order not to be discovered?"

"Yes, but that's the whole operation — guerrilla warfare," he answered glibly. He certainly had presence of mind.

"How did you feel when you had shot all the people?"

"I don't know, I don't understand the question."

Not wanting to accept his answer, I asked how he felt about his last killing, the shooting of Stacy Moskowitz.

"Sometimes I do feel sorry for having killed her."

"So," repeating his answer, "sometimes you do feel sorry for having killed?"

"Sure" — emphatically.

"Who told you to kill?"

"The King, Sam."

He had told me, "I had a job as a hired gun. I ran away from them — the demons. They wouldn't let me stop. It got to a point where I hated killing. I got sick of it. I wanted to stop." Then, "I was glad in a way they caught me."

Strange. In one breath he told me he had been hired by the demons to kill, and had killed several people, and in the next breath that he was glad in a way they caught him. In saying he was glad he had been caught, he had in all probability meant what he said, but he hadn't said what he meant. A matter not peculiar to Berkowitz. What he meant was that he felt guilty. Consciously or unconsciously, he felt guilty for the murders. In his own mind he felt he ought to be caught so he could be punished. But this, naturally, he did not yet understand.

Still, he had said he was commanded by demons to kill, and when anyone imagines he is possessed by demons he is insane. One suffers either from paranoia, an extremely rare form of insanity marked by distorted beliefs that are impervious to reason, or from schizophrenia, characterized by confusion, memory loss, and an inability either to understand what is happening to or around one or to hold down a job. In short, a person who has a thought disorder has a disorganized personality. The discrepancy between Berkowitz's controlled personality and the apparent thought disorder puzzled me. During our dialogue he was perceptive, well oriented, coherent, lucid. His level of intelligence was bright, possibly superior. His memory was excellent. Yet he was emphatic in his assertion that he was possessed by demons.

The line between normality and insanity can, particularly at first sight, be thin. One doesn't know where one ends and the other begins.

Did Berkowitz have a normal mind that produced abnormal thoughts, or did he have an abnormal mind which conceived normal ideas?

Does a normal man exist?

The case, I thought, was certainly bizarre, but apparently not so mysterious that one could not unravel it. My years of work in psychiatric criminology have taught me that the more exceptional, irregular, and unnatural a case may appear to be, the less mysterious, within certain limits, it often turns out in the end. Indeed, I had first learned this lesson from my mother discipline — medicine. Consequently, the more bizarre and peculiar a patient's symptoms and behavior seem, the less mysterious his personality. In the end it was always a question of examining, examining, and more examining.

David Berkowitz was either sane or insane. He couldn't be both. What could there be between sanity and insanity? It was an intriguing problem, but there had to be a logical solution.

At this early point of my encounter with the defendant, it was already clear to me that Berkowitz did not exhibit the symptoms of schizophrenia. And the cunning with which he had selected the time and place of his murders, and the skill he had used to elude the greatest manhunt in recent memory, was not indicative of psychotic behavior.

Could he be playing insane? (Another Hamlet?) Playing, he had told me, was his earliest childhood memory. It was what made him happy.

As I pondered the case after this first interview, I realized that my preliminary task was to figure out, so far as was possible, the enigma of David Berkowitz's personality. Did he really believe he was the Son of Sam, or was his real self far more complex and manipulative?

2

THE TERRORIZED

MIND

As interview followed interview, the details of David Berkowitz's troubled childhood began to fall into place. In those details I was beginning to discern the seeds of his adult behavior. In the nightmares of a child might lie an explanation for what would become the nightmare of an entire city, and in the behavior of the young David Berkowitz one might see a pattern that would explain the acts of Son of Sam. The adult terrorist was once the terrorized child; the public knew the adult; I had to find the child.

One time, as Berkowitz watched me making notes, he became upset and suddenly interrupted with: "This is absurd—it's all a game."[1] Was he thinking of his own games? Was he "playing" again?

At another juncture I had to explain why I did not use a tape recorder. Only after I had read to him what I had written did he finally calm down.

His calmness, however, was temporary. His anger flashed when we talked about his family. Suddenly, violently, in a shrill voice, he asked me: "Why do you ask so much about my child-hood? It isn't relevant. My childhood was normal!"

When, on the following day, I asked again about his family, he again interrupted me: "I don't want to talk about my parents. I shouldn't even have said what I said yesterday about them. It is enough. . . . You write *bad* things about them!"[2] He screamed the word "bad."

"I only write what you tell me," I answered. Simultaneously showing a streak of loyalty toward his family, an honorable feeling, he had at the same time become quite antagonistic, one of they many times where his anger flared up, only to apparently disappear just as quickly. It was becoming clear that resentment and anger simmered just beneath his surface control. I felt that his hostile attitude toward me and my ongoing examination expressed feelings that were related to those he emotionally had been close to. I had established with David Berkowitz a trans-ference situation.

By transference we understand the transfer to the psychiatrist of feelings, impulses, wishes, fears, and fantasies which the pa-tient has experienced related to people whom he was emotionally close — parents, siblings, etc. In an interview — or treatment situation — the patient unconsciously thinks of the psychiatrist as the object of his repressed impulses. A person who has a dominant father (or mother) may become rebellious and defiant of all authority. He unconsciously identifies the psychiatrist as a father figure. By understanding the patient's situation, the doctor will try to make him accept the fact that his defiant behavior against him is unrealistic and that these feelings he originally felt against his father or mother are now no longer valid. Although the transference — a difficult part — was somewhat outside my present concern, even so, it was essential that I do an orderly examination of Berkowitz, though my time was limited, yet still bearing in mind that I keep the defendant at ease.

Berkowitz was moving around on his chair, restless. As a child he was chubby, he said: "I was teased about it. I always ate. I was nervous and bored and had to eat."

When did he come here? He looked at me, wondered a second:

"August 3 or 4." [It was August 11] He added: "Feels as if I've been here forever." He obviously was bored.

"Would you like to get out if you could?"

"Sure," his blue eyes turned brighter, "go home."

"What would you do if you could get out?"

Looking out the window for a moment and then turning to me, he announced slowly — putting himself into a fantasy of future serenity: "Just take it easy, take a long drive." He thought for a moment. "Get work. Start again one more time." The last words were followed by a wistful smile. "I could get a job. These interviews could be conducted in my home."

"Who knows?" I asked. "You might repeat what you did before."

"Maybe not. I don't think so. I wouldn't go back to Yonkers. I would go to Colorado, to Vermont. They wouldn't know me and I could start again." As he uttered these last words, he looked down, his hand limp in his lap. For a moment tears came to his eyes, then his anger burst out as he compared himself to a cornered rat. Realistically aware of his serious situation, he desperately wished to be free, yet he knew he was now confined to a cell and that the court had started its proceedings against him. Having made himself a prisoner, he resented his loss of freedom.

Did he, as a child, have daydreams? At first he couldn't remember, but then he admitted that he daydreamed about going into outer space. "All types of daydreams," he added hurriedly. "I just don't want to talk about them."[4] Clearly he felt threatened.

Understanding Berkowitz's preoccupation with death was one of the keys to understanding the motivation for his murders. Among children, concern with death is especially significant because it establishes a matrix for future behavior. Their anxiety may be a desire to die, a fear of dying or causing death to others, or the need to escape from the reality of life itself. Or it might be a mixture of all these feelings.

Death was of particular concern to the young David Berkowitz. "I've had many experiences with death during my earlier years that might have led to my fascination with it and at the same time caused me to question the value of life," he told me. "I always had," he later said, "a fetish for murder and death. I had homicidal fantasies as far back as I could remember. Sudden death and bloodshed appealed to me. I remember numerous car accidents in which people (young people) were hurt or killed."[5]

Enumerating a succession of encounters with meticulous attention to detail, he described these incidents in an animated tone, as if he was eager to re-create the sense of trauma he felt as he witnessed them:

1. A girl was hit by a car on the Bronx River Parkway and East 172nd Street. She died instantly. I was about 8.
2. A youth from school drowned at the Bronx River near Westchester Avenue. I remember him from school — his face not his name. I remember the police dragging the river. I left before they found him. (Age 9)
3. A girl and her Mom were hit by a car and killed on Bruckner Boulevard and Soundview Avenue. Both died instantly. My age 10. . . .
4. A boy was killed on Watson and Morrison Avenues when he fell from the side of the bus — I saw it. (Age 13)
5. My girlfriend Elaine Dickens was stabbed by three youths outside of P.S. 77 on Ward Avenue and East 172nd Street. I don't mean my actual girlfriend. I should say classmate.
6. One day I was going to the ballfield on Morrison Avenue when a cop car pulled up in front of an alley and the police ran into it. I followed them, and in the middle of the yard was an elderly woman lying in a pool of blood. The super yelled to the cops "she jumped." . . .
7. A man jumped off the roof of a building on Stratford near Westchester. I remember all the blood.
8. The neighborhood candy store man was stabbed to death in his store on Stratford Avenue near Westchester. The neighborhood talked about it for weeks. I remember the blood splattered all over the glass store front.
9. A man drowned in the Eastchester Creek by Co-op City Boulevard. I stood over him when the cops pulled him out. They didn't even chase me. I looked into his open eyes. I'll never forget it. . . .

The list goes on and on . . .

One gets the sense that Berkowitz wasn't only an observer of the gruesome scenes, but behaved as if he were a part of them. It may well be that he exaggerated what he saw, or that he has total recall. When he was really interested in a conversation he had had or an event he had observed, he could have almost perfect recall. This recall, as expressed in his recitation, was probably another evidence of his desire to show off.

"As a child," he told me, "I had tremendous fascination with death. When I thought about dying, I thought of being transported into a world of bliss and happiness."[7]

Did he ever think of committing suicide?

"No" — but he came close to it. "When I arrived at Stratford Avenue [in the Bronx] I used to stand looking out our window with a fantastic view. Throughout the year, rain, snow, or cold, I would look out the window and pray to God to kill me, that I would be hit by lightning. I begged to God for death. I used to sit on the fire escape and thought of throwing myself down, wanting to jump. But there was always the guilty feeling that if I did it would destroy my parents. It would have hurt my parents. The guilt about it would have been worse than the pain involved with death. I was between 7 and 13 years old when those thoughts came to me. After Pearl's death, after my [adoptive] mother died, I never had these suicidal thoughts. I still wanted to die, but with heroism, with honor. I wanted to die while saving lives, battling a blaze. This is why I wanted to become a fireman, helping people, rescuing them, and being a hero, or possibly dying in the blaze. My parents always wanted me to be a doctor or a lawyer and I said 'No, I don't want to.' I wanted to be a fireman and they didn't understand why. Now this is the reason why I wanted to be a fireman, because I wanted to be a hero and save lives."[8]

When I said he certainly could have saved lives by becoming a doctor, he did not have a ready answer. The suggestion puzzled him. He could possibly understand that one could save lives as a doctor, but that wouldn't be the same as being a visible hero — where people could notice him and learn about his heroic deed. In short, he wanted to call attention to himself, to wear a uniform, and to be in the limelight.

Did he have dreams at night?

He answered, quite eagerly, that he had had frightening dreams, but he couldn't remember any pleasant ones. But when he admitted that he had been dreaming about his father and his home, I asked if these dreams were pleasurable. He didn't answer; he only smiled.

Did he have nightmares as a child?

"Yes, several times I woke up frightened, woke up my parents."[9]

In describing his nightmares, he became emotional, as if he were reliving them. When I remarked that his father had told me he couldn't remember David ever having any frightening dreams as a child, he at once became excited, and gesticulated heatedly. David became irate, he shot back in a high-pitched voice:

"Yes, I had nightmares, many!" He yelled as if an injustice had been done to him, as if he had been deprived of something that had been an important and meaningful part of his childhood. For a second his face had become flushed; it burned with outrage. Then he became quite, seemingly satisfied that he had made his point.

How could his father have forgotten about his nightmares? It wasn't until much later — after I saw him at Attica Prison and after he had written me several letters — that I was able to reconcile his insistence on having had nightmares with Nat's forgetting them. For the moment this inconsistency remained a puzzle. Berkowitz anxiously continued:

"I had my own bed, which was on the opposite side of the bedroom. However, when I did have nightmares, they got so bad that I'd have to crawl into the large bed between my parents for comfort. I couldn't bear to sleep alone. At times my father would stay up and sit opposite my bed until I fell asleep. Other times I'd have to sleep between my parents.

Up until I was ten I slept in my parent's bedroom. After that my parents moved into the living room to sleep on the new Castro convertible. But the nightmares still continued. So I then went into my parents' bed to sleep. This annoyed my father. I woke him up and he had to get out of the bed to let me in so I could stay between my mother and him. After I got in, he jumped back into the bed and they went to sleep. I didn't fall asleep too quickly. My father snored, and it annoyed me. It also comforted me because I knew he was close by my side. This is very funny, especially if you could have seen it, but I used to tap and shake my father ever so often to see if he was still there. Boy did he get mad. It's so funny looking back at it . . ."

Berkowitz paused, reliving his early memories:

"As for my father not remembering," he said pensively then he must be covering up. How could he not remember? It happened almost every night."[10]

Two points were clear. David wanted to be close to his parents because he needed attention and affection. And the reason Nat didn't remember his son's nightmares was that he apparently was angry about David's behavior and *was* suppressing it.

Berkowitz continued, adding some engrossing details: "Nat used to sleep in my room in the bed next to me, until I was asleep. I always slept with the lights on. I was terrified of the dark. I would see shadows and ghosts and all kinds of monstrous shapes which terrified me. It got so bad that they refused to let me see monster shows, which were popular on TV. One evening when I was home alone and they had gone out, I saw a show called "Home on Haunted Hills." I was alone. I was maybe 8 or 9 years old. That night I had terrible nightmares. I went into their bedroom and I told my father that I had seen this horror movie and he scolded me. I've always had a wild imagination."[11]

Again, I felt I had moved closer to David's inner world. The shadows and ghosts of his vivid childhood imagination may well have been the first of the many menacing configurations he felt he was surrounded by. It was this seed that was to germinate and grow in him through his adolescence, ultimately transforming him into the Son of Sam.

Not unlike most parents, David's adoptive parents did not look into the deeper meaning of his nightmares. But we shall see later how his fearful child's imagination helped to create the stuff that demons are made of. Nightmares are always born of conscious or unconscious fears, and Berkowitz had more than usual. They played a predominant role in shaping his reactions and behavior as a child.

His early relationships with girls was a crucial part of his personality development. He wrote to me:

"I wanted to tell you of some unusual things that happened in my life that you may find significant. I never told anyone about this before.

"When I attended Shorehaven Beach Club in the Bronx (about age 7) I remember an incident that happened to my friend Bruce. We were by the water fountains in the hot sun when an argument developed between Bruce and the two older girls. I remember the girl with the long dark hair, without provocation, slapped Bruce in the face and nose.

"I remember how he screamed and bled from the nose. I never saw anyone bleed so much. The two girls laughed and left.

"The second incident was when I was about 5 years. I was playing in the sandbox when two older girls who were there began to put sand in a cup and then sprinkle it in my hair. Passively I played with them letting them do it. When I want back to my Mom (Pearl) to go home she saw all the sand and slapped me. It took several days for all the sand to work out of my hair. I also realized that they had made a fool of me."[12]

In both these instances, particularly the latter, Berkowitz felt taken advantage of. But although he was afraid of girls, he was flattered that they played with him. He was glad they had given him their attention.

His relationship with yet another girl is of interest to us:

"From my early childhood I used to take baths with a little girl by the name of Lory. I may then have been two, three, or four years old. I remember it from the pictures they took of me. Dad showed them to me. The girl was pretty. I've seen it from the pictures that I've bathed with her."[13]

Curious about this incident, I asked about his conscious memories, aside from the photo:

"I really have no recollection of my bathing with Lory. I only remembered it from the photograph I saw. But in the picture we were both giggling so I gather we weren't really aware of the physical differences between us."[14]

He had suppressed or repressed his conscious recollection of it. Aware of their physical differences, they were both defensive, and tried to cover up their embarrassment with giggling.

He later sent me a picture of his Bar Mitzvah party. The same girl, Lory, is flagrantly lying across his lap, flanked by two other girls, all innocently laughing and having a good time. This time he was not embarrassed by her presence.

Not so innocent is another memory of Lory: "I didn't tell you about the time I hit Lory over the head with the butt of [apparently a toy] gun. I almost split her head open. It was one of the most vicious things I ever did during my childhood. I was about five or six years old."[15]

Berkowitz's demon-invoking imagination was at work early.

"I've always fantasized about being close to young girls with whom I was sexually attracted to. However, in reality, I never had sex with them, much less talked with them. I was too shy to talk with them nor was I handsome or popular enough.

"All my childhood playmates were girls who existed in real life. But, as I said before, I never even talked with them. In my relationship though, my imaginary one, I had a wonderful relationship with them.

"I talked with them revealing my innermost desires, thoughts and secrets. I also made out with them often. However, I always knew that they were imaginary — that I had only fantasized our relationships. In reality, I never knew them. This is also why I won't reveal their names. They were real people and I don't want to embarrass myself. I also don't want to build up their egos.

"Even to this day, I continually dream up make believe relationships. I daydream of them every waking moment."[16]

Nowhere — in none of his interviews with me, nor in any of his letters — has he once mentioned that, as a child, he played with boys. When I told him that I had heard from a friend of his fathers's that at about ten or eleven years of age David played with this man's son, he could not remember it.[17]

Playing with girls, even if only in fantasy, gave him much

gratification. Deprivation in almost any area is probably the great mobilizer of our fantasy lives. What one cannot obtain in reality, one tries to achieve in fantasy. His fantasy life became a mechanism to help him compensate for his lack of real satisfaction — a mechanism he was to use later as a matter of course.

As a child, Berkowitz craved attention desperately. He had unconsciously to compensate for his dissatisfaction with himself, for his own uncertainty about who he was — something which was always gnawing away at him. Being illegitimate, not knowing his parents, now knowing his own identity, became one of the sources of his destructiveness. From his sense of loss arose a belief that he was different from others, that he awas not liked. These feelings had been rampant in him from earliest childhood.

"I hated school because I hated the kids in my class. Their laughing at me, their ridicule, the fighting after school the competition for grades and girls. Yes, I hated it. When three o'clock came, I ran home from school at full speed. Once I even got hit by a car doing it. Just wanted to be home with my mother and the neighborhood kids."[18]

His miserable time in school, he realized, had affected his later life. It "pattens me," as he put it.

Did he do his homework? He couldn't answer yes or no. "Sometimes," he said, "I did my homework . . . However, this was a rare occasion. Many times my parents had to force me to do it. Then, again, most of the time I just didn't do it, telling my parents that I had no homework."[19]

In 1964, when he was 11 years old, a teacher described him as a "*moody child. Can do good work if he wants to. Very easily upset, however.*" (emphasis added). In 1968, at age 15, in the 10th grade, he "shows more strength in understanding than in vocabulary."[20]

When I probed to learn about his high school years, he seemed anxious to give a full account.

"I graduated by the skin of my teeth. I was always a discipline problem, even when my mother was alive. I couldn't be controlled in class, I was wild, unruly, undisciplined; I was always

in the Guidance Counselor's office. I had to sit in the back of
the classroom because I had been so wild. . . .

"As to the schools, my teachers said *I was smart, but I was
too wild* [emphasis added]. I didn't sit down and study and read,
although I liked to read, but select literature. I didn't like to be
assigned to any literature. In those days I liked mysteries, sports,
and baseball. Now I have lost all interest in sports.

"I was the worst in school."[21]

Berkowitz seemed to enjoy presenting himself as a terror, even
though his school reports describe him as only "moderately
aggressive" with occasional temper tantrums.

He needed frequent encouragement in school. Highly interesting is a teacher's impression of David in 1962 – 63, when he
was ten years old:

Mrs. Berkowitz and I have met numerous times in an effort to aid
David. I have given him extra time after scool to improve his ability in
Math. He has improved. It's very important that David be shown
patience, but more so genuine warmth and interest or he cannot produce it seems. He has improved in all areas this year. His mother is
most cooperative.[22]

This teacher's observation was acute. Had she any inkling that
David didn't receive real love in his home, or had he intimated
it to her?

In February 1960 the school tested David and found him to
have an IQ of 118, a "superior level."[23] Obviously his problems
were emotionally rooted. His mother had taken him to a psychologist once a week. He remembers saying little during these
sessions. The one thing he remembers well is that her husband
was very kind and gave him cookies. He recalled only what gave
him gratification. But he resented the psychologist's intrusion
into his private world — his thoughts and feelings.

He didn't want to be dictated to. He rebelled against being
hemmed in. He often played hooky. When he first told me this
I was almost sure that the truancy had been chronic. As a matter
of fact, his records from the Board of Education in New York

City showed that from kindergarten up to and including high
school, he was often absent.* Throughout his school years,
Berkowitz played two different and contradictory roles. De-
fiantly truant, at the same time he gave his adoptive father the
impession that he was a good boy, and always went to school.
He showed two contrary sides — an ambivalence which we shall
later see became a hallmark of his general behavior.

It is understandable that his truancy went undiscovered after
his mother's death in 1967. His father could not supervise him,
since he had to take care of his business. But how was it possible
for him to be absent from school while Pearl was still alive and
at home every day? It is remarkable how he manipulated her:

"I got to stay home a lot when I was in public school. Most
of the time, however, I wasn't sick. I just played sick. In the
morning I'd say, 'Mom, I don't feel well.' She would put her
hand on my forehead and say, 'It does feel very hot.' Then I'd
get to stay home. You see, I had this trick of pressing my head
against the radiator before I went over to my mother with my
'sickness' complaint.

"Sometimes my mother would make me take the thermometer
into my rectum. I used to tell her: 'I'll put it in myself, leave the
room, you're embarrassing me by standing here and watching
me.' Then, after she left, I'd run over to the radiator and put the
metal end up against it. I did this for a minute, often counting
up to sixty. Then I'd run over to the bed and put the thermometer back in. When my Mom checked it, sure enough, I had a
fever.

"I loved staying home. My mother, Pearl, thinking I was sick,

---

* In kindergarten in 1958 [age five], he was absent 46 days; in the fourth grade in 1962,
28 days. At Christopher Columbus High School, in the 10th grade, February 1969 –
June 1969, he was truant 36 days, described as "*excessive.*" Failing all subjects that
term, he had to repeat several of them.[24] When he told his father, "I think I have to
take some classes over," his father went to the school and discovered that David had
been playing hooky. David had to take two subjects again, during the summer of
1969, at James Monroe High School. "We rearranged his program," his father told
me, "so that he had enough credits to graduate. I picked up his diploma in 1971."[25] In
the last semester he was absent 12 days but was able to graduate with a good average
of 83.3.[26]

would wait on me hand and foot. Every hour she would bring me tea with lemon or hot cocoa. Plus, she always had a variety of cookie snacks on hand. I felt like a king. I got to watch television all morning long. Staying home was great. But I laugh when I think about it. Boy, what a con artist I was.

"Getting 'rock candy' was another special treat. Everytime I stayed home, my mother ran off to . . . get a box."[27]

As a child, David was already a con artist. He played his role to the hilt and loved it. His supreme enjoyment was dominating others so that he could be the center of attention.

A common reason for truancy is a strong dependency between mother and child. In David's case the reason was not only dependency, it was also jealousy and possessiveness. He didn't want to leave her. What did he fantasize about her doings while he was away at school?

"When I did start school (kindergarten) I used to fight with my Mom when she tried to take me. I hated to leave her because I didn't want to miss anything. . . . Pearl had to take me to school and make sure that I went in. Naturally I sometimes used to cry and make a fuss . . . going to school and forcefully at that, was my being rejected. To me, and even until this day, I feel rotten in a school building. To me school was like a dumping ground. This is how I visualized it when I was in public school but it was unconscious back then . . . I always felt that my mother was simply sending me to school to get rid of me."[28]

Truancy is an important early indicator of criminal behavior. About 60 percent of all criminals, thieves, rapists, muggers, murderers, or robbers have been truant from school, manifesting their preoccupation with their own desires which interfere with their attending classes and reflecting rebellious or defiant attitudes toward parental authority and the law.

As a child Berkowitz had begun to act out his anger against authority in the form of vandalism and arson at school. He recalls: "I destroyed a lot of property in the school. I always went on 'PASS' to the toilet but en route I would take out a magic marker and deface the walls. I wouldn't write anything but just scribble.

"I also did this by myself — no one else knew about it. There was no motive."[29]

"I set hundreds of fires when I was a child. Many of them were not serious (fires in vacant lots), but the Fire Department had to be called. I also did this myself, I had no motive except I loved to cause the excitement. I *NEVER* got caught."[30]

He set fires in his home (Stratford Avenue).

His antisocial and destructive feelings apparently dominated most of his activities. "I was destructive, I killed and tortured animals. I killed my mother's parakeet Pudgy. She loved the bird with a passion. I killed thousands of bugs, tortured them, burned them glued them with rubber cement. I was killing maiming and destroying since I was a child."[31]

It seemed that he may have tortured animals because he himself felt tortured. He himself may have felt he had been treated like a bug.

How and why did he kill his mother's parakeet, the bird that was her pride and joy? Was he being hypocritical when he told me how much he loved his mother? Berkowitz was at first unsure of his motivation regarding Pudgy:

"It was I who killed him by giving him very small doses of kitchen cleaning materials that I found in abundance under the sink cabinet. After I started to put the poison in his food cups, within three weeks he was dead. My parents took him to the veterarian but the vet said he had developed some type of cancer. They never brought the bird home again because they (my parents) said it had to be destroyed. My mother never got another bird."[32]

I suggested to David that he resented all the attention Pearl gave Pudgy. He wrote me:

"Yes, you're very perceptive. I didn't like all the attention he was getting. My mom would spend hours messing with that stupid bird. She cleaned his cage and removed all his droppings. She washed his cage and constantly fed him. When I tried to touch him he would always snap my finger. He was nasty to me. We both hated each other. When my mom used to spank me, she would talk to Pudgy who used to have his cage in the living room and tell him how naughty I was. She did the same thing with our dog, Lucky."[33]

David thought of himself as the unquestioned favorite. When anything interfered with his status, as happened with the bird, he brutally removed the obstacle. His mother cried and wept and he wept with her. Nobody knew that he was the real culprit; he never told anyone that he had killed the bird. Sharing Pearl's sorrow over Pudgy's death, he played to perfection the role of innocent — a role that was to become his trademark.

And it became routine for him to steal whenever the opportunity offered itself.

"I stole from my parents often. Just nickels and dimes mostly. I'd rifle their piggy bank and my mom's purse. I always had plenty of candy money and money for baseball cards. I had a huge collection of cards too."

"The most I ever stole was a dollar bill, but I stole these bills pretty often. She never knew if a buck was missing. She used to leave her purse in the kitchen. Carefully, without upsetting anything, I would remove her change purse and pull out a single dollar bill. Carefully, I would place the small purse back in the pocket book, trying to place it in the exact same spot. It always worked. I feel bad about this. Sometimes, I felt good when I got away with it and I always did. I get pleasures out of my craftiness.

"I used to steal from my friends and their parents all the time. Sometimes I'd steal something that had no value, such as lipstick, paper clips, soap, a packet of thumb tacks, etc. I did feel good after I did it though. I can't understand why. When I got back to my room, I often just threw the stolen item away. This stuff had no value.

"My grandmothers were also often targets of my sneaky attacks. I frequently remember breaking up their boxes of matzoh. I used to crush their boxes of matzoh and saltine crackers just for the hell of it. They seemed to think that they got that way in the store. They never knew that I was [the] one who always crushed the products."[34]

Not to be detected in his wrongdoings, small or large, had become a central problem for Berkowitz. "A troublesome aspect of my life," as he says, "related to the crimes in general."

"When I broke windows and car antennas I did it alone. When I overturned a gallon can of white paint in the stairwell, I did it alone. This act caused a lot of damage and the super raised hell, but he never knew it was me. You see, I was coming down the stairwell of my building on Stratford Avenue, and several house painters were working in an apartment on the third floor. Apparently one of them left an almost full gallon of paint outside the apartment doorway. The top was off it, and then when I walked by, I felt a strong urge to turn the can over and let the paint spill over the hallway. So, listening carefully for noises in the apartment, alone and without anyone looking, I quietly turned the can over and went on my way."[35]

Berkowitz couldn't explain why he did it.

"I know of no motive. But I had a compulsion to do this and mess up the hallway. And this act was one of a multitude that I did throughout my life without any rhyme or reason. Also, I think I was about eleven or ten years old during this incident. Further, I didn't even know the person who lived in the apartment! . . .

"When I was truant from school it was the same thing. When I didn't go to school I either took long walks or stayed home watching television or merely spending aimless hours. Then at three thirty I'd telephone my father at his store to tell him that I just came home from school, even though I never went.

"Most of my friends did mischief from time to time. But it was nothing in comparison to my actions which they never knew about. Of course, I was careful not to tell anyone of my secret ventures into other neighborhoods to set fires, and to share my almost precious and joyful acts of thievery with others."[36]

Not being detected or even suspected gave him a feeling of power, he told me, even omnipotence. He had made himself invisible, a phantom. This may well have been one stimulus for his later murderous career: his early experience encouraged him to believe that he could get away with it without being discovered. At a very early age, David Berkowitz had come to feel he stood outside his family, outside the law, outside of society itself.

He had gone into great detail about his destructive activities. I asked: Had he never done anything good in his life? "Much to people's surprise," he answered, "I do have a 'good' side."

"I often gave to charity an amount much larger than what others would give. When the ladies would come around my apartment in the Bronx, I would often give five or ten dollars to their polio crusade while others only gave a dollar at the most. Doing this made me feel very good. When I gave I felt very humane and nice. I actually felt this.

"I did favors for several of the elderly tenants of my old Bronx building, such as carry out their garbage of go to the store for them. Their favorite store was Olinsky's, a supermarket on Lydig Avenue.

"In Yonkers, I gave the newsboy nice tips for my weekly deliveries of the local paper and a nice tip on Christmas. His name was Frank and he lived in the apartment next door with his sisters and mother. They were wonderful people. A rare breed."[37]

Hearing about the good side only reminded me of one of the most striking aspects of Berkowitz's personality — its duality.

"People think that I look honest but I'm not. I have an innocent face but I'm not at all innocent. I must admit that I do love my face. I mean I can fool anybody with it. It's above suspicion so to speak. My face, my lips and my blue eyes are like weapons which I sometimes use to my own advantage. I don't consider my facial features handsome. To me they're just innocent looking.

"... I was very aware of its usefulness during my crime spree."[38]

When I looked at Berkowitz, I was beginning to feel that I was seeing two faces.

3

ALWAYS ALONE

Murder often begins at home. The forces that molded a troubled youngster into the Son of Sam were generated in part by a web of family circumstances. The tragic fact that the people caught up in it were decent and well-intentioned cannot belie the fundamental importance of these early and intimate ties.

Richard David Falco was three days old when, in June 1953, Pearl and Nathan Berkowitz picked him up at the hospital and took him to their home at 1105 Stratford Avenue, part of the old Soundview neighborhood in the Bronx. They had made the adoption through a doctor. Nat was 43 and Pearl 37 — a rather late age to be taking on the upbringing of an infant whose origin they did not know.[1]

Of his father, Berkowitz had told me at our first interview at Kings County Hospital that "We didn't get along that good, but we didn't get along that bad." I suspected that it was more bad than good. He initially was not willing to pursue the subject. Nat told me: "David was much closer to my wife than to me. I spent most of my time with my business which was 15, 20 minutes away, worked 6 – 7 days a week."[2]

In fact, as David Berkowitz was to make clear in later exchanges with me, he was a very antagonistic son, with most of his hostility directed toward his father. He gave me a photograph of his parents dancing:

"The picture of my father and mother dancing brings back wonderful but sad memories. I cry sometimes when I think of how I had made my father's life so miserable when I was younger. Once I had abused (verbally) and tormented him so that he locked himself in the bathroom and sobbed like a child. I had no feelings for him back then. I was a cruel monster.

"Yes, what I say here is totally true. I had my father so saddened that he just charged into the bathroom, locked himself in and cried. I sincerely believe without a doubt that had he not done this he would have killed me. Of course I would have deserved it.

"After he locked himself in, my mother and I heard his sobbing all over the house. Next, my mother ran into the bathroom or rather to the bathroom door and was pounding on it. I think she feared that my father would hurt himself. But he eventually let her in and she consoled him. I, of course, got chased away into the next room. My mother chased me. I really can't go on with this because it is so upsetting."[3]

Unlike many other little boys, David disliked and resented his father because "he had my mother. He (father) made me leave the room when they wanted to be alone. I resented this."[4]

David was a rival to Nat. Often he talked to me about the love between his parents. "My adoptive parents were extremely close. I would say that they had a near perfect marriage with the exception of my father's job. This took a lot of his time away from me and my mom."[5] This incestuous rivalry is frequently a universal cause of the conflict between a boy and his father.

What interested David a great deal was their sex life.

"When I was a child and until I was nine or ten, I slept in the same room as my parents.

"I do remember sleeping in the small bed in front and about six feet away from them. But something happened and of this I'm sure. Every night, after we all went to bed, my father, after about a half hour, would come to my bed to ask me if I were asleep. Sometimes he would shine a small flashlight in my face. Then he'd ask if I were sleeping and go back to bed.

"Obviously, I wasn't always asleep. I do remember that if I was awake and replied to his question that he'd be angry. His anger must have frightened me because I became an expert at feigning sleep. He'd walk over to my bed, shine the small flashlight and ask the question. Often, his head was only inches away from my face but I kept my eyes closed and I lay still.

"He'd go back to bed and that's all I remember. Now that I understand it, I guess it was then that sex occurred. Honestly, I don't remember. I think I heard something, but I can't be positive. Anyhow, I'd remain motionless for several hours. Sometimes, if I had to urinate, I'd hold it in because I was afraid to move and make my dad angry. However, I never wet in my bed. . . .

"The light in the bedroom was always off with the exception of a small light by my bed which only illuminated my area."[6]

Nat wanted to make sure his son wasn't awake when he made love to Pearl. But the young boy, even when he was awake, heard no suggestion of intimacy. Apparently he repressed what he might have heard or seen, particularly because he himself unconsciously had designs on his mother. Only once did he say: "I guess I did hear voices and sounds from my parents' end of the bedroom, but I can't remember."[7] In his fantasy, he alone was her beloved.

When David was about ten years old, his father "purchased a convertible couch. So, both he and my mom moved into the living room to sleep. I had the whole bedroom to myself. From then on I slept alone."[8] Thinking he had prevailed upon his parents to give him their bedroom, this young boy must have been filled with a sense of power, and was perhaps aware of the fear he engendered in his parents.

Much stimulated by the sexual situation at home, sexual feelings, conscious and unconscious, came to play an important role in his mental makeup and his behavior.

"I saw my mother and father in the nude numerous times. When I was young, I went to Shorehaven Beach Club in the Clason Points section of the Bronx. I went from age 1 to age 17. Until I was 5 I shared a locker with my mother and her friend Bea Wyman. My mom used to take me into the shower and bathe me at the end of the day. So I saw her naked often. In fact, I saw hundreds of naked women. They were all over the place.

"When I reached age six, I started to share a locker with my father and his friend Mr. Leventhal. Now I saw my dad in the nude and also hundreds of other guys. However, I never saw my mother and father in actual embrace, nor have I ever seen them together in the nude."[9]

Four years before David was born, Pearl had had a breast removed because of cancer.[10] And when he was 11 she had another mastectomy. Recalling that he had seen her in the nude when he was young, I asked David how he felt about it.

"Truthfully, I never noticed my mother had only one breast. She always wore a heavy housecoat. As I told you before, I used to shower with her in Shorehaven Beach Club. But once I reached about age five I then went to the men's locker rooms with my father to shower. At age five I don't think I really knew what a breast was. But I do remember that my mother was always covered. She was very self-conscious about nudity and privacy. When I was growing up and when only my mom and me were in the apartment, she always locked the bathroom door so that I wouldn't intrude. We were alone, yet she bolted the bathroom door with the sliding bolt."[11]

He contradicts himself about his mother being nude or covered up. That he says at age five he didn't know what a breast was betrays his suppressed knowledge. His power of repression helped him to cope with his anxiety provoked by the breast situation.

In sharp contrast to this "forgetting," he remembers well a particular episode from before his fifth birthday. In the light of his later, adult behavior, it obviously made a deep impression on him.

"I will never forget the day that an elderly maintenance man walked into the locker area. The screams and shrieks were beyond belief. I realized then that a man, just one man alone, had tremendous power. He has tremendous power over the woman when he catches her off guard or in a compromising situation. I'm serious.

"When this guy walked into the lockers, all these women

started to run and scream. It was funny but also interesting."[12]

From this incident, the young Berkowitz learned that the element of surprise was something that could be used to gain the upper hand.

Charles and Ruth,* neighbors of the family, recall the young David Berkowitz. Their son had been friendly with him, and Charles too had taken a special interest in him, realizing that David's father didn't seem to have time for the boy. They were aware of the often silent, yet telling disaffection between father and son. Charles saw David as a "normal, good child."

"I would take the kids to a ball game, down to the gym. Several times we went mountain climbing. At one stage of the game he became interested in mountain climbing. So one day I took the two boys and we took a ride. We went to Bear Mountain. The three of us climbed up Bear Mountain. I'd take him to Shea Stadium to a ball game. I introduced him to the manager of the San Francisco Giants, who was a friend of mine — we were boys together. It was a little lark. They didn't believe that I knew the manager of the team, Charlie Fox. I said oh yeah. So we went down there and called him over and of course we talked. We were kids together. We came from the same block. And on Saturdays they used to have Father and Son day at the YMCA and I used to go downtown to 23rd Street and I'd take my son, and I would take David several times. He was very good at weight lifting. And they'd go swimming and things like that. So the boys were very close together. . . .

"As they got a little older they would go to this summer camp, it was a pool with athletic facilities there, and they would play some kind of ball game. David was always the winner. He taught my son to accept defeat. I think if they played 600 games in the season, David won 600 games."[13]

David's athletic prowess impressed Charles, and he suggested that the boy try out for the Little League team, but David resisted. Charles felt "the reason he was reluctant was the he was afraid of becoming a failure in front of people." But when he finally did join, he was the best ballplayer on the team.[14]

* Pseudonyms

Berkowitz was surprised when I told him what had been said about his excellence in baseball. He denied it adamantly.

"I don't think," he wrote, "I was 'very good,' but I played well enough to be chosen into all the neighborhood ball games.

"Sports was my life during those childhood and teenage days. School meant nothing to me and I spend my days in the classroom causing disruption and/or daydreaming. I couldn't think or concentrate about school studies — mainly because I didn't want to. I loved sports — all types — baseball, soft ball, punch ball, stick ball, slug, football, paddle ball, hand ball and tennis. My days spent at Shore Haven were filled with playing ball."[15]

It was his good luck that Charles often acted like a father to him while Nat was busy in his store. The strained and distant relationship between David and his father was in direct contrast to the ties between David and Pearl. "I called her 'Mom' . . . or 'Mommy.' . . . Pearl was my real mother, she made an impact on my life."[16]

Cousins on his father's side were a threat to the growing boy: "They excelled in everything. They had physical good looks. They had good marks in school, and their schools really were good. . . . I had an acne condition when I was young and I was fat. I had it until I was 18. I had difficulty getting together with girls. My cousins were popular — tall, slim, they had a lot of girlfriends."[17]

A strong sense of self — a genuine, healthy self-esteem — was conspicuously absent from David's personality as a child. He remembers he was frequently critizcized by his parents. "I wanted to have praise. Praise for heroism. Instead I got criticized," he later told me. "I never could meet their standards."[18]

Berkowitz found respite from all this unhappiness in long bicycle rides. In this *solitary* activity, he felt strong and independent. "All the kids had bicycles and often rode them but only around the neighborhood. I rode my bike all over N.Y."[19]

From his home in the southern end of the Bronx (Stratford Ave.) he used to ride all the way up to Armonk or Valhalla, which was right next to Kensico Dam (his favorite spot) or Tarrytown, New York. "Believe it or not," he said, "and I swear on my mother's grave, that I rode this distance almost every weekend by myself. Rye Beach was another of my favorite spots that I peddled to dozens of times a year.

"The furthest I ever traveled was to Armonk (New York), Cos Cob, Connecticut on U.S. Route #1.

"Just me and my bicycle — we were a team, I was once planning on riding my bike by myself to Montauk Point, Long Island. This, of course, would have been an overnight trip and I swear, I could have done it back then. My dad would have let me, too. Honestly, I was so mature in many ways, so grown up. I mean I could survive on my own. My dad trusted me and treated me like a man."[20]

Unhappy, lonely, obsessed with rejection and neglect, caught up in fantasies of self-aggrandizement, the teenage discovered another activity through which he could vent his feelings *and* develop some much-needed discipline, concentration, and self-control: the sport of mountain climbing, where one misstep can mean death. He writes:

"I was a lot different than other kids my age. I did different things — things other kids never dared to do.

"First, I climbed for the thrill of it and the challenge, huge, formidable cliffs. At the age of 14 or 15 I was an avid rock climber. I had a host of mountain climbing gear. I used to get on the Trailways bus and head up to New Paltz, New York, where the 'Shawangunk' mountain range is located. The 'Gunks,' as they were nicknamed, are located in the town of Gardiner, nine miles east of New Paltz.

"It was fantastic — that close walk with death — challenging God or fate. I used to bring a sleeping bag, food, equipment, climbing gear, etc. I climbed with Leon Greenman who once owned a very large Outdoorsman store on Spring Street in New York City. Plus I joined the Appalachian Mountain Club.

"When I scaled these cliffs — I mean I really did it — by myself on the end of a rope — I just loved it. I also loved to repell off the top. Repelling is sliding down backwards on a single rope.

"My dad never objected to my going rock climbing even though it was dangerous and could possibly cause my death should I have fallen. However, all my friends thought I was a fanatic and a nut. These 'Bronx Boys' couldn't understand my passion for the woods and nature. All they wanted to do was play ball. I did this too. But mountains were my true love."[21]

Whatever positive in this activity, such as love for nature, this mountain climbing seems to indicate in part Berkowitz's unconscious tendencies to want to hurt himself. He had an unconscious and conscious wish for death and his mountain climbing was, as he said, "that close walk with death — challenging God or fate," expressing an unconscious desire to harm himself which ultimately might lead to death.[22]

What kind of people were they who had adopted the baby David?

Berkowitz described Pearl's family as being fine people. Pearl had been extremely close to her parents, and her mother had moved into the building after the death of her husband. Pearl had two brothers,* Harry, now dead, and Ben who, as David says, "got me the job as a sheet metal apprentice and to whom [sic] and his wife I am very close."[23]

"Harry was the emotionally troubled one," said David.[24]

"My Uncle Harry," he went on to say, "I loved very deeply. He was such a wonderful, quiet and mysterious man. Rarely did he venture out of the house except to go for long walks. When he went walking he was gone for days. He loved the solitude and the mountains and this is where he went. Harry was a most amazing fellow. However, all his life he never had a friend. He was a total loner and a recluse. Uncle Harry died alone and was buried alone. He was friendless."[25]

It may well be that through his close relationship with Harry he learned to love nature, particularly the mountains. This particular relationship may also have sharpened his sensitivity to troubled people. With his impressionable mind he seems to have imitated Harry, perhaps picking up the same fears and anxieties.

From his aunts, Berkowitz learned that as a young girl Pearl

* Both names are pseudonyms

was extremely attractive. She was one of the younger girls in the neighborhood, and the men and boys would flirt with her. This, of course, made the older girls jealous. "They teased her and pulled her hair. They also did other things to torment her as would be expected from vicious children. My mother, I was told, often ran home crying. Her older brother often went to her aid and they were close companions."[26]

I asked Berkowitz whether Pearl was a flirt. "No," he answered. "I said that because she was very attractive, the boys in the neighborhood always made passes at her and gave her all their attention as opposed to the other girls who teased her out of jealousy."[27]

Pearl "went to college for a few years. But she never graduated. She fell in love with my dad (Nat) and she went off with him into the service. They both served together down south in an Army base. She was very devoted to this nation and to my father. I believe it was called the woman's army corps back then. She was assigned to a clerk's job and worked in an office. My father was a Master Sergeant. Because of his skill at keeping books and storing surplus, he was assigned to the Quartermaster Unit."[28]

A photograph of Pearl shows a handsome woman with high cheekbones, her attractively curved mouth turning to a smile, and welcoming eyes, in which one can feel some flirtatiousness and seductiveness. She was, according to Berkowitz, "an average dancer, but she always enjoyed dancing with me and my father. She was also very outgoing while my father wasn't. Pearl was often known as the life of a party. She wasn't shy and she had a sense of humor."[29]

Charles' wife Ruth, who had known Pearl since David's adoption, says: "We were very good friends. . . . she was almost like a sister to me, we were so close. . . . She didn't confide in me that much. But just closeness. . . . We liked each other and we played cards, we played mah jongg. . . . We'd see each other every day. . . . As to confiding with me about her private life, she didn't do that."[30]

One of the few favors Pearl asked of her friend Ruth had to do with David. Pearl didn't want him to attend Evander Childs

High School, the district school, because it lacked a good academic program. Ambitious for her son, she wanted him to go to Columbus High School on Pelham Parkway. She asked Ruth "if I could say that he lives with me, so he could get into that high school. So I said, of course, so he used my address."[31]

Ruth did not know whether Pearl was unhappy about not having children of her own; Pearl never talked about it. "We knew that he was adopted but we never mentioned anything to him. I don't know if that was good that Pearl told David that he was adopted. The adoption probably bothered him all his life."[32]

Young David regarded being an only child as a form of discrimination:

"I always begged my parents to get a brother and sister. I was the only one on the block who didn't have any brothers or sisters. My father told me: 'Mommy can't have any other children.' But I didn't understand it. . . . I always wanted someone."[33] He desperately needed company and attention.

As a young child, however, he actually did have "someone" — his mother. Pearl reflected the ambivalence of many parents toward their children: she feared as well as loved him. That she was an older mother, inexperienced with children, and forced to cope with this wily and intransigent boy, aggravated the situation. When in doubt, she overindulged. When David showed his hostility by smashing toys, she simply replaced them. The message to him was clear: she could be taken for granted.

A trip to the supermarket left some doubt as to who was taking whom:

"I used to love accompanying my mother on her food shopping trips. . . .

"I had her buying everything in the store. When I pointed to something that I wanted and she decided to say no, I'd just pout and/or throw a tantrum and get it anyhow.

"Best of all, I loved the sour pickles. I always managed to get me one. . . . They would have these pickles floating around in a big wooden barrel. I'd grab one, take a quick bite out of it, then my mom would have to pay for it — five cents."[34]

Her money could, to some degree, bribe him into obedience, even obsequiousness, but to buy love and affection was another matter. His lack of that affection for her notwithstanding, Pearl doted over the boy:

"Both my parents followed my growing up . . . and they also took an abundance of photos — especially home movies.

"Yes, they both fussed over me constantly. As you could see by those photos that I was dressed up and not in play clothes. This is because my *mom always made me wash and change clothes everytime a picture was taken.* She really cherished the photos and I remember her taking them to her marjon (not sure of spelling) meeting. . . .

"When the neighborhood women came over to the apartment to play, my mother always called me out of my room to meet the ladies. It was annoying but I know that she was only showing me off because she was proud of me and loved me. Of course I didn't see these reasons back then. All I knew was that it was annoying."[35]

Another of David's furtive activities involved food. The only thing he liked about Pearl's games were the snacks:

"My mother purchased all sorts of candies, fruits, nuts and cakes around the living room and in the kitchen. So I had the opportunity to nosh on all sorts of goodies. Another funny thing (I'm laughing now) was when I started to overeat all the snacks. My mother would scold me and tell me to stop eating. But all the other ladies would sympathize with me and then they would tell Pearl to let me be and to continue to nibble. So my mother would always relent."[36]

Endowed with a natural charisma, Berkowitz used it to his advantage. His charm and mischievousness appealed to these middle aged ladies as it appealed to his parents. His innocent-looking, pixie face helped him to get whatever he wanted.

The furtiveness surrounding his eating was entirely consistent with the furtiveness that surrounded most of his other activities:

"My nicknames, as sometimes said by my adoptive father, Nathan, are 'Sneaky, Snoop, and Spy.' I couldn't even get food from the kitchen when someone was in that room. I had to wait, despite hunger pains, sometimes an hour until the kitchen was vacated before I'd move in for a snack.

"This is peculiar I know. But I can't explain it. When I did go into the kitchen, I often crept in, then I would quietly open the ice box and gingerly remove the selected item. Like a phantom, I snatched one 'devil dog,' and careful not to upset the box, I rearranged the remaining cakes to make it appear that no one was there."[37]

He felt guilty over the excessive eating, which to him had become a ritual. Whatever was edible, he *had* to put in his mouth — incorporate into himself. When, at our first interview, at the prison ward of Kings County Hospital, I asked about his eating habits, he didn't reply. Instead, he announced, *"I always ate. I was very nervous. I had to eat."* All enunciated with distinct pauses between every word.

Any food in particular?

"I liked meat, cooked carrots. I didn't like potatoes."

"What about fish?"

"Yeah, halibut. But it has little nutritional value."[38]

David's anxiety about food was associated with two distinct fears. One would think that he ate as if he were afraid the food might get away from him. but this fear might also work in reverse — an unconscious fear that he might be eaten. And such feelings are not uncommon in children. In his case, guilt about his sexual desires for his mother and his hatred of his father may have helped to maintain and strengthen this fear. With a child's imagination, he always was willing to embellish his fantasies. For example, this fear of being overwhelmed to the point of being eaten, of being destroyed, comes out in his demon story. The polarity between these two fears was one source of his ambivalence.

The oral stage of emotional development lasts for the first year of a child's life; if the infant is either too frustrated or too overindulged during this period, some part of him will remain "stuck" in this stage for the rest of his life. We may find this in many adults who eat, drink, smoke, talk until the crack of dawn, or bite their nails. Such people have not outgrown their oral needs. They often are dependent, helpless, and need to be the center of attraction.

For David, uncertain about his origin, food provided security, love, and *immediate* gratification. To him, postponement of gratification became synonymous with rejection and pain. He *had* to "nosh on all kinds of goodies," because denial of that gratification was like a loss of love.

His fantasies of omnipotence from eating and incorporating the food into his body seemed already to have been at work during the first year of his life. We notice that behind his behavior as both child and adult were the feelings of a person who has been defrauded of what was rightfully his (in this case, his real parents), and concomitantly *had lost the love that should have been given him*. He was, unwittingly, always seeking this love.

Other traits, such as David's compliance and his secrecy, may have stemmed from the time when he was between one and two-and-a-half years of age — the anal stage of emotional development. During this time of toilet training he, like other children, had to learn self-control, self restraint, and to hold back. To the family and to the world, a person with anal traits may appear to be submissive and cooperative. In David's personality, co-operativeness translated itself into compliance and secretiveness, a trait which was to become predominant in his character.

People generally possess a mixture of oral and anal characteristics. The oral traits make them generous, kind, ambitious, self-righteous, cooperative, passive, calculating and willful. Anal people are cautious, thrifty, ambivalent, and orderly. They are also manipulative, impatient, rigid, perfectionistic, controlling, and cruel. While some of each of these traits are necessary for a mentally healthy development, in extreme form they can create a personality which is destructive to others and themselves.

Through frustrations and neglect, Berkowitz's childhood traits became exaggerated and entrenched. His oral traits, often sadistic in nature, were his avaricious appetite (as shown also in his being overweight), overeating leading to biting,* foul lan-

---

* His biting tendencies are further explored in the account of his relationship to dogs. See chapter 4.

guage, his desire for the limelight, and his indulgence in oral sex. His anal traits were his suspiciousness, hospitality, manipulation, ambivalence, impatience, cautiousness, control, and cruelty. All these were instrumental in establishing his emotional readiness for the brutal killing of innocent women. Eat or be eaten. Kill or be killed.

On my first interview at the Prison Ward of Kings County Hospital, Berkowitz had told me that as a child, he got into many fights. Yet, he added, "I didn't want to fight." Later he described how these fights happened:

"When I was a kid, I often got picked on for being Jewish. There were plenty of fights between me and the Italian guys, but they were the aggressive ones. And as a result, as a child I was very ashamed of being Jewish."[38]

His feelings of rejection and isolation because he was Jewish went very deep.

"I never felt Jewish. Whether I was in a synagogue or not — whether it was a holiday or not — I never felt Jewish. Rather, I rejected my Judaism because of all the ridicule I faced in school. There were many anti-Semitic remarks. Those Catholic kids were always passing nasty remarks about the Jews. To be with the crowd, I had to rebel against my own Jewishness. But I'm not proud of this.

"No, I never felt Jewish at my Bar Mitzvah. I tried to fast on Yom Kippur but without success. I fasted for about one hour. Then by seven in the evening, I was heading for the refrigerator. However, my parents never saw me take any food. I snuck into the kitchen and stole a knosh [*sic*]. They always thought I held out my fast until the morning at least."[39]

Did he have an anti-Jewish feeling because he was adopted? Was he rejecting the religion of his adoptive parents as a way of separating himself from them? David seemed anxious to reply:

"This may be true what you ask. I can't say for certain why I developed a dislike for being Jewish when I was a child. But I did, and my father knows this too, often ask my parents if my natural parents were Jewish. I remember asking this often. However, back then my adoptive parents assured me that I was totally Jewish.

"I also remember as a child that I felt proud to hang around with the Gentile boys. When I hung out and played ball with the non-Jews this caused my grandparents to get upset. My adoptive father's mother was always putting the Gentiles down. But I continued to befriend them and reject Judaism."[41]

I asked him if his mother observed the Sabbath.

"Yes, she lit these Sabbath candles faithfully every Friday evening and whenever a sacred Jewish holiday came about. I remember how she put a towel over her head, then opened up a tattered prayer book and quietly recited some verses. She did this as she was lighting the three candles and immediately after she finished. Obviously my mother was very religious as far as observing rituals.

"She also kept a kosher house and we had separate silverware for dairy and for meat. When she died my father gradually discontinued this practice as it was too confusing and inconvenient. As for my father, he never went for this candle lighting stuff. He is somewhat of an agnostic, and like me, he sees no value in religious ceremonies.

"I remember, too, that we ate baked potatoes often with meat. Me, I always liked butter on my baked potatoes. So when I tried to sneak some butter onto them, my mother screamed her head off. "No butter with meat, David!"

"It was kind of silly. If she saw butter on the potato which was on the same plate with the meat, she'd practically throw out the whole meal. What a waste."[42]

David went to Hebrew School and he had a Bar Mitzvah. This occasion was a catered affair with abundant food and drink. There was rock music. He recalled that he danced the "twist" with Pearl. David appeared happy and triumphant. He was the star.

On the surface he was in tune with the gaiety of the event — and of its solemnity. He had been in the synagogue — the House of God and prayer — that very same Saturday morning and had, according to the Jewish religion, recited the *Haftorah*. He had been blessed and had given a blessing. He had been inaugurated as a new member of the Jewish faith and as an adult in the Jewish community. All this, despite his confession that he never felt Jewish, whether in or out of the synagogue, or on the Jewish holidays, or, indeed, at his own Bar Mitzvah. Again we are reminded of the profound ambivalence of David Berkowitz's personality, the schism that divided his feelings from his actions.

Two months after his Bar Mitzvah, Pearl's cancer came back and she was hospitalized. Berkowitz gives this dramatic account:

"Mom and Dad were at a Chinese restaurant in Parkchester. I went to sleep at 11 o'clock and fell asleep. I woke up at 8 A.M. and went into their room and saw that it hadn't been slept in. I called my neighbors and nobody knew anything until about 11 o'clock, when I learned that my Mom had fainted and had been brought to a hospital. They took tests on her. She stayed there for two or three months. I couldn't see her because I was under age. This was about two months after my Bar Mitzvah and she was transferred then to the terminally ill ward at James Ewing. And I went there, everyone could go there. At that time I was able to see her. I never can forget the way she looked. Previously she had been beautiful. But she was now hairless, all features gone, distorted. She was pale and in pain. Hair was almost gone. All puffed up. Her face looked like a balloon. Her arms were as thick as logs. There was a smell."

Berkowitz was not told about the seriousness of her illness until she was actually dying. He appeared visibly shaken, though, while describing her condition to me. Then he stopped talking, the pain of the memory still lingering within him. He looked pale, his eyes sad, his mouth drawn. When he was able to continue, he said that "Pearl was in a cancer ward. All dying patients around her. I had never seen anything like it; screaming and moaning and pleading to God, like a sick chorus of death: 'Please God, please Jesus, Oh God help me.' They didn't even know what they wanted, begging to God in agony."[43]

His voice faltered. His eyes were filled with tears. Suddenly he burst out: "This made a terrible impression on me. My mother wasn't as bad as the other ones, yet she died before them."

"My mother was cognizant of me. She saw me, while the other

patients were delirious. She was aware of what was going on around her, however, she died before all of them. She didn't know she was going to die. She said to me, 'When I get better I'll take better care of you.' She loved me and I loved her."

Tears were rolling down his face. He went on:

"I go to her grave all the time. Since Dad remarried he never goes to her grave. I resent it. I went four or five times a year and cleaned up the grave."

By now he was sobbing loudly.[44]

David Berkowitz had lost his anchor in life. His father told me that David "cried a lot at her funeral."[45] Ruth and Charles recall that "he was struck hard by it," but add that "he must have cried, but not outwardly."[46] I couldn't help recalling the ambivalent feelings he had expressed about his mother in our first interview — that she was "nagging," and "sometimes a pest," and that her death left him both "happy and sad."

Ambivalence notwithstanding, his mother's death left him angry and rootless. His father took him on a long trip to New Paltz and Lake George, N.Y. They were together for about 14 days, but on returning to the city his loneliness intensified.[47] Nobody took care of him; he was completely alone. His father was preoccupied with his store; and to make things worse, their relationship had deteriorated even more.

In 1970, they moved to Co-op City, the huge housing development in the Bronx. Berkowitz was upset that the "girls in Co-op City didn't find me attractive. I began to hate girls and wanted to join the Army." Before he enlisted, however, he became an auxiliary fireman and an auxiliary policeman at the 45th Precinct. He was thus able to partly fulfill his dream of being a hero in uniform.

In the spring of 1971 his father married a woman by the name of Mary who had a 25-year-old daughter, Carol (both are pseudonyms). On the surface Berkowitz appeared to accept his father's remarriage, but in fact he was very unhappy about it. Nat told Ruth that after he remarried, "David used to go into his room and play records all day long. Never came out to talk."[48]

Charles said that Nat's second wife was "very nice. He seemed happy; he was unhappy that he didn't get along with David. It looked like they [Nat and David] were going to separate because he was going to Florida and David didn't want to go, he was going to stay up here. That made him feel unhappy, but he had his life to lead."[49]

Berkowitz enlisted in the Army in 1971. He wanted to "die for a cause." Toward this purpose he signed up with the infantry. He was, he says, "fanatically patriotic." That he might have wanted to die should come as no surprise. But there were also other reasons for his enlisting.

The depression caused by Pearl's death was profound. He felt something important go out of him. "After Mother's death I lost all feelings and emotions. . . . I lost the capacity to love."[50] He thought that perhaps the military would supply the kind of support that would allow him to feel human.

For David, the uniform had a huge symbolic importance. In giving him an increased sense of self-importance, it enabled him to leave his father's house. And the Army offered him a substitute for the family that had disintegrated after Pearl's death.

Berkowitz had hoped to be sent to Vietnam so he could perform heroic deeds. Instead, he was shipped to Korea and never saw combat. Bored (although he managed to find some pleasures), he claimed to have had the sexual favors of a number of women and to have used marijuana, mescaline, and amphetamines. He also claimed ten LSD trips, taking only half the amount that others took. (The half dosage may suggest a fear of losing control.)

Berkowitz stayed in Korea from December 1971 to January 1973, at which time he was sent to Fort Knox, Kentucky. His military records show that on March 9, 1972, he was caught stealing food in the mess hall. He was also twice cited for not moving with his unit when he was supposed to.

From Korea he wrote to his father at least twice a month. In these letters he often mentioned an officer with whom he had a great deal of trouble. Nat Berkowitz has told me that his son soon lost his initial "gung ho" attitude toward the military,[51] and this apparently was what led to his problems with the officer. Nat feared that in a combat situation, David might try to kill his superior; his son had, in fact, expressed a fear of being court martialled. It occurred to me that he unwittingly substituted the officer, the authority, for his parents, who had always criticized him for his wrongdoings, and for which he fantasized punishment. The military equivalent of this would be court martial. His court martial fantasy might be yet another expression of his fear of abandonment which he may have felt as punishment, reminding him of his being neglected by his real parents, Pearl's death, and Nat's prospective move to Florida.

On March 24, 1973, he was given a general rating. He was found to have "been in this unit for over 1½ years and has proved himself to be an outstanding and dependable soldier. He is enrolled in an education program to better himself and improve his performance."[52] While one might question the Army's inability to see through his behavior, it must be stressed that David always put his best foot forward when he was under scrutiny.

At about the time of this evaluation, Berkowitz began to attend a Baptist Church in nearby Louisville. "All the sermons were about demons (!), sin, hell, eternal damnation, etc." he later wrote to me. "They had a bad effect on my life and mind."[53] His description of his religious activity suggests a frenetic attempt to escape from reality, from his own real trouble.

"At Beth Haven Church I enrolled in every program. I went to church on Sunday, getting up at 6:00 A.M. I stayed in church from 9:00 A.M. until 10:00 P.M., all day Sunday. I went to the Wednesday night service, the Thursday "soul-winning" outing, the Friday night meetings, etc. I listened to religious broadcasts constantly—seven days a week. I read dozens of religious books. I was enthralled with the doctrine of the Apocalypse — the end of the world and the ever-lasting punishment of sinners. "Hell" fascinates me. I spent my days telling my peers and superior officers of the need to be "saved" and the tragic increase in sexual immorality and permissiveness of our day."[54]

Berkowitz began to proselytize in the streets. He seemed bent on converting the world. But, as usual, what he really wanted was not what he said he wanted. His real wish was that his prospective converts (especially women) "would refuse to accept Christ and thus suffer even more in hell for their deliberate rejection of the Gospel. . . . I just wanted to see the men get to heaven," he wrote to me. "They're all hard working, clean cut men, patriotic men. Who the hell needed those sluts, those go-go dancers. Too many women in heaven would spoil it."[55]

What did he need women for, anyway? As he said "at 5:00 P.M., when the work day ended, I couldn't wait to get back to my room in the barracks and masturbate."[56]

As a preacher, as with many other things, David was a failure. If he ever did save a soul, nobody knows.

Berkowitz's frantic search for something to hold onto, something which could give his life some direction, and his failure to find it, was devastating to him. He felt guilty for having let himself be baptized, and angry at those who had persuaded him to take such a step. Living in a duality of heaven and hell, and with all his antisocial acts weighing on his mind, he had now become more guilty and depressed. He was afraid he was going to be punished for the ill deeds he had committed in reality — and in fantasy. As Berkowitz himself explained: "When I worshipped God, it was out of terror."[57]

Nat Berkowitz, now all the family David had, was upset by his son's conversion. For his part, David's mixed feelings about his father became sorted out with the passage of time. A letter he wrote to Nat from Korea indicated the problems these feelings created for David. He felt an enormous need to reassure his father of his love for him; yet the language of the letter is inflated, as if his sentiments were not genuine. A range of feelings — love and hate, guilt and innocence, anger and well-being, reality and fantasy — all merge into a basic confusion and chaos, and yet a sense of candor:

Dad, although I'm your only son, you must admit we have never been close. Actually, it's all my fault. I mean before I was just too stubborn and immature, Dad. I know I often hurt you but I didn't know better. I didn't mean to do all the things I did because I've always loved you and Mommy. I just didn't know how to say it. I know I was adopted, but I'm grateful for you because you gave me all you could. The love you and Mom gave me was more than I ever deserved.

When you married Mary, I was very happy although I never expressed it. I was cruel to her. I don't know why. I'm really very very grateful to her because she has given you a new life. After Mom died you became a vegetable, Dad. I felt sorry for you because you didn't deserve it.

. . . .

I'm glad that you enjoy life. You should, because you deserve it. You have really been a good father. You've worked hard and done your share.

. . . I just can't explain my ideas and philosophies to you. You wouldn't understand. It's all too deep. I feel like a saint sometimes. I guess I'm kind of one. Dad, believing in God is wonderful.

It's very hard for me, Dad. The lifers don't understand me. I'm just not army stuff anymore.

Well, I'll make out okay. I got this thing called faith.

To be honest with you, I have never really told you anything about myself. I really can't now. But just trust me, please. Everything's fine (not really). I hope to see you soon. Just be happy and please try to forget about me, Dad. Make believe you don't have a son please. It's better this way because we may not see each other for a long time.

I hope things are okay in the store. I'm sorry that I can't live up to your expectations. I'm sorry that I'm nothing in society, that is I feel sorry for you because you don't see my point. I'm happy with the way I see things. It's wonderful.

You know Dad, with you and Mary together you may as well be honest with yourself. You know you can be just as happy with yourselves, without me around. I've been a burden to you all your life. Well, I won't be anymore.

I've been too much trouble to you all along and I'll be even more trouble with you now. So please try to forget me Dad, please it will be easier on you. I'm very content with my thoughts. Peace to you.

Love to you.
Love all of you.

Sincerely,

Dave[58]

Following his discharge from the Army in June 1974, Berkowitz lived briefly with Nat and Mary, but it did not work out. He perceived Mary as a threat. He was very suspicious of this new graft on the family tree. He felt the need to check up on Mary to make sure his father had made a good match. "Nothing," he says, "missed my inspecting eye. I do have to make it clear, though, that there was nothing of a fetish here. I mean I never fondled her panties or anything.

"In fact, after I snooped in her dresser drawers I immediately washed my hands . . . my only interest was to check out her personal papers, books, bank book, photos, letters, etc. I did want to ascertain her motive in marrying my Dad and to make sure that there were no other men in her life. I didn't trust her one bit."[59]

His resentment against Mary was understandable. She had invaded his territory and had taken Pearl's place. His overt approval of his father's remarriage was not convincing. He merely echoed what was expected of him. a compliant son's concern with his father's unhappiness.

There were other factors which added to his resentment. After marrying Nat, Mary brought her 25-year-old daughter, Carol, into the family. Carol was smart and had many friends. She was held up to him as a model of good behavior against which he was to be measured. Not only did David perceive his father's remarriage as an *apparent* rejection and abandonment of him, but he was now threatened by two women who dominated his home. As his feelings of insecurity grew, he blamed Nat. Angry and rejected, Berkowitz began to move away from the place he had known as home.

In the autumn of 1974, Berkowitz began to attend Bronx Community College, working briefly as a cab driver in order to support himself. An old friend remembers him at this time as "quiet" and "friendly." "We used to meet him on the corner. He was good company. He was reliable. Often he would laugh to himself." "Berky," as his friend called him, "used to disappear for a few days at a time." When asked where he had gone, he would reply, "I took a walk."[60]

In January 1975, Berkowitz moved into a building on Barnes
Avenue in the Bronx. Fay Stick, who characterized herself as the
"Official Mayor" of the building, recalls seeing him frequently.
She said, "I know everyone, so I talk to people. I like people
very much. The day Berkowitz moved in, the door was open. I
walked in. His father was in the kitchen. The apartment had a
large room and a kitchen. I saw David come in and I wished him
good luck. I was told that he was a college boy in Bronx Community College. He looked very pleasant and that was it. I saw
David many times, whether in the lobby or in the elevator when
I was with him. He had a large laundry bag with him, coming
or going. Whenever I saw him, he was immaculately dressed,
very clean . . . a chubby, kind young boy, blue eyes, very good
looking, very, very pleasant."[61] Another friend of his, however,
saw a shadow behind this pleasant façade. He remembers Berkowitz as being "in his own world, preoccupied with himself."[62]

Attending college, holding down a job, living in his own apartment, David Berkowitz took on the appearance of an adult. On
the surface it seemed that the disturbed childhood might be put
aside for at least a measure of stability and that he would be
able to function reasonably well. But below the placidity was
the maelstrom. And he was about to release the maelstrom.

4

PROLOGUE TO
MURDER: SEARCH
FOR MOTHER

Who was David Berkowitz really?

Adopted children, without exception, have in their innermost soul strong fantasies about finding their real parents, the biological family to whom they can give their love. Because being adopted is a circumstance not of their own making, they often withhold love from their adoptive parents; they are saving it for the true parents. Their love and allegiance are divided between the family that has adopted them, and the "real" parents they have created in fantasy. Thus, ironically, adopted children frequently harbor hostility (as well as love, if their upbringing is gratifying) toward the people who took them in.

Such was David's case. His loyalty, like so many of his other emotions, was painfully split.

In one of our first interviews David said that he was about six or seven when Nat and Pearl told him he was adopted. Nat, however, told me that David learned about it before his third birthday. He was told that his mother had died in childbirth, and that his real father was unable to take care of him. Having told him once, the Berkowitzes thereafter avoided the subject. David picked up their signal, and although the topic was always on his mind, he brought it up only when he was bothered.

David recalled being "confused and surprised" by the information. His confusion really centered, however, around the meaning of adoption and its consequences. No child likes to have a mother and father who are not of the same flesh and blood as he. He intuitively feels that something is wrong. But why talk about it? Thoughts can be annihilated with words.

Hating being an adoptee, David looked more than once at Pearl and Nat, and wondered what his natural parents looked like. What had he inherited from them? From whom had he gotten his secretiveness, his black hair? Who had bequeathed him his blue eyes? The situation obsessed him. Was he trying to figure out the interaction between heredity and environment, between nature and nurture, between original and aftereffects? Of course he didn't use these terms.

That David learned about his adoption before he was three is significant. If adopted children are told at an appropriate age, 7 – 9 years old, the majority of them assimilate the information about their origins, and mature with few problems. But adopted children who have been told too early often feel shameful, anxious, and confused. They may show hate and rage, and often establish poor family relationships and retreat into an intense fantasy life. Frequently they are troubled and distrustful, with their intelligence disturbed.[1]

Why couldn't David "belong" to his adopted parents? The causes go back to earliest childhood. During the first three years of a child's life, mother and infant are merging in a unique symbiosis. The infant is dependent on her for the gratification of all his needs, physical and emotional. During the course of normal development, this symbiosis is then gradually attenuated — during three stages of what Margaret Mahler has called "separation-individuation."[2] During this time, the mother begins to cue, prompt, and encourage the child toward the formation of *his own individuality,* and toward *emotional separateness.* Although still dependent on mother, the child, by the culmination of this process, should be able to sense himself as a separate individual. This rapprochement period lasts from 1½ to 2½ years of age.

What happened to David was that long before he was actually told he was adopted , he had already sensed it — probably in part from unthinking exchanges between Nat and Pearl in his infant presence. This emotional shock prevented him from being able to rely on his mother to help him maintain his psychological balance during the critically sensitive time of emotional separation. As a result, the process was never properly completed, and mother and son failed to make the separation. This failure led to a lack of understanding, or alliance, between them, and little or no ability on the part of the child to accept his parents. Separation anxiety became one of David's predominant emotions, which in its wake carried a deeply unresolved relationship between child and mother — the pull between them manifesting itself in their Oedipal relationship. . . . All this unresolved conflict was to make the adult David intolerably vulnerable to the emotional problems normally encountered in the course of a life.

How this showed itself will be clear if we recall young David's behavior with Pearl. While wanting to be on his own and asserting his independence, he was nonetheless extremely dependent on her. He was willful, obstinate, attention-seeking and aggressive — then, alternately, meek, clamoring for her good graces, desperately needful of her, and fearful that he would lose her. The foundation of his behavior was not love. It was anxiety, uncertainty, fear.

Although unable to show genuine love, Berkowitz always feared losing it. This fear, plus resentment at the dependency it caused, engendered a constant anxiety that was never far from his conscious mind. At an age when he was unable to differentiate between fantasy and reality, he had learned of his adoption. Growing up with two sets of parents — one fantasized, the other real — he lived in two different worlds simultaneously. This conflict provided the paradigm for the ambivalence that pervaded so much of his life. Much of the two-faced, hypocritical, manipulative aspects of his character were probably rooted in this situation.

The lack of empathy between David and his adoptive parents was also of crucial importance. His response to Pearl's death was striking. "I was happy and sad," he told me. "Pearl was a pest, sometimes she was nagging." He felt she had intruded on him, watching and spying on him. He felt he wasn't trusted. She knew nothing about him, his anger, or his alienation; and he didn't understand how she could be so possessive of him. Overpowering his sense of self, there was little if any emotional understanding and responsiveness; little if any empathy between them.

This lack of empathy was much of the foundation of narcissism — self-love — in David, who expected and demanded that everyone fulfill his wishes. Having no independent sense of self-love, he was seeking this self through the use and abuse of others for personal benefits. Unable to establish any lasting relationship because he was unable to identify with others, he craved admiration, and used his charm and seductiveness to mask his insensitivity and cruelty.[3]

Because of the ambivalent relationship with his adoptive parents, and the lack of family empathy, Berkowitz was not able to negotiate the rocky passage to adulthood. Yet, in his fantasy, he clung with unusual tenacity, and not abnormally, to some hope of change in his life situation.

We all need our fantasies to give us hope; if we lost them, something inside us will die. And David held on to his fantasy. But when, in December 1974, Nat Berkowitz announced that he planned to move to Florida, all David's old fears of abandonment, rarely far from the surface of his consciousness, were once again aroused. Now he was impelled to turn to the fantasy that had sustained him all his life. He would try to find his real family.

"I found a pamphlet about The Adoptee's Liberty Movement Association" (ALMA — an organization dedicated to helping adopted children find their real parents) he told me, when I later asked him how he had traced his real mother.

"And then?"

"I called them, got an application form, and paid the membership fee of twenty dollars," He paused and looked at me. Leaning toward me, "I had a deep desire to know my natural family, but [stressing every word] I had absolutely no knowledge of how I should search for my family. About a month later I attended my first meeting in the auditorium. There were several hundred people. Later we were divided into small groups — 12 to 20 people around a table; I didn't know anyone. I told them I would like to look up my natural father. 'Why not your natural mother?' they asked. My mother, I said, had died at my birth. They laughed. What was so funny about that? I thought. Hadn't they heard of such a thing before? They then explained that they laughed because every adoptee is told the same story. Later on I confronted my (adoptive) father about it, and he acknowledged the falseness of the story. He said 'She just couldn't take care of you. She was poorly off financially.'

"Mother didn't really die. She just couldn't take care of me."

Berkowitz had become quiet. He moved around on his chair, uneasy. Pulling himself together as if aided by an unseen force, he slowly spoke.

"I always believed she had died, and I felt guilty, torn apart."

"I thought I was responsible for her death."

As he spoke, he wrote down the words on a long yellow pad with a firm hand. He had become silent. I was waiting. Then:

"I always believed she had died, I felt guilty about it, I had that feeling constantly, that I somehow caused her death. My life had been chosen, and that somehow I was responsible for her death."[4] Tears came to his eyes. He sat, self-absorbed, as if experiencing his enormous guilt for having caused his mother's death.

Previously, at our very first interview, when he had described how he went about finding her, I had complimented him. But this time, when he responded to my praise with indifference, I began to suspect that finding his mother hadn't been everything he had fantasized it would be.

A few days later, he wrote me:

"You see, Dr. Abrahamsen, it was at this time, and never until then that I first realized *I was an accident, a mistake, never meant to be born — unwanted.* I always believed my adoptive parents' story that my mother died while giving birth to me and that my natural father put me up for adoption because he had no choice. He wasn't able to care for me without his wife.

"The previous story, while seemingly truthful, caused untold guilt for me during my childhood until age 22. It caused me guilt because I always believed that I had somehow been responsible for Betty Falco's death. But she wasn't really dead after all."[5]

David Berkowitz's feelings about the phony story are, to this day, typical of many of his feelings about his adoptive parents:

"I wasn't angry at the Berkowitzes for telling me the 'death' story. They sincerely meant well. They were also told to say this, and after all, numerous other adoptees were told similar things. So, as I said before, I wasn't angry with the Berkowitzes."[6]

This statement has the same quality as all his other statements about people who were central to his life. His denial of negative feelings may be consciously sincere, but the statements are not credible.

This sudden disclosure of the truth about his real mother had the same effect as a lighted match on a powderkeg. A desire to find her exploded within him.[7] His need was immense and immediate. He embarked on a feverish, compulsive hunt.

David, determined to find his roots, worked frantically, almost hysterically, during late 1974 and 1975 to reach his blood relatives. At last he would even the score. At last he would feel equal to all those people who had real parents. At last he would feel emotionally secure. His search expressed his burning desire to make reality match fantasy. No matter how much he tried to understand his mother's reasons for giving him up at birth, more than anything he wanted to confront her with his outrage, to take her to task.

He was aware of the huntlike quality of his undertaking: "There was something deeper than just searching for my 'natural' family. I mean there were hundreds of ALMA members who were searching too. However, I don't think very many of them sought out their roots like I did. I had totally devoted myself to that hunt. It took everything out of me and I worked around the clock.

"In my hunt, I divorced myself from all other cares, except the basic ones. I neglected my studies and just spent my time running down leads and day dreaming what it would be like to see my natural family and what they looked like.

"Finding my mother was a necessity, an extreme one, that I cannot fully explain. Obviously, it was more than just locating her, it was much more."[8]

A copy of his "David Berkowitz" birth certificate gained him access to information at the Manhattan Bureau of Records. There he discovered that his real name was Richard Falco. He called Nat in Florida, who said he didn't remember the name, but authorized David's uncle to go to the family safe deposit box, get the real birth certificate, and deliver it to David. At this point he recalled that David had a half sister, and told him so.

The birth certificate listed his parents as Betty and Tony Falco, his birthplace as Brooklyn. At last, a real lead.

David called all the Falcos in the current Brooklyn telephone directory but did not find the one he sought. Discovering a Betty Falco in the Staten Island book, he drove to her house and rang her doorbell. She was not the right person, and she was not pleased to see him. In fact, she "almost called the cops."

An ALMA counselor suggested he consult the old phone books at the New York Public Library. The 1965 Brooklyn book listed a Betty Falco, but the listing appeared only for three more years. Following a hunch, he called information and asked for a Betty Falco at that address. He was told that the number was unlisted.[9]

Taking a chance, "I went," he said, "to the Brooklyn address with a Mother's Day Card." "I couldn't find her on the broken building directory. But I found the name Falco on a mailbox."[10] On the card he had written, "You were my mother in a very special way." He signed it R. F. "Then," he goes on to say, "I placed the letter which contained my telephone number in the mailbox."[11]

"I still wasn't certain that this was the Falco I was looking for

— remember the tremendous lead in Staten Island which suddenly dissolved."

"Several days later the woman in whose mailbox I left the letter called me. After questioning her, I discovered she was the person I was searching for."[12]

When I interviewed Betty Falco, she confirmed that she had found a card in her mailbox the day after Mother's Day (5/12/75), signed "R. F." Not knowing who it was, she called her daughter, who at once guessed who it must be. That he signed the card with the initials R. F., and not his legal ones, D. B., may have been another indication of his divided loyalty and identity. When, several days later, she called him, she was surprised to feel that she could recognize his voice. She became excited, almost hysterical with joy.[13]

Berkowitz could not fully grasp the reality of it all. Was he really, finally going to meet his mother? He was to meet her at the apartment of Betty's daughter, Barbara.* What if only Barbara were there? Suppose Betty didn't like him? What if couldn't stand her? He couldn't back out now! What should he tell Nat? That he made a mistake? He was going to meet his family! Should he kiss them, hug them, shake their hands? He had known too much fear, too much being alone. Too much not knowing anyone he could call his own flesh and blood. He had suffered loneliness every day and every night, but now he was going to know the truth! Nervous and excited, he had no idea what was in store. With his wild imagination he had created a whole new world for himself, and for this he cannot be blamed. We all try to create lives that are attuned to our needs and sensibilities. What we cannot have or fashion in reality we make up for in fantasy.

This is what Berkowitz did too. Maybe, he thought, he should have been satisfied with what he had. But now, on the threshold of meeting his real mother and his sister, it was too late to turn back. The existence he had lived until now — he could hardly

---

* Berkowitz's half sister. A pseudonym.

call it a life — had come to an end. This was another life, one rooted in reality.

Berkowitz seesawed back and forth; his casual statement that "by the end of the week I was on my way to meet my natural family for the first time" was infinitely more simple than the actual experience was. In fact, he approached the momentous meeting with tumultuous feelings. This encounter was to be the culmination of his life-long dream.

In one of our early interviews, I had asked Berkowitz to describe his real mother. He cast his eyes down, as if afraid of what I might see in them. Then, at last having thought of an answer, he looked up and burst out with a triumphant, hearty laugh: "She is like a Jewish mother." He went on: "— average looking. When she was young, she was good looking. She used to be a professional dancer in the Ziegfield Follies."[14]

This noncommittal reply to the question had given me this basic information: the historic meeting with Betty Falco had been a crushing blow, an unbelievable disappointment. Later, in a letter, he described the meeting in detail:

"I suppose I was fearful of being rejected, that I was the one that they wouldn't like. This didn't happen, however. Yes, I looked forward to meeting her.

"The first time I saw her was at my sister's house. This is where we had the first meeting. My sister's house was clean and simple looking. The furniture was middle-class with plastic covering on the sofa and club chairs to extend their life to the fullest.

"My mother appeared to me to be a little on the heavy side, with her hair done but in disarray. In other words, she tried to do something with it, something cute and neat, but failed miserably. This was when I first met her. Lately she has a better hair style. She was plain looking and I was disappointed about this. She certainly wasn't as pretty as Pearl.

"Of course Betty was nervous but I was too.

"Her clothing was neat and I could see that she had carefully manicured herself for the first meeting. Actually, she looked out of place and comical. Her dress was ill-suited to her. It was a low-cut dress that left the tops of her breasts exposed and exposed even more when she bent down. She also wore too much perfume.

"All in all, she was nervous, friendly, cordial, shy, but ordinary looking.

"If I remember correctly, my mother greeted me with a kiss and hugged me shyly. It was a nice get together — friendly and amiable but clumsy and awkward.

"The first thing she started to do was apologize for giving me away for adoption. She also commented on the way I looked and seemed pleased that I appeared healthy.

"We sat on the couch in [Barbara's] apartment for quite some time and talked casually."[15]

What went through his mind when he first saw her? His thoughts raced. He was here because she was his mother. She bore him. He grew inside her. She brought him into the world! How was it when he was born? Did he lie on her stomach? Did he get her breast?

It preyed on his mind when he learned that she had given him up for adoption while keeping Barbara. Angry feelings welled up in him.

Betty talked to her son about herself. As a young bride, she and her husband Tony Falco (her maiden name had been Rebecca Broder) had operated a fish store in the Williamsburg section of Brooklyn. Tony had left her after only a year;* he ran off with another woman — the widow of the store's previous owner. After Falco left (he was never heard from again), Betty took up with a man named Joseph Klineman.[16] Thirteen years later, in 1953, David was born.

Berkowitz was staggered. Tony Falco — listed on David's birth certificate as his father — was not his father at all! Barbara, his half-sister, was the only child of her marriage to Tony Falco.

What a hoax! Using the name Falco on his birth certificate, when Klineman, her lover, was his real father! Rejected on two

---

* Betty later told me it was after four years.

counts! Not only was he illegitimate, he got a fake name on his real birth certificate! He didn't even get his real father's name!

Later, I asked him to tell me more about his initial reactions to his mother. His reply:

"For your question about my mother, no, it isn't the least bit painful to talk about her. I think my first reaction was one of disappoinment. I don't know what I expected. I had fantasized a beautiful woman. But all I found was a totally ordinary person. There is nothing about her which stands out. She was a nervous and frightened little woman. I felt sorry for her. But she is a kind and friendly person who has been savaged by a lifetime of extreme guilt. Everything she says and does has an apology at the end of it and at the beginning. She is a chronic apologizer. 'I'm sorry, I'm sorry.' I hear this over and over. Every letter she sends has an apology in it. 'I'm sorry for this. I'm sorry for that,' etc.

"No, I wasn't shocked. I wasn't scared. I was disappointed."[17]

Despite the anticlimax of the meeting, and the crushing news about his real father, David's finding his real mother was a considerable achievement. While there are no statistics showing how many adoptees succeed in finding their biological parents, we do know that their numbers are small, particularly because of the emotional and legal obstacles they encounter. Several states have stringent laws specifically designed to hinder such reunions, although the State of New York *now* encourages them. Berkowitz told me that many in his group had given up looking because it was too much work and took too much time. He was an exception. The singlemindedness of his purpose gave him strength and perseverance.

His anticipation of meeting his mother had been overwhelming, and his disappointment when he saw her proportionately frustrating. But his disappointment had nothing to do with her physical appearance. Nor did it have much to do with her personality. Berkowitz could not have been satisfied with any mother he found, no matter that she might look like Elizabeth Taylor and behave like Mother Teresa. The reason was, simply, that she had given him away, a matter which could not be forgiven. And, to add insult to injury, it had been done because he had been born illegitimately.

"Obviously my adoption," as Berkowitz himself said, in a classic understatement, "caused me mental and emotional problems." His feelings of shame, guilt, and hopelessness about his origins turned into a saga of struggle and vanished hopes.

"I still, to this day, have negative feelings for my mon, Falco. Despite her nice and friendly ways, I don't have it in me to totally forgive her. I told her when I first met her and a great many times afterwards that I forgave her. But this isn't really the case. . . .

"I went through too much with this adoption business to simply say "all is forgiven, Mom." I had so much agony over the thoughts that I somehow caused her death. So many years I believed the story about my mother's dying at birth. I believed that my father (whoever he was) gave me up for adoption because he couldn't handle me by himself. However, I believed that my father (my natural father) had nothing but hatred for me (because the doctors let me live instead of her). Of course I found out that this story wasn't true. My mom didn't die. It was all a hoax. Still, I lived with this guilt for so very long. I lived the story as if it were true. I mean I retained this death guilt for so long. It's hard to get rid of it.

"And as I told you before, when I found out that Betty really didn't die, then I was relieved in one sense, but upset in another. Then the question came up as to why I was adopted. I had to find out. I had to find out someone from my real family. I needed family real bad—a mystical and perfect family—a blissful family—a perfect relationship. Of course this wasn't to be. I guess this was one pathway that eventually led to murder. My dream family didn't exist. It was my last hope."[18]

I wanted to talk with David's mother Betty, to hear about her reaction to her newly returned son and to learn first-hand what kind of a life she had had.

Until Berkowitz was 22 years old (in 1975), she had nothing to do with him except to give him life and deliver him to his adoptive parents. Still it would be informative if I could learn what kind of people she and David's father, Joseph Klineman, were.

After long delays, and with David's help, I was able to locate her. On the phone, as we arranged for the interview, she sounded most friendly and anxious to talk to me. A few days later, in July 1980, she came to my office. About 5 feet tall, dressed in blouse and pants, nice face, blue eyes similar to those of her son, she confirmed what he had told me about her marriage with Tony Falco, her daughter Barbara, and that Tony had left her for another woman.

As to her own background: her father was born in Austria-Hungary and her mother in Poland. They had met in the United States, and Betty, one of nine brothers and sisters, was born in 1914. The family lived in Brooklyn, the father was a tailor who tried to do his best for the family. As the children grew up, they all had to go to work. Betty went through grade school, then went to work in factories and offices. Herman,* her oldest brother, is still alive and lives in Florida.

At 16 she became a chorus girl and danced in the Ziegfield Follies. She was asked by Moishe Florenz Weiz to join the Jewish Theater on Second Avenue, but nothing came of this because her brother objected. A year later she was again asked to join a theatrical troupe, but again her oldest brother refused to give permission, and she had to decline.

In 1936, when she was 22, she was married in the Brooklyn City Hall to Tony Falco, whom she had known for two years. Her Jewish family was dead set against her marrying a gentile. (She had once had the marriage certificate, she told me, but Tony took it with him when he left.)[19]

Brooklyn District Attorney Eugene Gold later made a strenuous attempt to locate her marriage license, but it could not be found. When I mentioned this to Berkowitz, he said he thought it was because she had called herself Falk; hence the misplaced license. Why then did she now call herself Falco? I wondered. Why has she never officially divorced Tony? Was she in fact ever

---

* A pseudonym

really married to him? If she later tried to marry Klineman, as she claims, she would have had to have a divorce. Her marriage seems a mystery.

Indeed, much about Betty Falco seems a mystery, as David Berkowitz notes: "My mother . . . is a very secretive person, who drowns herself in little white lies. She's always hiding something and every time I ask a question, if for some reason she feels threatened by it, gives me a stupid answer. She treats me like a child and a little baby. She'll write a two-page letter yet, say nothing. Like me, she's a sneak."[20]

Betty told me that when she became pregnant with Richard (David) she had been "living" for quite some time with Klineman. They "had a good life." Although he was married to someone else, he would stay with her in her apartment; she cooked for him and for his three children. He would spend the day with Betty, and in the evening would go back to his wife, where they slept in separate rooms. His children came to visit Betty, and they all ate together.[21] When her daughter Barbara married, Klineman made a wedding for the girl.

How did Betty feel when she got pregnant?

"I was happy about it. Klineman seemed to like it, too. When I went into labor, he brought me to the Jewish hospital in Brooklyn, where I gave birth to a boy named Richard Falco on June 1, 1953. He was a beautiful boy. Everyone said so."

Dwelling on what it was like to have an illegitimate child, she said she was guilty and ashamed, and two days later the child, through an intermediary, was given away. She felt terribly guilty, she said, about giving him away. As she spoke her eyes began to glisten, tears began to fall, and she dried them with her handkerchief. Repeatedly she asked, "What could I do?" She looked miserable. Again and again she brought up her son, whom she called Richard, and how bad she felt about his crimes, and the young women he had killed.

"After the baby had been taken away, I was in a fog. I didn't want to see anyone. I was depressed and upset, it was a tragedy for me. I felt guilty about it. Klineman took me away for a couple of days so I could rest." When they returned, they again took up their life together.[22]

Asked why she gave away her child, she couldn't answer. I elaborated on my question: "You told me that you and Klineman had such a good relationship. Why then did you give your child up for adoption, a child who was an expression of the love between you?" She looked at me but said nothing. Either the good relationship with Klineman wasn't true, or she herself lived in a fantasy world, believing she was married to Klineman. If she were depressed and upset—"a tragedy for me"—as she put it, why hadn't she used contraception, or had an abortion? Without knowing the facts, it is not farfetched to speculate that she may have wanted to have a child to force Klineman to marry her, but her scheme failed. Apparently he balked.

What could she tell me about Klineman? In contrast to her earlier reticence, she grew eager: He was very good looking, and very good with his hands; he was in real estate among other things; he was brilliant; their relationship was a makeshift one. She described him as a generous man who had money and gladly spent it on her so she could buy food and clothes, and have something left over.[23]

David, however, felt quite differently about the man, his opinion apparently formed by talking with his mother and half-sister.

"He was stocky, about 5′6″ tall and weighing about 200 lbs. He had a round oval head, similar to mine. He was stern looking, never smiled and was ugly. He always wore a hat which just came down over his eyebrows, looking like a sinister character. I have nothing good to say about him. He was a liar, he was cheap, devious. He had a great deal of money which he earned through real estate. He didn't leave my mother anything. They were shocked when they read his will. The will didn't have her name on it. She started to cry. He died in 1971. They had been together since 1950."[24]

Betty told me about Klineman's illness. "At the end he could hardly talk, he couldn't make himself understood, and when he did I found out that he had not written a will so I didn't get anything from him, except that his wife gave me the watch he had which I had given him and a few other things. We sat *shiva* [a Jewish ritual of mourning] at her daughter's place and his sons came there."[25]

Clearly there was intimacy not only between Betty and Kline-man, but also between Betty and Klineman's children—and this relationship had continued for over 20 years.

But now she was alone again, she said, and began to lament her small apartment, her radio and TV, how lonely she was with no one to talk to. However, since the story about Richard broke, she had wanted to disappear, to leave town forever. Hinting at her miserable financial situation,[26] she seemed defensive and was reluctant to mention anything that might harm herself or her family. I reminded her that following our first phone conversation, she had called me several times and asked many questions, which I tried to answer. I understood her precarious situation, but this was something which had its roots in the past. Before she left my office, she gave me her address. The two interviews had lasted about three hours.

Betty Falco is intelligent. She answers the questions in her own way, and in this respect she has much similarity to her son.

"Her story sounds like fiction," her son David noted. "But it's not." He describes Klineman's funeral, as it was told to him:

"When Joe died after a long illness, at the funeral parlor, my mother and sister went, with all due respect, but sat in the rear of the funeral home. As I said, the relationship was known by everyone in the neighborhood, and by Klineman's family. It was pretty open and perhaps scandalous, but it was accepted.

"By the way, my mother even mentioned to me that she and Joe's legal wife met face to face at the funeral home. However, nothing was said. This was also part of the arrangement."[27]

Of Klineman's children, Berkowitz said: "They loved Betty's *kasha* [a Jewish dish] and her split pea soup. I do have to admit that I tried this stuff myself and it sure was good."[28]

Except for one thing, all of this, as previously mentioned, was done openly. The only secret was Betty's pregnancy. Had it happened today, she might have kept her child. But in 1953, adoption seemed to be the only acceptable course of action. Nonetheless, there remained a certain amount of mystery about Berkowitz's real family.

For Berkowitz, the question was, how did it happen that he was conceived at all? It troubled him:

"My birth, I now know, was either out of spite or accident. Spite, as far as Falco tried to ger her lover Joseph Klineman to give up his legal wife, divorce her and marry Betty. She may have deliberately tried to conceive a child, me, in order to pressure Klineman into a marriage commitment.

"Or, I may have just been an accident. Carelessness or failure to use the proper birth controls caused my unwanted conception.

"Here I was, never wanting to be born in the first place, cursing the day I was born, only to find out that I wasn't supposed to be born after all. Here I was, miserable, unhappy, maladjusted, plagued with Death fantasies and suicidal hopes, only to find out that I was unwanted, an accident after all.

"Here I was, or am, causing all types of destruction and havoc. Yet, I'm not really supposed to be in this world.

"My mother, Falco, was sitting in those parked cars with Klineman. Greedy, wild-tempered Klineman. It was that bastard who I took after — his temper, his impatience, he hated crowds and probably people too.

"When I finally found Betty Falco I was told that Joseph Klineman had died. Not only did he die, but he died a horrid death. He perished from cancer of the rectum. From what my sister and Betty told me, he had quite a painful death. It was also a prolonged one. When I found this out I no longer had any anger at him. Fate, God, or whatever, had taken its course. He suffered. It's settled."[29]

For Betty, it wasn't quite "settled." He left his money to his legal, "frigid" wife. Betty got nothing, even though for over 20 years she had "fed him, clothed him, copulated with him, and waited on the irresponsible bum. After all these decades together he shoved everything back in her face."[30]

Berkowitz focussed obsessively on Betty's parents, especially her father. This man, whom he never met, evoked the same kind of angry responses he had to certain other people and events in his life. His account of his grandparents' death reminds me of the long list of violent incidents he claims to have witnessed during his childhood in the Bronx:

"I hated him by just looking at his picture. I also had the opportunity to stand over is grave which was overgrown with weeds. The cemetery was a Jewish one, real small and in Staten Island. He died by falling down a flight of stairs. He was in his 90's. My grandmother, also in her 90's, died by falling down the same flight of stairs a short while later. Both apparently died of broken necks — tisk, tisk, tisk.

"Betty tried to develop her dancing talents and she wanted to continue dancing and go into show business. Supposedly, she had a lot of talent. However, her strict father, Mr. Broder, who valued tradition over the needs of his children more than anything else, refused to let her fulfill her desires. He insisted that she remain a homebody, get married, raise kids, fix meals, darn socks, retire to Florida and eventually die, all according to Jewish tradition.

"That rotten bastard, who considered Betty the 'apple of his eye,' his favorite of all her brothers and sister, refused to loosen his grip on her. When he finally died and the grip, while not mentally released but at least physically released, was loosened, it did Betty no good. By now she was too old to begin a career and life had already past her bye. I believe he passed away in the early 70's.

"Coincidentally, I recall a picture of her and her father alone. The rest of the family wasn't present. Her dad was sitting in a wooden chair with a blank expression while Betty, in her dancing costume, stood beside him. She was very young then.

"Another reason I dislike my 'natural' grandparents (my mother's side) was because of their hatred of my sister. Because Barbara was only half Jewish, they completely excluded her from conversations and family activities.

"How dare these prejudiced scum treat her as an outcast. Meanwhile she turned out to be the best and most loving of the whole family. If there's a hell, I hope mom and pop Broder (my grandparents) are there.

"One last point. I've been told that the District Attorney from Brooklyn once tried to locate Betty and Tony Falco's marriage certificate. Well, I don't know the story and what transpired between my mom and Tony forty years ago. However, you can bet the marriage was held in secret. I know that the Broders with their traditional values must have had seizures when they learned my mother had married a gentile.

"I don't think my mom married out of love for they or rather Tony took off with another woman shortly afterwards.

". . . Barbara, my sister, was the black sheep of the family. But her heart is far from black. She's very loving and loyal — a typcial 'Jewish mother.' She always puts her family first before herself and would gladly die in one of her daughter's places if it ever came down to that."[31]

To all appearances, David was sharing the pleasure in his newfound relatives that Betty and Barbara felt in finding him. But when he "tried to feel something for them, something deep," he couldn't. The next time he saw them was two weeks to a month after the initial meeting. The final time was in February 1977. He cultivated a "deliberate niceness" toward all of his new relatives. "I seem kind, lovabie, amiable, but I really didn't feel anything for them. . . . Betty Falco doesn't even know me," he later wrote. He confessed that everything about the relationship was "phoney." The sentiments he had written to his mother ("Hello, keep well, take care, I love you") were "bull." In fact, he had been "really tempted to say the opposite."[32]

Berkowitz for the first time in his life was dealing directly with the secret source of many of his ambivalent feelings about life. Evidence of how rigidly he sought to maintain his emotional equalibrium was the growing tension between the surface and the darkness below.

His feelings about Betty: "Behind my mask (Ritchie, the nice guy) I was filled with anger and rage toward her. With absolute control I managed never to show or verbalize this."[33] He was trying to keep the lid on his volcanic emotions.

Discovering that his real mother had not died in childbirth certainly alleviated some guilt and relieved him of the fearful notion that his natural father hated him "because the doctors let me live instead of her." But meeting her shattered his primary fantasy of "a mystical and perfect family — a blissful family — a perfect relationship."[34]

Anger and rage that in the past he had been able to control

through suppression and creative fantasy now had nowhere to go. His mythologized mother turned out to be just plain Betty Falco. Out of mixed fear and respect for her he kept quiet, but inside he was boiling. He had seen through her. "A closer observation of her personality will reveal selfishness and excessive worry over 'what will the neighbors think.'"[35]

"When she gave me away, it was for *her* benefit, not mine . . ."[36] She had kept Barbara and abandoned him. He was given away because "he was not good enough." The truth was that he belonged to no family. His myths were expiring all around him.

At the time of his release from the Army in June 1974, Berkowitz had perceived something disturbing in himself. During that summer, "Things began to happen to me and with me. People began to sense something in me. I can't explain it. They were driven from me." Who or what was doing this to him? "It was a certain power, force, which chased people away. It was a mysterious force working against me. I felt bothered and tormented, 'De Schmutz.' (Yiddish for 'the dirty one')."[37]

Then, less than a year later, the already disturbed young man sustained two enormous losses: the loss of his father, when Nat and his wife moved to Florida, and the loss of his illusions, when he came face to face with his real family. Even Betty, in some way, understood this: "The shock of meeting me must have been too much for him, and so the rest happened."[38]

In Berkowitz's life there were now five women, all of whom he feared and hated:

His stepmother Mary, who took his father, Nat, away and left David alone again.

Mary's daughter Carol, his stepsister who outshone him and upstaged him.

His half-sister Barbara who was kept while he was thrown away.

His adoptive mother Pearl, who died when he was 14, abandoning him.

His biological mother Betty — he would make the world pay for what she had done to him.

Meeting Betty was both cruel and crucial. Of all the cruel

blows this meeting dealt him, the cruelest was that he now realized he was an *"accident, a mistake, never meant to be born —unwanted."*[39]

There were no rules or guideposts for such a being. There was no forgiveness for such rejection. His hatred toward women was becoming all-consuming, a fireball, and absolute.

A poem he wrote, titled "Mother of Satan," was dated September 22, 1976 — a month after his first murder:

Old Mother Hubbard
Sitting near the cubbard [*sic*]
with a hand grenade
under the oatmeal.

Who will you kill now
Daughter of Satan?

In the image of the
Virgin Mary — pure and innocent
The Great Impersonator —
Is that you? "Yes."
How many have you decieved — [*sic*]
lured to slaughter like a
fat cow?

. . . .

While several thoughts are evoked by this poem, the most potent is the deep hatred he experiences against his natural mother, "Mother of Satan," who has deceived him. But he doesn't express his hostility directly to her; it remains, instead, to be released in brutal and unspeakable fashion. By now his anger and rage has passed into a new dimension.

5

STALKING THE
VICTIMS

"I do love death. I've always loved it. I've wished for it, and tried to understand it. Death is fascinating . . . its power, its hold; it is wonderful."[1]

Berkowitz had been fantasizing about death since childhood. Now the time had come to experience death in reality.

Meeting his real family, particularly his mother, had undone him. He had thought that finding her would end his loneliness, hate, and hopelessness. But the psychological trauma of having found her had been too great. He was instead in the grip of despair, rage and utter self-pity.

All his life, from the time of adoption to the rotten job as nightwatchman he held until May 1976, his life had been a series of defeats and disappointments. And he was angered, enraged, because he couldn't find a girlfriend after he left the Army. His biological mother proved to be the ultimate disappointment and frustration. His murderous rage toward women, which until now he had been able to keep in check, was about to burst from him.

On Christmas Eve 1975, on Baychester Avenue in Co-op City in the Bronx, a 14-year-old girl was attacked and stabbed repeatedly in the back and side of the chest by an unknown assailant. Her screams attracted attention, and she was rushed to Jacobi Hospital. Her wounds, proving to be superficial, were treated, and she was released. For a long time afterward, she was beset by terror, nervousness, and nightmares.*

I was taken quite by surprise when, at an early interview with Berkowitz, he openly confessed to me that he had committed the crime. This was news to me; he hadn't mentioned it before.[2]

He told me: "I attacked a girl, I put a knife in her several times. . . . I realized I'd stabbed her. After the stabbing I ran to my car."

"When you ran away you must have realized you did something wrong?"

"Yes," he answered.

"How did you feel when you stabbed her?"

"Very strange, confused. I didn't understand what was happening to me. I tried to kill."

"That was a mess," he added. "It was a young girl. I had a small hunting knife with a blade 3½″ long. I used to go to the woods and go camping. It was late at night, about 10:30 or 11:00. I saw her immediately. In my first attempt to kill I didn't know how to do it. I stabbed her, she looked at me. I stabbed her again. It was terrible, she screamed pitifully. It wasn't like the movies when the stabbed person falls down and is killed. I kept stabbing her with the knife. She was trying to grab me. She screamed and I was getting sick. It made me sick. After a little while I just couldn't tell whether she was stabbed or I was ripping her coat. I wasn't going to rape her or take her money. I was only going to kill her. That's all."

---

* After I had read the police report, I talked with her father, in October 1977. He described his daughter's condition as still emotionally fragile, almost two years later. Accordingly, I refrained from interviewing her. On August 30, 1977, following the capture of the Son of Sam killer, Detective Gurra of the 45th Precinct asked the girl if she could identify their prisoner as her attacker. She was unable to, because he had come at her from behind, and although Berkowitz claims she turned around, she did not remember getting a look at his face. She was unable to remember his face or any physical characteristics; it had become too painful for her. She had developed amnesia.

"Isn't that enough?" I asked.[3]

He looked down, not wanting to meet my eyes. Scared of what I might see in them, he turned his head away without a word.

The room, of a sudden, felt smaller.

How did Berkowitz appear with his camping knife, which he had described as a hunting knife? This time he was not camping, he was hunting — for a victim. Terrifying the girl, he himself was just as terrified. The scene was grotesque; there was terror in the knife. It made him sick.

"I was getting sick," he told me. But watching him now, watching his eyes, he was not terrifying, he was pathetic. He who wanted to kill a young girl, a victim; but he, too, seemed to look like a victim.

His attempted murder occurred about six months after he had found Betty and Barbara. It was one of the precipitating events, if not the precipitating event, which activated his murderous, sadistic impulses.

At about the same time, it has been reported by Lawrence Klausner, he made another attempt, this on a middle-aged woman. In checking this information with Berkowitz, he told me: "I never committed the crime against the older woman on Christmas Eve. I don't know where he [Klausner] got it from. But if I said something like this . . . I must have been bragging."[4]

The bloodiness of that first unsuccessful attempt at killing caused him to now turn to a more impersonal weapon, a .44 caliber gun. In June 1976 he decided to go to Texas to see Dan, a buddy of his from Korea. First he drove his car to Florida to see his father. Then he continued on to Houston, met Dan, and persuaded him to buy the .44 caliber gun, with ammunition. He then returned to New York. Here are some excerpts from my first interview with Berkowitz about the trip:

Q. You went to Texas, to Houston?
A. Yes.
Q. And there was Dan. What did you want . . . how long did you stay with him?
A. About 2, 3 days.

Q. And it was with him that you bought this . . .

A. Gun.

Q. A .44. Is that called a Charter Arms gun, is that what it is called?

A. No.

Q. What is this gun called, does it have any special name?

A. Bulldog.

Q. I see. Had you ever used such a gun before?

A. No.

Q. This was the first time?

A. Yes.

Q. Did you buy any other guns in Texas?

A. No.

Q. What was the purpose of buying the gun?

A. I knew I was going to have to do something with it.

Q. What would that be?

A. I think it was going to be shooting people, you know.

Q. Shooting people?

A. Yeah.

In Berkowitz's interrogation by the Brooklyn District Attorney in the early hours of August 11, 1977, about the purchase of the .44 caliber gun, he was asked:

Q. You had him (the friend) buy the gun?

A. Yes, it was a legal purchase.

Berkowitz also owned a machine gun. Herewith the interrogation about this weapon:

Q. Now, the .45 caliber machine gun that you identified before as being yours. Where did you get that?

A. In a gun store in Brooklyn, New York.

Q. When was that, David? Do you recall?

A. Almost two years ago.

Q. Why did you buy that weapon?

A. I needed an effective weapon.

Locating his victims, then stalking them, was more complicated than he had anticipated. And for this we must be grateful. With his murdering mind and his arsenal of weapons, he could easily have gone on a spree and, in one incident, killed many people. Why didn't he do it? He was a cautious person, and shooting several people at once would certainly lead to immediate detection; he himself would probably have been killed before he got arrested.

One reason for his difficulty in locating and shooting his prey was probably rooted in his conflicted state of mind: to shoot or not to shoot, to kill or not to kill? He felt he *had* to do something. On the other hand, he also felt inhibited from doing it:

"There were times that I was troubled over my sudden urges after the shootings began. I used to visit my sister and when I did, my gun, maps, extra ammunition, and other related paraphernalia were always carefully stored in my car for quick use.

"After a visit but also almost daily, I left around ten or eleven o'clock and began making my rounds, so to speak. Yes, Queens was special to me — very special. But this I can't explain. Shooting someone in Queens was an obsession."

He goes on to say:

"When I got my bad urges about my family, knowing that my gun was so close, yet frightened by these thoughts, I'd just go take a long walk to release any mental tensions I had for the moment. Walking for me has always been very therapeutic."[5]

Berkowitz tried to fight off his murderous feelings. Unable to kill anyone in his family (his mother or half-sister), he turned to substitutes. There was no other way to relieve and release his unbearable emotional tension.

During the first three shootings, his ambivalence was manifested in the way he held the huge .44 pistol — in one hand. Why?

"Why did I shoot with one hand and when I missed, why was I frustrated, you ask. Well, the best answer that I could give is a 50/50 one. I wanted to take a life, yet I wanted to spare a life. I wanted to and I didn't want to. I spent a great deal of money in gas and oil. I purchased other guns before my .44 caliber revolver. A shotgun and a .45 cal. rifle already cost me almost

$500.00. Lastly, I spent a great many hours driving in search of victims. No.! I knew that I was going to commit the crimes that I set out to do."

This bit of accounting reflects his extraordinary egocentricity, his narcissism, and his total immersion in his killing. Because he had spent so much money on car, guns, and ammunition, he felt *entitled* to shoot.

He goes on: "I did not become subconsciously deluded — hence, mental illness. Rather, I am very much aware of the fact that I really deluded myself. I did this on purpose. I had taken many quiet and peaceful walks along Orchard Beach in the Bronx and also Ferry Point Park. I was determined and in full agreement with myself that I must slay a woman for revenge purposes and to get my back on them for all the suffering (mental suffering) they caused me.

"Of course you would disagree extensively with my immoral view. I don't blame you. Because I, too, realize that this was a poor excuse for all I've done. However, at the time I sincerely believed that I was justified. I believed that I had every moral right to slay a chosen victim. As gross and perverted as this sounds, it was my belief. I psyched myself up to believing this. But perhaps I didn't succeed in finally convincing my inner self — my deep conscience. Regardless of how I went about my justification for my crimes. It suited me then.

"I guess that shooting with one hand which I did unconsciously was a result of my inner conscience speaking to me and that secretly I wished I had missed. But outwardly I was angry when I did because I went to so much trouble to succeed and I took such huge risks."[6]

Berkowitz showed some resistance to killing and this apparently had some bearing upon the outcome. But his overwhelming egocentricity — his efforts to succeed and the great risks he took —directed his homicidal actions. His ambivalence notwithstanding, he was driven to murder.

Stalking the victims was an important part of the ritual: "I had no plans for attack, so to speak. However, I did have a general idea of where I would be going in search of victims. So,

I familiarized myself with the streets and possible escape routes from those central areas. Also, I managed to learn all the streets by repeated trips into the area. I mean that there were nights in which I travelled all through a certain area but it turned unproductive. Naturally, I got to know streets by this method, too.

"Towards the end of my spree, I developed a keen perception of police tactics. I began to figure out just where and when a cop car would pass or where a 'stakeout' car would be parked. I really got good at this — expert.

"After a while, I was able to spot an unmarked car regardless of its disguise. Some were taxi cabs, some were beat up old rattle traps, but they were police cars just the same, and I 'made' them. Unmarked police vans were also a frequent sight.

"I had developed a mental warning and caution device in my mind, and it worked."[7]

I was interested to learn just how he found his first victim, Donna Lauria. He told me:

"I saw her and another girl [July 29, 1976] sitting in a blue Oldsmobile Cutlass, as I drove past. I parked about two very short blocks away on a side street. I saw both girls sitting there, apparently talking. I circled the car at a distance like an animal stalking its prey. Cautiously, I was watching for movement from other people in the street. However, there was none. Then, from behind and on the sidewalk, I approached the car, took my revolver out of a paper bag, and stopped parallel to their vehicle. I faced Donna, aimed my gun in the general direction and fired all five rounds very rapidly. I saw the glass breaking into small slivers, the horn started sounding loudly, and I then ran full speed in the direction of my car. I stopped running within 50 feet of the car, then started walking briskly to it. I got in then drove off. I aroused no attention. I didn't know I had killed her until I read the Post the following afternoon. The shooting took place about 1 A.M.

"I went straight home and went to bed. I got up early the next day to go to work at the cab company in the same neighborhood (Pelham Bay Park). I was at work promptly at 6:45 A.M. That day I made out better than usual in both tips and fares. I made it my point to go to work so I wouldn't arouse any suspicion. But who would have suspected me anyhow? I didn't know the victims."[8]

How did he *feel* when he killed? He and I talked about the murders:[9]

Q. Do you often relive the shootings? Sometimes?
A. . . . (inaudible)
Q. Is that yes?
A. Yes.
Q. You have to say yes, because, you see, the machine [tape recorder] doesn't see you. I see. You do relive it. Can you describe for me, then, when you were standing there and you had shot, let me see, what was the name of the first girl you shot, Donna, and you shot, bullets went through the glass, and the glass apparently splintered, fragments, or whatever you call it, how did you feel about this?
A. I didn't.
Q. You didn't feel anything?
A. No.
Q. You were not confused or anything . . .?
A. Yes, I . . .
Q. . . . What kind of feelings did you have?
A. Nothing.
Q. Nothing?
A. Nothing.
Q. You mean that you shot her and killed her in cold blood, and you didn't feel anything?
A. Nothing to feel.
Q. Nothing to feel or fear?
A. I just saw the glass.
Q. Just saw the glass.
A. Thousand of pieces.
Q. Thousand of pieces.
A. Slow motion.
Q. Tell me more about it, if you can.
A. I pulled the gun out of the bag, see, and I just started shooting.

Q. Yeah?

A. I had the gun in one hand, held the gun in one hand.

Q. And you had the bag in the other hand?

A. Yeah, and I just started to shoot, at the window. And I just saw the glass come in, my eyes were transfixed to the glass. Thousand of little pieces, you could see them; you know. You could see . . . almost count every one.

Q. And your eyes were transfixed to the glass?

A. Yes.

Q. And you could see the little pieces?

A. Yes.

Q. You could see every piece, something like that?

A. Uh-huh. And I saw Donna, she had dark hair, she just as if she was covering herself from the glass, the flying glass.

Q. And what happened then, you just stand there, you were, so to say, transfixed?

A. Yes, I emptied the gun and I was still pulling the trigger and it was clicking, but I didn't know it. Then the horn, the other girl decided to blow the horn of the car. I just, you know, it shook me up, I was still, I found I was still pulling the trigger, and then I just, I don't know, it was like trance-like. . . . then I just, when the horn started blowing, I got, I just, I just ran away. I didn't know what else to do.

Q. Yeah, you ran away because, why?

A. It seemed like the only thing to do (laughs), I don't know.

Q. You didn't want to be caught maybe, is that the point?

A. Oh, I didn't want to.

Q. Yeah, but you said, the horn, the automobile horn began to blow you said?

A. Yes.

Q. The other girl had sounded the horn?

A. Yes.

Q. And then you ran away, because you said . . .

A. No, I was still pulling the trigger.

Q. You still pulled the trigger, yes.

A. And then it was just clicking.

Q. And this was the first shooting you did?

A. Yes.

Q. And you were not sure about whether you had killed her or not? Was that the reason you . . .

A. I wasn't sure I shot anybody. I wasn't sure I shot anybody. You couldn't tell.

Q. Because it was too dark, or what?

A. No, they just stood there, they didn't move.

Q. And then you ran away?

A. Yeah, I just went back to my car.

Q. Did you walk of did you run?

A. I ran.

Q. Let me ask you please, how far was the car away from . . .

A. About a block, a half a small block maybe.

Q. And that was, you wanted to get away then, you ran away in order to not be detected, or . . .

A. Nothing else to do.

Q. Now you said here, you mentioned to me that, you ran also because you had something else to do?

A. Yeah.

Q. What would that be?

A. More

Q. More? More killings?

A. Yes.

Q. I see. So there would be two reasons why you didn't want to, why you ran away then; one was that you had some more business to do, and the other one that you didn't want to be detected.

A. Right.

Q. You didn't want to be caught.

A. That's right.

Q. But wasn't it also a matter for some sort of survival you didn't want to be caught, because if what would have happened if you had gotten caught?

A. Nothing.

Q. You know . . .

A. I mean the police would arrest, and . . . nothing.

Q. What would happen if you would be arrested?

A. I guess the same things that's happened now.
Q. Yes, and that you would be kept here or some other place.
A. Yes.

Berkowitz was obsessed by his first shooting. Yet he didn't feel anything. His words, though, "thousand of pieces," "slow motion," "my eyes were transfixed," "trance-like," "when the horn started blowing, I just ran away. I didn't know what else to do," all show he was absorbed, preoccupied. He was bent on it, indicating that ambivalence or no, his muderous feelings were totally engaged. That he denied it, at this interview, was in order to demonstrate that the shooting was done without his conscious participation. But that he ran away from the murder scene indicates both his guilt, and his awareness of what he was doing. He was not insane.

When he says also that he ran away because he was going to do more shooting, it is hardly true. His pattern was to shoot only one or two victims at a time.

Charles and Ruth, neighbors from his childhood, gave me their reaction to berkowitz's murderous activities:

Ruth. You know it scares me. You know that first killing of Donna was right around the ccorner here. I was just coming home late that night, maybe an hour or two difference between the killing and when I came home.
Charles. That's something that bothered me a lot.
R. What would have happened if I saw him!
Abrahamsen. It was only one block from here?
R. Right around the corner, a half a block.
A. What was that address?
C. Buhre Avenue
A. I can drive around there and see.
C. Yes, you can walk right over, the corner building.
A. David knew at the time that you were still living here?
C. Yes
R. And I was coming home late that night, playing canasta. I was walking home from that building where he killed someone

else, the Hutchinson River Project, off the service road of the Hutchinson River Parkway.

C. He knew this area because he lived in Co-op City and it's just a short distance from here.

A. How far is Co-op City, can you see it from here?

C. Those five buildings over there.

R. You know he used this building as his address at one time.[10]

That Berkowitz located his first victim close to his childhood home is important. He killed Donna in surroundings that were emotional home territory — where, as a young man, he had always felt sexually frustrated. As Charles reflected: ". . . He knew this neighborhood. So his first victim was right around the corner from here, and he had another victim which was just two blocks away from there on Hutchinson River Parkway."[11]

Charles couldn't help repeating himself. "Suppose I had seen him running down the block, I'd say 'Hey Dave, what are you doing here?'" But Berkowitz was not discovered until a year later.

He used every means to avoid suspicion and one of his ways was to shoot women he didn't know. Berkowitz prided himself on his caution.

"I've always been a cautious person. There are people whom I associated with just prior to my capture—peers, family, neighbors, etc. After my arrest they said, 'I can't believe he's the killer.' Well, if they could have read my mind and seen my thoughts, then they would have known without a doubt that I was the Son of Sam."[12]

His remarks here swell with pride over his deceptiveness. Nobody was going to know that he was the Son of Sam.

Yet, he also wanted it to be known. He sometimes had an overwhelming, desperate wish to proclaim to the world that he, David Berkowitz, was the "Son of Sam" — the most feared murderer of recent times. "There were so many times that the temptation to share my hidden secret became overpowering," he later wrote me. "I often stared at my telephone, my hands trembling . . . as I thought of picking up the receiver, dialing, then saying to the party at the other end: 'Hello, is this the Son of Sam Task Force? Well, guess who this is?'"[13]

Again his duplicity played havoc with him. He was terrified to confess he was the killer. But he "wondered what they would think when they heard about it on the news at the time when the shooting took place." He anticipated that the world, not to mention the family of his victim, would be filled with horror, sadness, and shock. (His remark further reflected his revenge upon them and at the same time showed them what power this unknown person had.)

"After I killed Donna I felt happy. I felt some peace. Sang songs on my way home after killing Donna. That built up tension dissipated temporarily. While I didn't have a physical, sexual orgasm, I certainly had a mental one. After a shooting, it was like being in the woods again, I was walking on air.

"I got some revenge.

"I wasn't bothered by the killing; wasn't haunted by it.

"I felt powerful and cunning, especially when I put on my 'innocent' look. No one suspected a thing."[14]

The car that Donna was sitting in had been double-parked. He had to walk into the street to shoot her. I visited the murder scene myself, and was struck by his daring — to shoot someone in a double-parked car in an open street. It was a bold move, and belies the nervousness he later professed to. At the moment of the attack, he was able to overcome his fear. At the same time, he was cunning and compulsive:

"I knew what I was doing. I knew right from wrong, and I knew that my gun could snuff someone's life. However, I developed such an obsession to do what I did, all the laws or promises of the gas chamber couldn't get me to stop or turn back"[15]

Berkowitz was far from finished. About three months later, on October 23, 1976, he struck again:

"The second job was the DeNaro, Keenan one [Carl DeNaro and Rosemary Reenan in Flushing, Queens]. Both of them were sitting in a red Volkswagen and making out. This was my second murder attempt with my .44. I had approached them from the rear of the car, walked up to the passenger side window and opened fire. I was more frightened than they were. Only one bullet struck the young man and he really wasn't the intended target. I had fired with one hand and wildly. Boy did I mess up. But really, I was very nervous.

"After the shooting, I ran to my car, and drove off quickly to a White Castle (a hamburger place) on Northern Blvd."[16]

After the shooting he became hungry and anxious. He had to eat. DeNaro was seriously wounded. His skull had been splintered.

During his confession to the Queens District Attorney, Berkowitz was asked: "Did you intend to kill both the passenger and the driver?"

"Just the woman. I thought she was in the front seat, passenger's side. It was very dark." (At the time, it was thought that the killer was looking for young women with long, dark hair.)

"Can you describe the hair of the people in the car."

"It was like a blondish."

"That was on the passenger's side?"

"Yes."[17]

Later he told me: "This (shooting) took about ten minutes" —from the time he first saw the victim until he fired the gun. "I could have waited longer but I was anxious. I wanted to get it over with and then head home."[18]

The third attack was on November 27, 1976, in Bellerose, Queens. Donna DeMasi and Joanne Lomino were shot and wounded. The shooting took place within five minutes of choosing his victims. "I saw them on the porch. I drove my car around the corner and parked it. I then got out, walked directly to the porch up the street and fired."[19]

That Berkowitz was "nervous" during his first three shootings had as much to do with his vulnerable ego as it did with his fear of being captured and incarcerated.

"You asked me why I was so nervous when I did the first shootings. I guess it was a case of me being fearful of capture. But I also realized I was doing something that was not only illegal but also dangerous. I, too, could have been killed or wounded. The possibility of an off-duty police officer or a patrol car passing through the vicinity when the shots were fired was also taken into consideration by me. So I guessed I had a lot to fear.

"However, and most importantly, when I was about to commit my crimes, I was cognizant of finally being able to pass that point, in which a human plays God. Does this sound strange? Sure I was nervous. Why? Because I was about to commit the ultimate of crimes taking another's life. This was a very traumatic event."[20]

With his highly charged narcissistic love, Berkowitz proclaims that "he too" could have been killed or wounded. The man in the car might pull out a gun and chase him. Desperately wanting to be a hero, Berkowitz could hardly endure such a humiliation. He made it sound like a game. He had completely lost sight of who had started this murderous rampage.

The fourth shooting was in Forest Hills, Queens, on January 30, 1977. Christine Freund and John Diehl were hit and Christine died. Now Berkowitz's tone completely changes:

"This did result in a homicide to my joy at the time. However, this shooting was different than all the others for two reasons. One, because I used two hands to fire the gun. Two, because I didn't have any fear. This time when I crept up to the car and fired, I wasn't frightened and I remained calm and cautious. After the shooting I ran to my car and escaped into the freezing night. The next day I heard about her death and the police's theory that this recent shooting was connected to several others in the Bronx and Queens. Lastly, I cannot explain my change — a loss of fear, except for the fact that I was growing more 'cold-blooded' daily as my thoughts centered on murder and because my determination was increasing — my frustrations were building."[21]

He added: "I saw them get into the car and I walked up the street. I walked several hundred feet, turned around, and headed back to the car they were seated in with the engine running. I aimed and fired. This took about five minutes."[22]

He describes this murder as if somebody else did it. Cold-blooded, factual, he gives the impression that he would like to disassociate himself from responsibility for the crime. Later he adds:

"During the fourth shooting when I first used two hands, I guess at this time that I had further succeeded in justifying my crimes to myself and that I was more determined than ever. At this point I imagine I didn't care much anymore for I finally had convinced myself that it was good to do it, necessary to do it, and that the public wanted me to do it. The latter part I believe until this day. I believe that many were rooting for me. This was the point in which the papers began to pick up vibes and information that something big was happening out in the street. Real big!"[23]

He makes a telling point here. The public and the news media had by now become involved with the phantom killer. With so many headlines screaming from the newspapers, there was forged a link, not yet obvious, between victimizer and victimized. The world at large, in its fascination with his deeds, was unconsciously spurring him on. It was a game — Berkowitz pitted against an entire city. It was as if they would be disappointed if he did not now continue with his murderous deeds. The killer took public interest and concern to mean that they wished him to continue the murders. They were fascinated with his elusiveness. He held the public in his hand.

By his fifth attack, Berkowitz had become bolder, and had abandoned caution. On March 8, 1977, he shot Virginia Voskerichian to death on a street in Forest Hills. He says:

"Brazenly I travelled through that same neighborhood only a few weeks after the first shooting there. I spotted a girl walking up the street. She was pretty, slender, and dressed nicely. Without really looking about because my eyes were focussed directly on her only, I just pulled out my revolver from a plastic bag and I shot her once in the face. I had no fear with the exception of being caught and I was so transfixed on the shooting and my victim that I didn't notice my large plastic bag falling to the floor. I just left it there. I really didn't care.

"After the shooting, I drove straight home and I watched the news on the eleven o'clock news. The next day I purchased the

Daily News, Post, and Times. I remember the headline, SEC-
OND KILLING STUNS FOREST HILLS" (Daily News).[24]

How had he picked this person?

"I walked around for a long time—just walking and thinking.
I spotted this girl walking up the street. I raised my gun and shot
her once. This took only seconds. But during that evening I had
passed dozens of potential victims. I don't know why I chose
her. I could harldy make out her facial features in the darkness.
However, I was on the street for several hours — just walking,
thinking and prowling. Now that I look back on this, none of it
makes any sense."[25]

He's right, his murders don't make sense. But the way he
committed this one shows that by now he, at least unconsciously,
wanted to be caught. This was the only time he acted in the early
evening, at 7:30 P.M. All the other killings were carried out in
the dead of night, between 12 and 3 A.M.

The sixth shooting occurred just over a month later, on April
17, 1977. He shot a woman and a man, both of them strangers
to him.

"The sixth incident was in the Bronx. A double murder of a
young couple (Suriani and Esau) on the service road of the
Hutchinson River Parkway. It was my best 'job' because it re-
sulted in two deaths. Plus, I left my first carefully concocted note
on the scene. My shooting pattern improved greatly due to my
fearlessness which slowly developed and my two handed shooting method. Four shots were fired. Three hit the victims out of
four fired. The man was hit twice in the head. The girl once in
the face. Now, I was making the papers nearly every day. The
chase was on and the public was watching out for me."[26]

Now he gave the first hint of who he was, carefully omitting
his real name, only calling himself "Son of Sam."

How did he decide upon these two victims?

"This time I again had been cruising for hours — about six
hours. I was headed up toward Yonkers along the Hutchinson
River Parkway service road, when I saw two heads over the seat
of the car as I approached from behind. I then drove my car
around the corner and parked. I walked towards the car,

dropped a note at the scene, then opened fire. Valentina Suriani and Alexander Esau died."[27]

The seventh shooting was on June 26, 1977, in Bayside, Queens:

"Two (Judy Placido and Salvatore Lupo) were wounded and I was angry. I don't see how that girl lived. Again, I had no fear, I was alert and cautious. I ran to my car only as to quickly escape and I cunningly travelled up 35th Avenue and not on the main road, Northern Boulevard. This shooting was close to my sister's house."[28]

How did he choose these victims? "Again, I had been walking and staking out this area for hours. I saw them and just finally decided that I must do it and get it over with. Believe it or not, I had no real desire to keep at this. Yet, I did."[29]

Berkowitz contradicts himself when he first says he was angry when the two were only wounded, not killed as he had hoped, but then adds that he had "no real desire to keep at it."

This shooting was close to his sister's house, the significance of which he was unaware.

Berkowitz's eighth and last shooting, when he killed Stacy Moskowitz and almost blinded Robert Violante on July 31, 1977, took place in Brooklyn. He told me:

"I had come from work at 10:30 P.M. and stopped at a diner and had a little snack. Left the gun in the car. I don't think I had the rifle in the car. I went out to Queens and Brooklyn, and had to look around. There was nobody in Queens. So I moved over to Brooklyn."

At the time of this interview he was still standing by the demon story:

"I was driving. I got work to check out. I parked my car at Bay Seventeen, got out and walked around the neighborhood for 20 minutes. Saw a police car come down Bay Seventeen and stop alongside my car. I saw them give me a ticket, for my car was parked at a fire hydrant. The cops got back in their car and drove up the street. Just before they got to the corner, they double-parked the car on the left side of the street and they both got out by some other double-parked cars on the street. I couldn't see what they were doing. I stayed there for 10 or 15 minutes and I walked away, went over to the playground, sat down (on a bench) at about 2:30 or 2:45 A.M. Then I was told to wait there to kill somebody. Then I saw who it was going to be. They came. [I had to] change plans, two other people were to be killed. I walked 100 feet. Just walked up to it [car], pulled out the gun and fired into the car on the passenger's side. I fired four bullets."

I asked, "Did she move?"

"She sort of flinched. Cannot tell whether I hit the girl."

"Why?"

"Nothing happened. She didn't do anything."

"What did you expect her to do?"

"I don't know. She didn't scream, fly through the air."

"After I had shot, I ran to my parked car two blocks away. Just drove away."

"Were you afraid to be discovered?"

"I didn't want to be discovered."

"Why?"

"I had other killings to do."[30]

In a later account, he was more attentive to detail:

"I saw her and her boy friend making out in the car. Then, they left the car, walked over the walk bridge and went along the path by the water.

"After about 20 minutes, they returned to the car, made out some more and then came to where I was by the swings. I watched Stacy on the swing and then they stopped swinging. Her and her date then started to kiss passionately for several minutes. At this time I, too, was sexually aroused. I had an erection.

"Shortly after their deep kissing they went back to the car. If my memory is correct, they made out a little more and then just sat inside the car talking."[31]

The routine in the shooting of Stacy Moskowitz was the same. "It was guerrilla warfare," he told me at an early interview at Kings County, when he wanted to convince me of the demons.

"Yes," I answered, "but in guerrilla warfare one does not shoot innocent people."

Berkowitz had nothing to say. He sat staring out the window as if he were reconstructing in his mind the gruesome activities of the Son of Sam. His desire for revenge notwithstanding, what was common to all his murders was that his intricate mind raised obstacles for his killing, and this was not only limited to shooting the victims, it was also in finding them. "Despite all my crimes," he told me, "I failed to find a suitable victim 99% of the time."[32] Yet he spent a good deal of time "stalking" and "watching."

"I walked around the block several times. I checked out alley ways. I looked up to windows of all apartment buildings to see if anyone was looking out. But" — and this shows his resistance to killing — "I was secretly hoping that they'd drive away."[33]

But did he really want to be discovered? Not overtly. "I suppose that I didn't want to be discovered. The conditions had to be right. Obviously, I couldn't shoot with someone standing around the corner but in sight of me. I couldn't do it if a police car just cruised by a few minutes ago and eyed me as they went past."[34]

We find a grim example of his "stalking and watching" his victims when, one week before he was arrested, he was on a "mission to Long Island." "I went out," he told me, "to the Hamptons in the first week of August. I had instructions to kill many people in Southampton. In the afternoon I looked at a map to drive out there. I had the guns with me and came to Southampton (in fact, it was East Hampton) late in the afternoon. I drove to the beach, Asparagus Beach, Amagansett. I sat on the sand a couple of hours. I had to wait until nightfall. It started to rain and I had to go then. The operation had to be postponed to the following weekend. Disappointed. Ten o'clock. I was very tired when I came back to town and had something to eat and went to bed."

Then he added: "The beach was a medium-sized beach. When it began to rain, people left."

"And you?"

"I left, too."

"You had intended to kill someone and you couldn't kill because it began to rain?"

"Yes."[35]

It is clear that he was careful about risking his own neck. It is also clear that he wasn't a man who killed only upon orders of demons. They had ordered him to go out that August day and kill, but he had decided otherwise. Thus, he was in control of his murderous impulses, and his behavior had been deliberate and voluntary. I finally concluded that the signal, the command to kill which he said he received from the demons had, in fact, been his own invention.

All Berkowitz's victims were strangers to him, and except for one early evening murder, they had all been done in the middle of the night. While he was nervous and fearful at the first shooting, he also took great pleasure in it. In dooming his victims, he enjoyed an intense sense of power and mastery. He alone knew who the killer was. He was omnipotent. The "demons" had transformed the unassuming and quite ordinary David Berkowitz into one of the most sought-after killers of modern times.

The women he had killed had been killed by the revengeful and omnipotent child in him, by the child he had once been — and still was.

6

MADMAN
OR MALINGERER?

The demons made him do it, the son of Sam said when he was arrested on August 10, 1977. His discourse on demons, prima facie evidence of insanity — or so he believed at the time — was given thorough coverage by the news media. For the first time, the papers were able to print Berkowitz's own words. For most of them, this story was the best they had had in years.

In truth, it was an intriguing story. Who had ever heard of a criminal claiming to be possessed by demons? What *were* demons, anyhow? Evil spirits? Monsters, blood suckers, vampires? They belonged to that mysterious netherworld of the occult, which so endlessly intrigues us. By allying himself with the supernatural, Berkowitz had put himself in a very special role — that of a wizard.

Here was a slayer of young women, a monster who had managed to elude the police, and, what's more, was possessed and propelled by demons! No wonder we were so fascinated with him. He was all-powerful, omnipotent! Ironically, the young man who had gone through life feeling totally power less now had millions hanging onto every detail of his wierd story.

Devils and demons notwithstanding, the state now had in custody one of the most notorious mass murderers since the time of Jack the Ripper, who was never caught. He had confessed. What was to be done with him? Nothing could possibly avenge the families of his murdered victims, or appease the bitterness of those he had left living but maimed. Still, justice had to be honored, but what kind of justice? That he would be locked up somewhere was understood—New York State invokes the death penalty only when a police officer is killed. But where? For how long. How would justice define and judge his crimes? Was he accountable for what he had done?

As it happened, the outcome of the case hinged on a judicial procedure, known as the Dusky Rule — a competency hearing —to be held prior to the formal trial. Indeed, this hearing would in fact determine if there was to be a trial. If found to be incompetent, the defendant would be placed in a mental institution until declared sane for trial.

A single judge would decide on Berkowitz's competence to stand trial. In reaching his decision, the judge would have to know the following: Could Berkowitz recall the details of the crimes? Had he sufficient faculties to know who he was and where he was? Did he understand the charges against him? Could he stand the stress of a trial? And, equally important, was he capable of cooperating with his lawyers in formulating his own defense? Under the law, a defendant could be emotionally ill yet if he met these criteria he would be competent to stand trial. Even if Berkowitz was found competent to stand trial, he still might later, at the trial, be found not guilty by reason of insanity at the time he committed the crime. Whatever the final result, the decision to stand trial would finally rest on the judgment of one man, abetted by the opinions of consulting psychiatrists.

The Court appointed two psychiatrists, Dr. Daniel W. Schwartz, Director of Forensic Psychiatry, Kings County Hospital, and Richard L. Weidenbachker Jr., also of Kings County, to examine him. They began their examinations two days after the arrest, and spent a total of eleven hours interviewing him. They also talked to his adoptive father, and were shown relevant statements, letters and photographs "It is the opinion of each of us," their report stated,

that the defendant is an incapacitated person in that he, as a result of mental disease or defect, lacks capacity to understand the proceedings against him or to assist in his own defense. The details of our report are as follows: 1. Diagnosis: Paranoia; 2. Prognosis: Guarded

The eight-page report supporting this conclusion said that his adoptive mother had been "murdered" (Berkowitz told them that cancer had been "inflicted" on her by the demons), that after his first attempted murder, he was ordered by demons to get a gun. After describing the homicides Berkowitz had committed, the psychiatrists characterized his mental status as "alert, attentive, responsive, courteous, and cooperative."

Berkowitz was surprised that we should even ask questions about his delusions, convinced that we already know this information. . . . His mood and stance convey a feeling of relaxation and relief, which he attributes to the fact that since his arrest the demons have stopped harassing him because he is unable to do their bidding. In his appearance and manner he is quietly subdued and resigned, consistent with his belief that soon enough the demons will kill him. . . . He also demonstrates a strange capacity to shift suddenly from one emotion to another. He is close to tears — the only time he reveals such a feeling — as he talks about the unfairness of youngsters dying; the next moment, however, he enthusiastically describes himself as loving death. One moment he is angry about having been forced to come home tired and late from high school; the next moment he is chuckling as he recalls the fights they had on those crowded buses. All these emotional displays are very short-lived . . . the patient is engrossed with and mesmerized by his all-encompassing, fairly closely organized pseudo-religious system of grandiose and persecutory delusions, with associated illusions and hallucinations. Sometimes he can become so engrossed that he breaks contact with reality to a significant degree. For instance, during one interview, he became excited as he hears a dog barking in the distance, and he even prepares to leave the hospital building, briefly oblivious to the fact that he is under maximum security confinement on a prison ward. Despite his rampant psychosis and profound disorder or emotionality, the speech and thought disorder characteristic of schizophrenia is never manifest: loosening of associations, predicative indentification, etc. are not discernible. The details of his delusional thinking are clear, there is nothing in his statements, oral or written, that is not comprehensible.

As for his inappropriate behavior, they stated:

. . . the patient is, considering the reality of his present legal situation, inappropriately concerned with superficial cleanliness. . . . he refused to let a young female secretary take notes during an interview, not because he felt ashamed or guilty about what he might say but because he felt dirty and unclean in his physical appearance. Several times thereafter he complained about not having shampoo. When his father first visited him the patient remained silent because he would have preferred to have been seen "under better cirumstance," meaning, "if I was like neat and clean." Immediately after his Supreme Court arraignment in downtown Brooklyn he said he would not appear in public again unless he had clean clothes.

The patient is well oriented and appears to be of at least average intelligence, with a reasonably good vocabulary but rather simple sentence structure. His skill at precisely dating past life events is not the greatest but his ability to recall visually the details of every one of his alleged offenses is striking.

They then proceeded to justify their specific diagnosis:

Despite the presence of a rather elaborate paranoid delusional system, the question of this defendant's fitness to proceed is not that simple. He is well aware of the charges against him, understands that by society's standards his acts were criminal, and has the intellectual capacity to learn whatever there is about legal proceedings that he does not already know. The problem is that his psychosis prevents him from assisting in his own defense. In the first place he feels so emotionally dead that the outcome of his case is totally immaterial to him. "I don't have the strength to fight. It's too much. My work is done. . . . I don't care what the proceedings are." A trial ought to involve some reasonable degree of active defense, some emotional involvement on the part of the defendant, but this man is so indifferent that he does not even care which attorney represents him. Secondly, he is so engrossed in his delusional thinking that he cannot avail himself of the only chance he has for acquittal, the so-called insanity defense: "No, it would be worthless because it would not be accurate." He objects to being called insane because then the world would not recognize the danger of Sam Carr. Thirdly, under minimal pressure he has already shown even further withdrawal from reality, including the loss of his own identity. When on August 24, 1977 Supreme Court Bronx convened in the Kings County Hospital Psychiatric Center and the defendant's appearance was simply for arraignment, he nevertheless seemed to some observers to be in a trance and responded to a question that he was not David Berkowitz. Later he informed us that he was Craig Glassman and that there were times when Craig Glassman took over his mind and body. It seems likely that under the greater stress of an actual trial in a regular courtroom such withdrawal might be more frequent and more sustained, precluding any degree of assistance in his own defense.[1]

When I read their report in preparation for interviewing Berkowitz, their diagnosis took me by surprise. Paranoia in such a young man, 23 years old, is so rare that in over 50 years of psychiatric practice I have never seen a case of it. If such a condition as paranoia (deluded, systematic beliefs) exists at all, it occurs in persons of about 40 to 50 years old. Furthermore, hallucinations (seeing or hearing things that are not there) are rarely, if ever, a symptom of paranoia. For all practical purposes, the presence of such hallucinations excludes a diagnosis of paranoia. A mental illness in which hallucinations may be manifest is paranoid schizophrenia, a psychosis. But this condition is characterized by thought disorder — a disorganization of the personality, including loss of memory, inability to know what is going on — symptoms Berkowitz did not exhibit, a fact acknowledged by the two psychiatrists in their report. Something was wrong — their findings, their diagnosis, or both.

Nevertheless, their report, when made public, led to the widespread belief that Berkowitz, believing himself possessed by demons when he killed his victims, was insane.

At 10 A.M. on August 30, 1977, Judge Gerald Held, presiding at the hearing at State Supreme Court building in downtown Brooklyn, opened the psychiatrists' report and began to read it aloud. Curiously, he had not checked to see if the defendant was in the room. In a criminal hearing the defendant, by law, must be present in court, unless certain circumstances make his presence impossible. Berkowitz was not present. Notified of the defendant's absence, the judge held up the proceeding, waiting for Berkowitz to complete his trip from Kings County Hospital, sirens blasting on his 10-car caravan with a helicopter hovering overhead.

On August 15, 1977, District Attorney Eugene Gold of Kings County had called me into the case, and Judge Held issued a Court Order authorizing me to examine Berkowitz. My interviews with him began shortly thereafter.

During my extensive practice as a psychiatrist, I have frequently examined defendants to determine their mental competence to stand trial. Often the cases have centered on hallucinations that allegedly prevented the defendants from obeying the law. The essential task in such cases, as was true in the Berkowitz case, is to determine if these hallucinations are genuine. Do they really exist in the defendant's mind, and do they control his actions? If so, then he is psychotic and unable to stand trial. Or are these hallucinations a conscious, deliberate invention? If such is the case, then he himself is in control of them, and is competent to stand trial. The responses quoted below all took place at interviews with Berkowitz at Kings County Hospital in August and September 1977.

At the first interview I asked him when was the first time he experienced demons.

"I began to hear them just after I moved to Yonkers," he replied.

He had moved from an apartment in the Bronx to New Rochelle in February 1976, and then, three months later, to Yonkers. But at an earlier session he had admitted to having tried to murder a young woman with a knife on Christmas Eve 1975. If he had not experienced the demons until 1976, then he had made his first murder attempt without being so "commanded."

"Who told you to kill?" I asked.

"Sam."

"Where did you get the idea about Sam Carr?"

"A long story," he said curtly. Then, for the first time, he became flustered, and started to fidget. The bravado with which he had answered my previous questions disappeared.

I repeated my question: "How did you get the idea about Sam Carr?"

He finally replied: "I met Sam Carr in the distance. Not everyone gets too close. He's very reclusive. It looks like a dog; he talks through it. He hears it."

"How do you know this?" I asked.

"How?" he screamed. "You wouldn't understand" I can still hear his screams.

I tried again: "How did you get the idea about Sam Carr?"

"I went down there," he mumbled.

"Where?"

"Down the street, where his house was."

"How did you find his house?"

"I saw it," he finally confessed.

"You saw it from your window, isn't it so? You live high up on a hill, and Sam Carr lives down, far down below, possibly 200 feet from you in a direct line of vision."

As I spoke, Berkowitz looked at me quizzically, probably wondering how I knew all that. I hadn't told him of my trip to his apartment house in Younkers, or to the small house of the real Sam Carr.

I asked, "What did you do then?"

"I went down and looked at the house and saw his name and address outside the house."

"So you found Sam Carr. He exists in reality."

Berkowitz nodded. It was a dramatic moment, for he had previously denied this fact, insisting that Sam was a demon.

In fact, he had been at Sam Carr's house several times.

"Why did you go down to Sam's?" I asked.

From his apartment, he said, he had heard some howling and barking and wanted to find out what it was all about.

"What happened then?"

"When I stood outside Carr's house, I couldn't hear anything, but when I came back to my apartment, I again heard a dog barking."

This was news. The voice of the demon came and went, depending on where Berkowitz was physically located. It was as though he could determine its actions by his own movements.

The demon didn't control Berkowitz; he controlled it. Earlier he had told me that the voices of the demons had become weak and even disappeared when he went to Florida and Texas, only to reappear when he returned East.

"Have you seen Sam?" Berkowitz suddenly asked me.

"No. Why do ask?"

"I was just wondering." His voice trailed off.

I pondered the reason for his question. He was shaken. Had I talked in person with Sam Carr? Had I discovered that he was not only a real person, but also, that he was not a demon?

Finally I said: "Would you like me to see him?"

He didn't answer.

Berkowitz had become evasive. By asking whether I had seen Sam Carr, he was trying to make me believe that he believed in the demons. He was trying to get me to buy the demon story.

A psychiatrist, trying to determine whether or not a person charged with a crime is insane, often cannot be satisfied with interviewing only the defendant. He must investigate all the circumstances of the crime situation. In this case that meant looking at the matter of the barking dogs. Berkowitz had so far succeeded in making the two above-mentioned psychiatrists believe that he had hallucinated, in the barking of dogs, commands to kill. Oddly, nobody had probed further into these strange phenomena; and it was precisely this dog story which was making me suspicious of the demons' authenticity.

I visited Berkowitz's landlady in New Rochelle and was surprised to see that she had two dogs tied up in her garden. When Berkowitz had come to ask about renting her attic apartment, she told him about the animals. He had blurted out, "I don't like dogs."

"Take it or leave it," she countered. "The dogs are going to stay."

He had meekly accepted the arrangement.

The two German shepherds lived in the garden which faced the window of this attic apartment where he lived for two months. Their barking was continuous. And there was a similar situation in Yonkers, the last place that Berkowitz lived, from

April 1976 until his arrest on August 10, 1977. From his apartment window on the top floor of a seven-story building, he could see and hear dogs bark. Facing several houses, some 200 feet below, he could on the right see the house of Sam Carr, who had a dog, Harvey: on the left side was the home of Mara Neto (18 Windsor Street), who also had a dog — which Berkowitz shot. I have never seen so many dogs in one place as on that street in Yonkers. Their barking never stopped.

I also took a trip to the Bronx and talked with a former neighbor of his. About 30 feet below his previous apartment there was a fenced-in yard in which a very large black German shepherd had been tied up; it barked and howled unbearably. My informant told me: "I didn't know what to do. Once I called the police about it. But there was nothing they could do. They got many complaints from other neighbors. Berkowitz's windows faced the yard."

As if this wasn't enough, the job that Berkowitz had held through May of 1976 — after his first attempt to kill — entailed further involvement with dogs. He was employed as a night watchman at I.B.I., a large security firm, and assigned to patrol a warehouse at West 31st Street and 10th Avenue in Manhattan. For company on his nightly rounds he had three large dogs.

"I loved those dogs. We were buddies. I took care of them, fed them, bathed them."

He mentioned, however, that one of the guard dogs had bitten him on the left arm, drawing blood.

What did he do? I asked. "I bit him back," he said, laughing.

"You what?" said I incredulously.

"Oh, no," he said. "I was only joking. I gave him the chains. The dogs were off the leash; I was usually by myself . . . I liked the dogs. I didn't want to leave them."

Joke or no, the notion that he had bitten the dog revealed how much he wanted revenge. His professed love notwithstanding, he was afraid of dogs. The contradiction between this purported love and his actual fear was striking. They seemed to be a kind of fearful refrain in his life.

If Berkowitz had actually heard the dogs talking to him, he

would have had true hallucinations. A genuine hallucination originates from within. Here, there was ample evidence to suggest that the stimulus was external — it came from real dogs.*

In all my interviews, Berkowitz never mentioned feeling anxious or panicky the first time he hallucinated. But it is an elementary observation in psychiatry that a person is frightened the first time he hallucinates, because he does not know what is happening. Berkowitz, however, never mentioned feeling fright or anxiety when he heard the howling of the dogs. But since they were not human voices who were commanding him to kill, it was a rather unusual clinical manifestation of hallucinations; it seemed more like an illusory experience. And then, too, it took additional mental footwork to change the barking sounds into words.† Berkowitz's explanation had grown more and more suspicious. What was the validity, if any, of his sensory experience — his "hallucination?" Had he made it up?

My field research took me to the post office in the Bronx where Berkowitz had worked from March until the end of July 1977, a week before his arrest. In the large office where he had worked on the mail sorting machine, there was a tremendous, constant noise, so it was difficult to carry on a conversation. I recalled that Berkowitz had complained that he was sensitive to excessive noise. In my interviews with seven different postal employees, each told me, "There was nothing wrong with him." One young woman said, "He showed no disturbance, didn't even blink an eye when I mentioned the .44 caliber killer. [He was] just like any other person. He is the last person I would suspect. He was always courteous. If we had to lift anything heavy, he helped us. He was a gentleman, opened the door for you, and he was never vulgar.[2]

I asked a young woman who had worked with him whether

---

* These discoveries reminded me of the psychologist who had examined Berkowitz at the Kings County Hospital a few weeks after his arrest and who reported that when Berkowitz heard a dog bark outside he became upset and frightened, but calmed down soon afterward. This incident, which had previously been assumed to be a hallucination, was simply incorrectly interpreted.

† This was also the consensus at the colloquia of the American College of Psychoanalysts, May 1979, and May 1980 and May 1981 at which I presented a paper on the case.

there was anything peculiar abut him. "No," she said, "He even walked us one night to the car. We got off at 12:30 A.M. My friend was parked on a deserted street a few blocks away. We were glad to have someone walking with us to the car. We were afraid of going there because of the Son of Sam. He was parked on the opposite side of the street. He waited for us to start our car, and we waited for him to start his, and then we left."

"How did you hear about the arrest?" I asked.

"I had heard they arrested a suspect. When I saw his face in the newspaper, I didn't want to believe it was him. I was shocked. I couldn't believe it."

These interviews provided additional proof that Berkowitz behaved normally at work, and was known as a good and reliable employee.

In my early interviews with him, he confessed that sometimes he felt remorse about the killings. I recalled a police report that when he was arrested he had said, with a slight smile, "You finally got me. What took you so long?" Underneath the obvious irony I detected both guilt and relief. This suspicion was later confirmed when he said to me: "I was glad in a way that they caught me."

These guilt feelings were of the greatest importance in understanding his twisted personality. How could I get to them? The challenge was immense.

"Have you had any dreams here in the hospital?" I asked him one day.

"Dreams?" he countered defensively. "No." Then, "Yes."

"I dreamed I was swimming in the East River, and that somebody was after me in a boat. I was swimming around Manhattan. I got up on the pier in Manhattan. I was wet, I got to change my clothes somewhere. I went to Gracie Mansion, to meet the Mayor, to shake his hand."

He interrupted himself. "It's very noisy here. I don't sleep well —I haven't had bad dreams here. The shower feels good."

Berkowitz was in no mood to continue. I returned to the dream in the next session, to his shaking hands with the then-Mayor Abraham Beame.

"Were you perhaps asking for forgiveness?" I asked.

"I didn't want forgiveness, " he answered flatly. "Who needs that?" he screamed. I had to know if he had any free associations to the dream. I asked:

"Have you ever seen the Mayor?'

"When I was arrested."

"Where?"

"It was in Rockefeller Plaza, I don't know, in Police Head-quarters." [He meant No. 1 Police Plaza.] "He stopped and looked at me, and then he just walked away."

"How did you feel about that?"

Berkowitz shrugged.

I persevered: "Did you feel important that he was there?"

"No."

"Do you know why he was there?"

"Yes, he was there because of me. He had a press conference."

"While you were sitting there?"

"Yes." Then he corrected himself: "No, he had a press con-ference downstairs."

"How did you know he had a press conference?"

"The cops told me at Police Headquarters. I stayed all night long. Was talked to by District Attorneys."

"Then what?" I asked.

"They took me to Brooklyn to detention."

This effort to divert me was significant; he had avoided elab-orating about the dream. He feared that he was exposing some-thing dangerous or revealing. But he had told me the dream, that he had met Mayor Beame, from whom he sought forgiveness. His long swim to reach the Mayor, the "somebody following or chasing him in a boat" (an authority figure), shows clearly that he was anxious to get to the Mayor, to make up to him in order to relieve his feelings of guilt for the murders he had committed in New York City.

In his dream, Berkowitz tried to obtain absolution for his homicides (as if the victims could be brought back to life). Dreams, which often tell us of our carefully guarded or repressed feelings, bring what is in the unconscious mind to the surface. I suspected Berkowitz intuitively knew what he had unwittingly, revealed to me. Thereafter, each time I asked him to tell me about his dreams, he refused. The transference reaction here was negative.

Dreams do not lie. Berkowitz had revealed his true feelings, and if he wanted to repent, it meant he had feelings of guilt — which in turn suggested that he was not insane, and that his story about the demons was fiction. The evidence I was gathering was pointing to a conclusion far different from that of the other two psychiatrists.

A psychosis cannot be turned on or off at will — unless of-course it is a sham.

One day I asked Berkowitz: "Do you think one can talk oneself into a mental condition?"

He replied: "Yes, one could talk oneself into something, but I didn't do that." The very language of his response suggested that he knew what I was referring to. In fact, I concluded, Berkowitz had constructed the demons in order to provide himself with an explanation for his own violent emotions. He personalized and equipped the demons with terrific power. They were like wild dogs, and he knew their volatile nature because they were his own violent emotions.

It was in this way that he tried to concretize his emotions and sexual urges. He had to identify and give his unruly emotions names, and so he called them demons. They were a product of his conscious, deliberate thoughts; they came at his beck and call. He was their creator rather than their subject.

On September 28, 1977, I completed my first series of examinations with the defendant. District Attorney Gold requested my written report. In it I cited Berkowitz's suspicion of me as an agent of the Brooklyn District Attorney's office. I went on, quoting Berkowitz:

"I knew it (the shooting) was wrong in accordance with the laws of society. But it doesn't apply. These demons and angels fight. I was told to fight. I was told to shoot. The demons sometimes looked like people."

"Do you hear the demons now?"

"I hear them now once a week. Sometimes I do feel sorry for her [Moskowitz] being killed."

He says he knows he is charged with a crime, has talked with his defense lawyer and is able to help out with his defense. He also says he is responsible for the shooting: "I know I did the shooting."

. . . .

He says he feels the jury has decided "I have to be destroyed." Asked whether he feels the same way, he answers: "I guess so. I didn't fight hard enough [against the demons]." This may well mean that on some occasions he did have sufficient resistance to fight his own murderous impulses. "I don't really have any remorse. It seemed to be unrealistic — it was real, too. I knew it was me. People are against me." He feels sorry about having killed. "I still have some humanness left in me, some basis."

In my conclusion, I stated: "The defendant's face has an innocent, child-like expression. Throughout the interviews there is a tendency toward seductiveness that one senses rather than being able to pinpoint.

An examination of all the facts available to me indicates that the defendant can be cunning, shrewd and calculating, pitting his power against the authorities. He is very sadistic but when necessary, is able to conceal it and be quite ingratiating, appearing rather innocent.

... He functions intellectually on a bright level, is well informed, and understands all questions very well. He was quite perceptive and at times understood my question almost before I asked it. Memory was good for present and remote events, and his ability to repeat several digits forwards and backwards was excellent. During all interviews he always talked in a well modulated voice, except when he became excited and raised his voice. Smiling sometimes, which almost always was appropriate, he also could become angry or disappointed, which he showed. He exhibited few, if any, anxieties, undoubtedly because they are deeply repressed and isolated. He showed some manipulative traits.

. . . .

Another time, he complained to his lawyer that I had not talked much about his delusions or his demons, which had been such an important topic in the other psychiatrists' interviews. Apparently Berkowitz felt that his distorted beliefs were of such importance that all other topics should be relegated to the sidelines. The purpose of such a tactic would appear to be obvious. His main excuse for committing the crimes is his delusions. Thus, the examiner's concerning himself with these delusions (rather than with the general, more logical aspects of his personality and behavior) could give the defendant a feeling of drawing support and credibility from a psychiatric authority.

Noteworthy was that his claimed delusions seemed to be more transitory and situational rather than constant. They may, in fact, be exaggerated by him. He stated that sometimes his hallucinations became weak and even disappeared for periods, even while he stayed in Yonkers, all indicating that they did not have sufficient influence upon his mind to interfere with his intellectual capability to understand the murder charges against him, and to aid his lawyer in his own defense. Another point speaking for the fact that his mind is free is that there is no thought-disorder, which is so characteristic of a psychosis of schizophrenic origin. Nor has there been any deterioration of his emotional or intellectual abilities. His emotional involvement in his case is also shown by his concern over having had to dismiss Attorney Mark Heller, with whom he had developed a good relationship not only as his lawyer but also as his friend.

His reaction to this change of lawyers caused him anger and annoyance which, in my opinion, he expressed through restlessness and irritability during my interview with him following the dismissal of Mr. Heller.

While the defendant shows some paranoid traits, they do not interfere with his fitness to stand trial. His ego, directed in part toward pleasure, in part toward reality, is strong and he can well understand any stress of a trial. It should be remembered that every defendant is under stress in the courtroom.

It is my considered judgment that the defendant, David Berkowitz, understands the charges against him, is able to aid in his own defense, and is able to stand trial.[3]

The competency hearing was two weeks away, with a showdown impending. David Berkowitz could not be the person portrayed in both reports; one of the reports had to be mistaken. Berkowitz exhibited symptoms that did not fit any category of mental illnesses known to psychiatry. He had, so to speak, doctored up his own mental condition. His delusions were manufactured.

The competency hearing had been set for October 20, 1977, and Berkowitz's attorneys had requested an advance look at my findings. Shen Sheldon Greenberg, Gold's first assistant attorney, came to my office to receive it, he sat down and read it right then and there. When he had finished, he looked up and said with a smile, "This is dynamite."[4]

7

THE BATTLE OF
THE PSYCHIATRISTS

To avoid the hoopla that would occur when transporting David Berkowitz halfway across Brooklyn, the competency hearing was held at the prison ward of Kings County Hospital. Officials judged that Berkowitz could be protected from vengeance seekers if he remained in his temporary quarters.

October 20, 1977, was a raw day. The wind gusted erratically through wet streets and reverberated off high buldings. The stormy wind and pelting rain created, I thought, a howling, angry backdrop entirely appropriate for Son of Sam's demons. It didn't enhance the day when I saw several staff members from the District Attorney's office at Borough Hall in Brooklyn stubbornly trying to negotiate a large lectern into a small car, which, along with several heavy volumes of court records, they felt was indispensable at the improvised courtroom at Kings County Hospital. That the bulky objects clearly would not fit into the tiny car made no difference; they stubbornly refused to give up.

As we approached the hospital entrance and drove slowly toward Building G, where Berkowitz was being held, a horde of news people with tape recorders, cameras and videotapes attached themselves to us. My persistent "No comment," was of no avail. In the building entrance our I.D.'s were carefully scrutinized, our envelopes and briefcases opened and searched. The guards were looking for guns, bombs, or other weapons, terrified that Berkowitz might be hurt or killed; public opinion was so strongly against him. A few days after his arrest, there had been a demonstration outside the hospital, the demonstrators chanting "Kill him, kill him!" I was later to learn that one of the people clamoring for Berkowitz's life was the mother of Stacy Moskowitz. In view of the situation, one could hardly criticize the security personnel for their concern.

The air was heavy with tension in the makeshift courtroom, where separate tables had been set up for defense and prosecution lawyers. Because the case was so important the prosecution would be conducted by District Attorney Gold himself. Gold was a short man with alert eyes and a smiling, persuasive face. Sitting beside him was Sheldon Greenberg, First Assistant District Attorney, who had been with Gold for fifteen years, and who had worked with me for three months on the case. He was agile and moved fast, reflecting an astute mind. More than once he had exclaimed to me about how extraordinary the case was, and had warned me of the difficulties that lay ahead. He always ended by saying: "There is *never* going to be another case like David Berkowitz."

Beside Greenberg sat the Chief Assistant District Attorney Robert Keating, who persistently questioned me on the fine points of Berkowitz's psychology, posing many questions which were not easy to answer, particularly at the onset. He raised, always, the problem of a rational explanation for Berkowitz's crimes. I would say to him, "This is why I must delve into his childhood — because there lies the key to his behavior." Keating nodded.

Also at the table sat Belman Brook an assistant District Attorney, and Stephen Wax (who would examine me during the second competency hearing). In the front of the room sat the reporters and the artists who sketched defense and prosecution lawyers, judge, psychiatrists, and finally the defendant himself.

In the back were five rows of chairs for press and selected public. In the crowd, I recognized a tall figure, the mother of Stacy Moskowitz. It would be for Stacy's murder that Berkowitz would stand trial.

As the Son of Sam entered the courtroom, flanked by two guards, all strained their necks to see. He attempted to smile, but his ashen demeanor betrayed him — his face was taut and pale. Had he at last begun to realize the seriousness of his situation? He took his seat between two well-known defense lawyers, Leon Stern and Ira Jultak. No words were exchanged among them.

Judge John R. Starkey, a towering, black-robed, gray-haired man in his sixties entered and seated himself on his bench facing the crowded room. He addressed the lawyers, reminding all present that "I have told Mr. Gold and Mr. Stern that we do have a presumption of sanity. It is the position of the defendant that he is incapable of proceeding at this time, and it will be the duty of the defendant to come forward with some evidence, to overcome the legal presumption of sanity. Then, that having been done, the burden will shift to the people, to prove sanity beyond a resonable doubt." (He would later amend "beyond a reasonable doubt" to "a fair preponderance of evidence.")

"When I am using the word 'sanity' I am using it loosely."[1]

Dr. Schwartz, a psychiatrist, was the first witness for the court. After describing his sessions with the defendant, he stated that during the previous week he had conducted an additional, unauthorized interview with Berkowitz, which he had taped. Over the prosecution's strenuous objections, the defense was given permission to play the tape, a decision Judge Starkey would later regret as the courtroom at once lost all semblance of order. The playing of the tape led to a free-for-all: reporters scurried around, talking and gesticulating, tripping over cords and wires in their haste to place their tape recorders as near as possible to Dr. Schwartz.

The Court: This is the tape, as I understand it, of Dr. Schwartz's conversation with the defendant on Monday of this week. Is that correct, Doctor?

The Witness: Yes, sir.[2]

Whereupon the tape, Defendant's Exhibit B, was played for the court, all counsel and the defendant. For Dr. Schwartz it was a godsend; a way, at an early point in the hearing, of demonstrating to the public the fantasy world of Berkowitz's demons.*

Here is some of what the court heard on the tapes:

A. Berkowitz: You (Dr. Schwartz) said I was emotionally dead or something.
Q. Schwartz: Hh-huh.
A. Berkowitz: Well, in a way I guess I was, maybe it was hopelessness, you know. Then I saw the situation I was in. But now I see that there's hope. Not for me.
Q. Schwartz: Uh-huh.
A. Berkowitz: I'm willing to go, uh, to jail, you know, forever—that's all right. [Berkowitz talks about Glassman, the neighbor who "fingered" him on the night of the arrest.] I don't know, now he's getting all the credit for the arrest. When really, he was the cause of the shooting in the first place, along with Sam. I'm the Son of Sam. It's not me, it's Sam that works through me, uses me as a tool. But the Son of Sam, we're not the same people. Now I want to be David Berkowitz only. They use my body.† Sam did it through me. He used me, he made me go out there and do it. And now he's [Glassman] getting the reward money. Not only that, but he's writing a book which will distort the truth even more.§ After my dad left for Florida, you know, I was on my own. I mean, I just came out of the Army. I had saved up over $5,000; saved up to support a car, an apartment. I had the apartment furnished, wall to wall carpeting. I wanted to go to school and make good and everything. Had a job as a security guard. I wanted nothing but to live a normal life, you know. Then Sam came. The demons came, the two things came in. I went along only because they forced me and my heart was never really in it, although sometimes they — I said yes, it was. But it really wasn't you know. Serving Sam was all it was — in the end, but I hated

---

* It was obvious that Schwartz had already read my report, and that in an effort to counteract its effects he had, without the knowledge of the court or the District Attorney, once again interviewed Berkowitz.
† Berkowitz was very much aware of who he was. He was changing at will, consciously and deliberately.
§ This book—fiction—was published in the summer of 1980.

it.* ... You know, I was very disappointed in that other doctor, you know. Dr. Abrahamsen, because he didn't want to listen to me.† You know, this was very disappointing. Because without Sam I'm nothing. What are you doing, we're wasting time, you know. What's the purpose of everything? ... I was punished on the outside being the Son of Sam. It's the people that said the unkind things about me. Like for instance, the day I was arrested, they caught me smiling. I was smiling all day, I was really happy, I was happy that it was over. . . .

Q. Is there any way in which I can convince you that your best chance lies in the so-called insanity defense?

A. No, no, because I know I'm a normal person. I could work, I could, you know, balance my checkbook, I wipe myself after I finish the toilet bowl.

Q. (Laughs).

The entire tape ran for about 45 minutes in all, after which the court recessed for lunch. When Judge Starkey returned, somewhat delayed from luncheon, there was a conference at the bench by Gold, Stern, and the court. Then the judge stated to the courtroom that both defense and prosecution had concurred with his prohibition on further playing of tapes.

Mr. Jultak, a young and rigorous attorney for the defense, called Dr. Schwartz to the witness stand.§ The questioning went as follows:

Q. Dr. Schwartz, has your opinion changed in any way via the tape we just heard?

A. No, if anything, the examination I conducted this week strengthened my earlier conviction, my conclusion, that the defendant could not properly assist in his defense.

---

* Here is evidence of Berkowitz's ambivalent feelings about his killings. Three or four days following his arrest, he knew well that he had killed and that he hated it. Although it was suggested that he was confused, he wasn't so confused as to be unaware of what he had done. His monologue reveals his clarity of speech, although he tries to wrap his words in a strange way to cover his deeds.

† I did indeed listen to him, but was unconvinced of his demons.

§ Since this (and the following) competency hearing became the crux of the case, it is necessary to go into details so the reader may see how Berkowitz tried to protect himself against the aggressiveness of both defense and prosecution lawyers.

Q. Doctor, can you point specifically to which parts of that interview have led you to this conclusion?

A. Yes. . . . he is suffering from a delusional set of beliefs, the delusion that is relatively permanently fixed. Certainly, by no stretch of the imagination, could it be called transitory and that because of these delusions his judgment is quite distorted as to assisting in his defense. . . . He sees his primary purpose now as warning the world against Sam and the other demons and he is willing to plead guilty so that people will more readily believe him and see that he has no ulterior motive. This is so uppermost in his mind that it distorts his judgment as to what his defense in his own self-interest ought to be and because of this I believe he cannot assist in his defense in a rational manner.

Q. Doctor, in your professional opinion, is there any doubt in your mind that this defendant is sincere, is stating the truth as he sees it, rather than creating a situation of fiction?

A. There is no doubt in my mind whatsoever.

District Attorney Gold, in his cross-examination, went after Schwartz's notion that Berkowitz was "emotionally dead." He also wanted to shake Dr. Schwartz free from his belief in the demon story. The questioning was clever and pointed:

Q. Well, now, Doctor, coming back to your report which was issued at the end of August and the interviews you had with the defendant prior to preparing that report, isn't it a fact, Doctor, that during the course of the interview with him he exhibited sadness, love, loneliness, compassion, anger, excitement, fear, humor and curiosity? . . .

A. Do you want to go over them one by one?

Q. Sadness?

A. Yes, there was one point when I said he was —— I though he was close to tears.

Q. Love?

A. He expressed love for his father?

Q. Loneliness?

A. He spoke of loneliness, yes . . .

Q. Compassion?

A. That one I don't recall.

Q. Do you recall his expressing ——

The Court. About knowing people would die ——

The Witness. Yes. Yes.

Q. Anger?

A. . . . I am trying my best to recall a specific instance, that's all.

Q. . . . I quote from page 6 of your report, one moment he is angry about being forced to come home tired, and later from school. Do you recall that now?

A. Yes.

Q. So he showed anger?

A. Yes.

Q. Excitement?

A. Yes.

Q. Fear?

A. Yes.

Q. Humor?

A. Yes.

Q. Curiosity?

A. Yes.

Q. Would you say, Doctor, these are the marks of an emotionally dead person?

A. If you consider how short-lived and infrequent these emotions were in the total context of eleven hours of interviews, yes. When it comes . . . to the question of whether or not . . . his future meant anything to him, Mr. Gold, I think the overall impression had to be one of emotional deadness.*

Q. . . . Doctor, isn't it a fact that most of the discussions you had with the defendant during those eleven hours dealt with demons?

A. . . . There are whole sessions there that we had, I believe, that dealt with his past life. I did learn from him about his childhood and his past history.

Q. Wasn't it during the discussion of his childhood and thinking about the past that he chuckled and he laughed; isn't that so? . . . Isn't it so that where appropriate the defendant expressed anger, where appropriate he expressed love and sadness; wouldn't you say that's so?

Dr. Schwartz questioned whether any of these feelings, in view of Berkowitz's six homicides, really could be appropriate. To which Gold asked:

---

* It was not emotional deadness. Berkowitz was depressed, but for one reason only: he felt guilty.

Q. Now, are you suggesting, Doctor, that one who faces these kinds of charges should not ever express fear?

A. ... If the man is facing life imprisonment, I think that might well be a source of fear. But his fear had to do with demons and other things.

Q. Isn't it a fact, as well, Doctor, that he told you that the demons had disappeared while he was in this institution pretty much?

A. Pretty much, but we know they haven't.

Q. I said pretty much, Doctor.... Would you agree with that characterization?

A. Most of the time, yes.

Q. Isn't it a fact, Doctor, that during the course of your questioning of him he told you that the demons occurred to him *once a week*?

A. Perhaps.

Q. Well, once a week would mean almost all of the time he is not confronted by the demons, wouldn't you agree with that?

A. Yes, but I don't understand——

Q. Doctor, I must tell you frankly, neither do I!

The district attorney's answer had the force of a Mack truck, because he had led Schwartz into admitting that, in fact, most of Berkowitz's life was "demon free."

Gold then proceeded to demonstrate that Schwartz and Weidenbacher's claim that Berkowitz was not "inordinately concerned" with his personal hygiene, *was* not the case. He also showed that Berkowitz's reason for not having talked with his father when he visited at the prison ward was because there was no privacy. Gold's intention in bringing up these two matters was simply to prove that the defendant was responding rationally to his situation.

The district attorney then got to the heart of the matter: Berkowitz's capability to cooperate with his lawyers in his own defense. Gold quoted from Schwartz's interview in which, asked about what kind of defense he would offer, Berkowitz had replied: "I don't know." He had then elaborated: "I don't have the strength to fight it too much. My work is done. I don't care what the proceedings are." Gold read these words to Schwartz: "That's in your report ... is it not?"

A. Yes. And that's some of the statement I was referring to when I wrote at the time the patient was indifferent to ——

Q. Now, Doctor . . . continuing, there is another sentence which you left out. "There have to be certain formalities they have to do, let them do it." Do you remember that?

A. Yes.

Q. Would that indicate to you that he understands that there have to be proceedings brought against him?

A. Oh, yes. Mr. Gold, I have never questioned his understanding, but I think what you have quoted is an excellent section to illustrate how indifferent he is to these formalities.

Q. Would you say that he would be indifferent if he says that he will permit his lawyer to put in an insanity defense for him?

A. The last time I spoke to him, which was the tape that was played this morning, it was my distinct impression that he would not allow such a defense.

Q. Now, doctor, relating directly . . . to your last response, I want to read to you a part of the conversation on August 18, 1977. . . . "Soon enough there is going to come a question of what you shall do about these legal charges. What would you see yourself doing? Answer: Go to trial, answer the questions, whatever they want, play their games. Question: You don't seem very interested. Answer: It is just a matter of politics. They want to see justice prevail, you know, the victims' survivors." Do you remember asking those questions and the defendant making those answers?

A. I think so.

Q. . . . Then you continued, "What will your defense be if you go to trial? Answer: I don't know. Question: Do you think you were insane at the time? Would that be a viable defense, would you go along with such a defense? Answer: No, I think I can add, subtract. I don't sing to myself." Then you continued, "Do you think any of the stuff you told us might defend you?" and the defendant responded: "No. It wouldn't, people don't want to hear that, they don't want to know." Do you remember asking the defendant these questions and the defendant making those responses?

A. Yes, and we continued along that line.

At this point, Schwartz wanted to take over reading from the examination, but Gold stopped him.

Q. I will continue, Doctor. Have no fear. [Still quoting]: "Supposing Mr. Stern or whoever your attorney is would argue that question you did all this, that at the time you were not criminally responsible because you were suffering from a whole host of delusions and hallucinations, and the defendant responded, "That's what people want to believe they were, to be safe. I suppose it is better for them than the truth. Question: Well, whether they were or not is immaterial, the question is would you allow Mr. Stern to argue this way? Answer: I suppose, yes. . . . I will do what he says. He is the lawyer." Do you remember that, Doctor?

A. . . . Yes, I did at one point, Mr. Gold, get this brief, short-lived willingness on his part. [An important admission from Schwartz.]

Q. . . . And then you say, "Maybe you should think more about this and talk about it again, it is important; isn't it? Answer: The end is the same. . . . They will put me away forever. Question: You will be (put) away forever, you don't care where it is? Answer: It is no different, it is the same. Question: Some people would prefer a mental hospital to a prison and vice versa. Answer: I have never been in either one, both are just as bad." Doctor, would you say those are rather rational responses to the questions you put?   ⸙

A. Rational, yes, but indifferent, too.

Q. Well, is it indifferent to say, "I have never been in either one, both are just as bad?"

A. It is indifferent to say that he, in effect, doesn't care, that it makes no difference to him.

Q. Are you saying that it is indifferent to say that a mental institution is a bad place to be; isn't that what he said?

A. . . . As I understand it, he is saying at that point that it makes no difference to him . . .

Q. . . . Would you say, Doctor, that when he uses the word "bad" he is expressing some kind of an emotional reaction to being in prisons or a mental institution?

At this point there was an interjection from one who had not yet been heard.

Berkowitz. I don't mind being here, sir. In fact I have enjoyed my stay quite a bit. I am serious. I don't mean to be disrespectful, it is true.
Mr. Gold. Thank you.
Berkowitz. Okay.

The Court. In effect, Mr. Gold, I think that the response indicated that incarceration is bad, either kind of incarceration.

Berkowitz. But I was incarcerated outside too, your Honor, and I just want to make that clear, your Honor.

Q. Now, Doctor, you have stated that the defendant is emotionally dead; is that correct?

A. At the time I examined him in August, he appeared that way, yes.

A. Is he emotionally dead today?

A. Now, I would say this week he is — shall I say is more alive than he was then. He is more enthusiastic about the prospect of being able to tell his story to the world.

Dr. Schwartz had been compelled to retreat from his earlier position.

District Attorney Gold then brought up the matter of some 40 pages of notes that Berkowitz had made about his murders. Berkowitz was concerned about the disposition of these notes, and Gold interpreted this concern to mean that he was interested in building a defense — in contrast to Schwartz's position. He insisted that all of Berkowitz's energies were directed not at defending himself, about which he was "indifferent," but rather at warning the world against the demons. "Send me to jail for life," Berkowitz had told him. "Lock the door and throw away the key. Even electrocute me, if you will, but the important thing is to understand my story about the demons."[3] For that reason, said Schwartz, Berkowitz refused to plead insanity.

Dr. Weidenbacher who followed Schwartz to the stand, gave testimony corroborating his colleague's. He found the defendant to be "earnestly insane. . . . The picture is all too coherent to one, clinically speaking — progressive, initially insidious, and then flamboyant, madness, and more particularly, paranoid psychosis."

The next day, when Schwartz (who it seemed to me had been acting more as a lawyer giving legal advice than as a psychiatrist offering a professional opinion on the defendant's mental condition) returned to the stand, he contended that the "defense should be insanity, if there be any defense at all."

Schwartz was trying to have it both ways: his position was

simply that if Berkowitz wasn't willing to plead insanity, then he must be, well, insane.

It was my turn to testify. Called to the stand by District Attorney Gold, I first reviewed my initial encounter with Berkowitz. When I told the Court that the defendant had read my book *The Murdering Mind*, Gold elicited from me the fact that a competency hearing had been the issue in that book.

I went on to talk about Berkowitz's childhood. When I suggested that the defendant had ambivalent feelings, negative as well as positive, about his adoptive mother, Berkowitz blushed and burst out, "Your honor, that was a lie. What about the gravesite when I cried. . . . This is my mother you are talking about!" The judge quickly silenced him. Eager to pursue the point a bit, I remarked that although he had indeed often visited Pearl's grave, he had also sought out and lingered over the graves of young women who were complete strangers to him. I then proceeded with my report without further interruption.

My conclusions — "That the alleged delusions the defendant states he has do seem to be more transitory and situational ratherthan constant. In fact, I believe they were exaggerated by him —"[4]

I was cross-examined by defense attorney Ira Jultak.

Q. Dr. Abrahamsen, I take it, and I am not trying to be facetious, that you disagree with the conclusions and the diagnosis formed by Drs. Schwartz and Weidenbacher?
A. Yes.
Q. Sir, do you have any independent diagnosis of this defendant?
A. . . . I do believe that this defendant has a psychopathic personality with some paranoid traits.
The Court. Will you explain that, Doctor?
The Witness. . . . A psychopath is a person who is very narcissistic or egocentric, selfish; always thinking of himself — often, frequently unable to get along with other people or has been in trouble and wants, very often, immediate gratification. He cannot wait to obtain satisfaction, but has to get it at once.

He is impatient, he is intolerant of other people, and also very often gets in trouble, either with his family or with the law. Because of his desire for immediate satisfaction, he has to act out his desires in various anti-social or criminal acts. But such a person, this psychopath, is not psychotic or insane. He has very few anxieties and his conscience is very little developed. (Although he is capable of feeling guilt.)

This is, in the main, the picture of a psychopath.

Q. Then am I to understand that in the final analysis you feel that David Berkowitz is not in any way psychotic?

A. That is right. . . .

Q. Doctor, you sat through . . . two days of testimony listening to Drs. Schwartz and Weidenbacher, and you have heard their conclusion, based upon the findings they made while examining this defendant?

A. Yes. . . .

Q. . . . If I could ask you, in the hypothetical, attributing to a defendant those behavioral characteristics that Dr. Schwartz has attributed to David Berkowitz through his, what he calls delusional scheme, exhibiting those traits and expressing them as he did in his reports; if you were to apply those criteria or those behavioral traits which you seem to disagree exist, would you find a psychosis?

A. . . . If those delusions were true, then it would be a psychosis, yes.

Jultak next asked why I had not taped my interviews with Berkowitz, something he said the defendant had been anxious for me to do. I explained that it impeded the establishment of a good rapport with the person I was interviewing. Then, too, Berkowitz's desire that I use a recorder indicated his awareness of his precarious legal situation and that he was seeking to build a case. The key point, Jultak said, was that his client was simply afraid of being misquoted. He also suggested a recording might have made it easier for me to catch revealing inflections in Berkowitz's voice, to which I responded that I had been practicing psychiatry for forty years and felt quite capable of discerning a person's feelings while I was speaking to him.*

We then turned to the matter of Pearl Berkowitz's death:

Q. Doctor, did he tell you that his mother was "infected" with cancer?

---

* It should be noted that originally defense and prosecution had agreed that the defense attorney should see my notes following my examination. Later, however the defense attorneys requested that they be present at my examination of the defendant, and also that a tape recording be made—both requests in total breach of the original agreement.

A. It might very well be that he used such a word.

Q. Well, did he . . . elaborate? Did he say she was inflicted with cancer by the demons so that he would be isolated?

A. No. This he didn't tell me. I don't remember that.

Q. Don't you find this significant in the range of a delusional scheme?

A. No. . . . When you talk about delusions and a delusional scheme, I do believe that you have to see what kind of personality you are dealing with. David Berkowitz is a person who likes to be dramatic. He likes to have attention and he likes to dramatize situations which he has done for me sometimes.

Q. . . . Doctor, on page 8 of your report, right, "He says he likes goodlooking girls." I am reading: "I would like to make love to them, not shoot them." . . . This (was said) in a conversation you were having with him about two girls that he approached and shot while (they were) sitting on a stoop? This was in the context of a sentence in which he was saying Sam made him kill, that if it were up to him he wouldn't have killed, he would make love to pretty girls, not shoot them?

A. Yes.

Q. Doctor, nowhere in your report do you mention his delusional scheme in reference to that sentence, either, do you?

A. It doesn't look like it.*

Q. Doctor, on p. 10 of your report . . . I am reading: "As a matter of fact, at the end of 1976, in the Yonkers area, where he lived, he shot two dogs, one fatally and the other which survived still has a bullet in him." Doctor, did David . . . say he shot dogs or did he say he shot demons?

A. . . . We were talking about dogs and to me it seemed that he somehow had an idea that they were dogs, not demons.

Q. Doctor, "dogs" is your language, not his language; the idea of "dogs" is your language?

A. No, I would not say so because he has used "dogs" very frequently in conversations with me. . . .

Q. Doctor, page 11 of your report, I am reading: . . . "first week of August, on a weekend, he set out for the Hamptons but returned the same evening, without shooting anyone. He had been to control his sadistic and murderous impulses."

---

* Berkowitz later told me that he had sexual feelings for his victims without being delusional about it.

A. Yes.

Q. Doctor, did he explain to you that it rained at the Hamptons that weekend?

A. ... He came out to the Hamptons [East Hampton], which I happen to know very well, and he went to the beach and he sat on the sand and looked around and looked at the girls. This is what he told me. ... Waiting and seeing how the situation was. After sitting there for two and a half hours or so ... it began to rain and he left.

Q. Did he tell you that once it started raining there was no one to shoot?

A. Yes, he said so. But I would also say this: that if he had not been in control of himself, he would have shot someone.

Q. ... Now, Doctor, we get down to the bottom of page 11: ... "At that time he lived in the Bronx but says he had to move away "because of the noise.'"

Doctor, did he not tell you that the noise, as you call it, was the howling of demons?

A. Yes. But I must also say this. ... He was on the fifth floor staying in the apartment and there was a dog on the ground floor which was barking day and night. And everyone in that building was complaining about that dog barking, and I took it that it was this dog he realistically heard.

Jultak asked me if, in fact, demons (barking dogs) drove Berkowitz from his Bronx apartment. He continued to press me to admit that the defendant really thought he heard demons speaking through barking dogs.

There followed some rather important sparring over the difference between halluncinations and delusions and their significance vis a vis Berkowitz's emotional state.

Q. A fixed wrong idea that cannot be changed by a confrontation with reality, would that fit the definition of delusion?

A. ... The question is, whether you are dealing with a delusion or whether you are dealing with a hallucination. This is the point. ...

The Court. What is the difference between a delusion and an hallucination?

The Witness. ... A hallucination is a perception arising without any external stimulus causing it, but a delusion is an erroneous belief impervious to reason.

Q. Now, Doctor, if David insisted he heard a demon and you say in reality it was a dog, and you cannot convince David that it was not a demon, is that a delusion?

A. No, I would not say so, because he even went in there to get the dog.

Q. . . . Tell me his language to you, did he go to get a dog or shoot a demon?

A. I cannot answer that question. . . .

Q. We continue . . . : "At the end of 1975 or beginning of 1976, he rented living quarters in New Rochelle, the house owned by Jack Cassara. He began to develop the main ideas that the master of the demons was 'General Cosmo,' again he says he 'could not stand the noise any longer' and moved to Yonkers." Doctor, did he express to you that that noise was howling and demands of demons.

A. Yes, he mentioned something to that effect, but after I interviewed him I found out there really was a dog on the second floor which was howling and barking.

Q. Doctor, if it is in reality a dog and David Berkowitz insists it was a demon, it that not a delusion?

A. I do know that he was complaining to this woman about a dog which was barking. He didn't use the word "demon" to her.

Q. Did he tell you Doctor, that the demons were bothering him at Jack Cassara's house?

A. Yes.

Q. This is not in your report?

A. No. I have talked about the matter of demons. "He says he tried to fight the demons, run away from them, but they broke me down, I'm a soldier in Sam's army. I was told by Sam, the blood monster." It is there on page 12.

Q. So here for the first time you express what he told you of the demons and you use his language about the blood monster.

A. Yes.

Q. Doctor, can you tell us . . . who is this "blood monster?"

A. The blood monsters were the demons, they were sucking blood, as he told me. And I asked him whether he had seen any blood. He told me, no, he had not. . . . I asked him, why should they suck the blood. And he said that it is blood they are looking for and want.

Q. Doctor, were those blood monsters hallucinations?

A. I think they were more hallucinations than anything else. Well, but distressing here is that we do have the so-called hallucination basis in reality coming from dogs, so there is here a mixture of both—not a mixture, but certainly there is a reality basis for it.

Q. Doctor, would it be correct to say that hallucinations may stop, a delusion continues?

A. If they're hallucinations, yes.

Q. Then it becomes a delusion?

A. Yes. (uncertain about the answer) . . .

Q. Well, now, Doctor, now you have expressed here an idea commencing in 1975 about demons that would appear to you and me as being dogs, which exists to the present date — we heard a conversation as late as last Monday played for us in court, in which this belief is adhered to and has yet to diminish. Now, is this not a delusional scheme? Has the belief ever ceased in David Berkowitz?

A. I do believe that this belief has changed in nature since he has come in here and also he changed even when he was on the outside, because if there is a . . . genuine real delusion one would expect it would be present practically all the time, particularly if based upon hallucinations.

Now, it makes me doubt the validity of his hallucinations as such.

Q. Well, now, Doctor, when you say a delusion exists all the time, need one vocalize that delusion twenty-four hours a day for that delusion to be present?

A. Well, this isn't really the point. The point is really here how much governed is he by that delusion?

Q. Well, Doctor, how about being governed to the point of killing six people and wounding eight others?

A. Well, I do not believe that he was governed by any delusions or demons here.

Q. Then, you feel this is all a fabrication, a line that he has invented?

A. I do believe this, that Mr. Berkowitz is a very smart man. He is, as I said, cunning, he is able to emphasize, or increase or exaggerate these symptoms in order to give them validity and also in order to be in the middle of things, to be in the limelight.

Q. Doctor, perhaps not the best language diplomatically, but are you then saying that Drs. Schwartz and Weidenbacher were fooled or taken in by David Berkowitz.

A. I wonder how many times I have had that question directed to me. And I'm a little surprised that both these two doctors, who are psychiatrists, have gone that far as to say and base their findings upon these delusions — these alleged delusions.

The lawyer asked why I did not dwell on Berkowitz's demonology in my report. I explained that what was more significant to me was why the defendant had been so anxious to discuss these demons. Berkowitz had told me, point blank, that he would be most cooperative in answering questions, if I would just stick to Sam, Cosmo, and the rest. I could have delved into the intricacies of his communications with the demon world, as Dr. Schwartz had done. But sometimes a dog is just a dog.

Mr. Jultak asked the reasons for Berkowitz's setting fires at the homes of two of his neighbors. I explained that he thought people hated him and he was afraid of them. Mr. Jultak, however, believed and suggested Berkowitz was ridding himself of demons.

Jultak asked whether Berkowitz understood the proceedings against him. I answered that he felt threatened by the court. Did Berkowitz believe that Sam Carr had determined what was going to happen? I thought so, but on the other hand Berkowitz was able to resist the demands of the demons or Sam Carr.

In later cross examination, Jultak wanted to know whether I had asked Berkowitz if the only defense he had would be insanity. His question surprised me, because I am a psychiatrist, not a lawyer.

Later Mr. Jultak was to examine me closely about the exact date I had been retained by District Attorney Gold. I told him it was some time in August — before the unsealing of Schwartz's and Weidenbacher's report. The following questioning then took place:

Q. Did Mr. Gold give you his views about the defendant's competency?

A. Yes, he mentioned this to me. But also I told him this: that I am an independent person, and I can only judge in accordance with my findings.

Q. But he told you what his views were?

A. Yes. He told me his views, yes.

Q. And, Doctor, on August 30th, when a psychiatric report was made public and it was determined that the two court-appointed psychiatrists had found this defendant incapacitated; at that point in time you know that the district attorney's view was to the contrary?

A. Yes.

Q. And on what day were you actually retained, that is, was a fee set and determined for you to examine David Berkowitz?

A. I do believe that I was retained a few days before August 30th [it was actually August 15].

Q. A few days before the result of the examination was known, Doctor?

A. Yes. I think so. I am not quite sure.

The Court. I think what counsel wants to know, Doctor, and I think you have answered him, you told Mr. Gold that you are independent. In other words, you were not going to return a report of fitness to proceed before you had made the examination.

The Witness. Yes, of course.

Turning again to David Berkowitz, Mr. Jultak asked me to confirm that Berkowitz had exhibited some paranoid traits. Then he quoted me as saying that a paranoid condition pervades one's entire personality. "This is not accurate," I answered. He then referred to a testimony I had given in another case. The issue there was whether or not the defendant was psychotic. In that earlier case, the person had been psychotic. David Berkowitz, in my opinion, was not. For this reason, the cases were not comparable.

At the re-examination that followed, I testified that Mr. Stern had actually requested a psychiatric report from me, and that is why I prepared one — because the District Attorney's office wanted to accommodate him. If the defense had not asked for a written report, I would not have written one.

Finally, the judge asked one last question: could rejection by girls have been a subconscious motivation for the murders. I said yes.

I had been on the witness stand for most of the second day. The judge told me to step down. The defense and the people rested.

The prosecution was agreeable to having the judge decide on Berkowitz's competency to stand trial without further argument, since the defense attorneys had already agreed to it. The judge's statement was:

Well, gentlemen, I think I can decide the case here and now. I am convinced by a preponderance of the evidence, and not only by a preponderance of the evidence that the defendant is fit to proceed, I am convinced of that fact, beyond a reasonable doubt, because there is — our law is now — the Appellate Division, Second Department, says preponderance of evidence. It is somewhat a gray area so far as other jurisdictions are concerned, but I'm convinced, beyond a reasonable doubt, after listening to the testimony of the three experts, and it is a very, very, inexact sphere, the science of psychiatry. Even in my lifetime there have been theories, and on the question of fitness to proceed, according to the textbooks, we do have various phases as distinguished from the law, which state that he has the capacity to understand the proceedings against him. I think that everybody is agreed that he understands the proceedings against him.

Now we come to the question of preparing his defense and the question is, is he oriented as to time and place and the answer to that question is, yes. Can he perceive, recall and relate? He can to a great extent. Did he have a rudimentary understanding of the criminal process in the roles of judge and jury, prosecutor and defense attorney? I think that must be answered in the affirmative. Can he establish a working relationship with his attorney, and that has been demonstrated. Does he have sufficient intelligence and judgement to listen to advice? Yes, to listen. There might be a doubt as to whether he will take the advice. But that doesn't interfere with his ability to listen to advice.

He seems to be a man of very positive thoughts and his mental state is sufficiently stable to withstand the stress of a trial without a mental breakdown. So I find, not only by a preponderance of the evidence, but beyond a reasonable doubt, that he is competent to go to trial.
Mr. Stern. Respectfully excepted, your Honor.
The Court. Your exception is noted.

Judge Starkey's decision was a surprise to the tense audience, because of its promptness and because of its consequences. He had rejected the findings of Kings County staff psychiatrists

Schwartz and Weidenbacher. Dr. Weidenbacher left the room and Dr. Schwartz moved nervously from spot to spot. The judge set the trial date at November 2. It was considerably delayed, however, because the defense made a motion for change of venue, as they felt Berkowitz could not get a fair trial in New York City.

This motion later denied, the defense made a motion for a new competency hearing, having now engaged their own psychiatrist, Dr. Martin Lubin. Further, the defense moved that the competency hearing be held *in camera* — a closed hearing — a step which the news media strongly protested.

But now, something new had happened. By December 1977, Berkowitz had begun to doubt his own beliefs in the demons. In February and March, 1978, Berkowitz told Dr. Schwartz and Weidenbacher "I have to plead guilty to the charges and face the charges and punishment like a man and then wherever they send me from there I'll work, I'll work for the Lord."

The two psychiatrists believed that his pleading guilty and taking his punishment was a belief close to a "commonly held, fundamentalist Christian theology."[5]

It would be much simpler to say that Berkowitz felt guilty and wanted to be punished — religious belief or no. To put crime, guilt, and punishment together didn't require religion.

While the two doctors in March 1978 found that Berkowitz still showed symptoms of paranoia, they had by now reversed their opinion and found him, although still psychotic,* mentally able to stand trial.

When I examined Berkowitz, April 1978, he told me he felt "fine, beautiful." He sounded elated, euphoric, as if he had been relieved of a great burden.

"You seem to be in a good mood."

"I never felt better in my life."

"How did you change?"

---

* To this one may say that, if Berkowitz had been so mentally ill, suffering from paranoia as they originally had claimed, he could not have become better so easily and so quickly as they believed.

"I found Christ."

"Jesus as Messiah or as healer?"

"Both, I read the Bible every day. I wanted to repent my sin, I wanted to unburden my conscience."

"Is it a desire on your part to repent what you have been doing, maybe? or —"

Berkowitz interrupted. "Yes, that's right, my conscience has been cleansed. It was the conscience that was destroying me, that was making me go crazy. I was on the verge of a nervous breakdown, about to lose my mind."

"Did you lose your mind?"

"No."

"You didn't?" I repeated.

"No."

Contemplation and recognition of his crimes had made Berkowitz feel even more guilty and upset than when I had first interviewed him in August-September 1977. This recognition is important, as the capacity of a person to come to this state of awareness usually reflects a well integrated ego.

I asked him when the change had taken place. He replied, "After Christmas." (1977)

"What happened with the demons?"

"They have gone," he answered matter-of-factly.

One of my last questions: ". . . suppose now then in the end that the lawyers feel that you should not plead guilty. That you should claim insanity?"

"I won't go along with them."

"Why not?"

"Yes, I'm the one who gave them the idea of pleading guilty. I told them I wanted to plead guilty in the first place. This went on a couple of months ago."

In April 1978 the second Competency Hearing was held *in camera*. During the course of the hearing I was granted additional interviews with Berkowitz during which, among other things, he asked my advice! Should he plead guilty? I declined to advise him; this was a matter to be decided between him and his lawyers. His question nonetheless made me realize that he had gained confidence (and trust) in me — a notion that later events proved true.

The second competency hearing lasted five long days. Dr. Lubin testified that the defendant was unable to cooperate with his defense counsel, because of a state of psychosis or legal insanity. "A particular aspect of his religion," the psychiatrist said, "is in fact a reflection of a psychiatric state often referred to as 'religiosity.'"

First Assistant District Attorney Sheldon Greenberg asked Lubin: "Your idea that the only way that the defendant can save himself legally is based on an insanity defense; are you making that judgment as a psychiatrist or as a lawyer?"

The Court interposed: "Isn't that a question of law for the court to determine?"

Later, Greenberg asked the psychiatrist where he found the definition of religiosity. After much sparring, Dr. Lubin avowed that it was "part and parcel . . . of symptoms and signs observed in a condition called paranoid schizophrenia." To which Greenberg answered:

"And all of the terms that you used as far as the three subtypes of a disorder, 'hostile,' 'grandiose,' and 'hallucinatory,' they all referred to schizophrenia, did they not?

"Lubin: 'They do.'

"And they didn't refer to religiosity as 'religiosity,' the word?

"Of course not."

Later at the cross-examination by Defense Attorney Stern, Schwartz was asked: "In the course of your experience with David Berkowitz, and predicated upon your experience as a forensic psychiatrist, with having made thousands of examinations, having conducted thousands of inquiries, having made thousands of diagnoses, is there any indication in your mind that at any time you ever spoke to David Berkowtiz, he was feigning or he was manipulating you?"

The answer was, "No."

After having changed his opinion that Berkowitz was able to

stand trial, Schwartz was unsure whether Berkowitz could stand the stress and strain of a trial, that it could lead to a mental breakdown.

Jultak, on re-cross, asked Schwartz whether Berkowitz "is always under a delusional psychosis," which the doctor affirmed.

In Jultak's cross-examination of me (saying that "this witness steadfastly maintains there is nothing wrong with Mr. Berkowitz").* I was then asked: "Can he [Berkowitz] be manipulated?†

"He might possibly be," I answered. "I do not know for sure, but I do believe also this: He has a strong ego."

Q. Doctor, in summation then, would it be fair to categorize your testimony that David Berkowitz is absolutely fit to proceed at this time?

A. Yes.

Q. Would it be fair to categorize your testimony that he is not now under any psychosis?

A. Yes.

Q. Would it then be fair to characterize your testimony as excluding any diagnosis of paranoid schizophrenia?

A. Oh, absolutely.

Q. There is absolutely nothing that would suggest to you that this man might be a paranoid schizophrenic?

A. Absolutely not.

Jultak's last question surprised me. I had told him that my testimony absolutely excluded any diagnosis of paranoid schizophrenia and now he repeated the question. Some time ago I had learned that David Berkowitz had undergone psychological tests in August 1977 at the Kings County Hospital. A synopsis of the highlights of the dynamic clinical findings is given here:

The psychologist first interviewed him before she gave him the psychological tests.

---

* I had said Berkowtiz was not psychotic; I never said there was nothing wrong with him.

† By the end of his cross-examination of me, Mr. Jultak had become quite exasperated and frustrated apparently because he was unable to pressure me to change my testimony.

The patient entered the office willingly and calmly. He exhibited a fixed, and highly inappropriate smile almost all of the time. He was unspontaneous, but made good eye contact. He readily answered questions and remained cooperative throughout.

He was aware of the charges held against him. When asked why he did what he is alleged to have done, he replied, "For lots of reasons." He talked about Sam, a 6000-year-old demon, sometimes calling him Sam Carr, who commanded him to kill. "It's simple, he told me. No hidden meanings." He described Sam furthermore as "a fallen angel come to earth to destroy." He knew about him, "Since I was a child (at age seven). I didn't really know him then. . . . It was like nightmares. . . . I was scared of the dark. Like demons around me at night or in the darkness of the day."[6]

"About one and a half years ago the patient came to know Sam. "He introduced himself to me in Yonkers. I heard him." (Q. Saw him, too) "I saw him only three or four times." (Q. How does he look?) "He looks like a normal person. An elderly man — average features, clean shaven, short white hair. He said, his name was Sam. But he has several other names." (Q. What other names?) "I don't know. Many names. I only heard him for one and a half years. And I saw him by his house (in Yonkers)." (Q. You say he looks like a real man. Is he a real man?) "In a sense, yes. He's in the form of a man. You could see him."[7]

The patient obtained on the Wechsler Adult Intelligence Scale a Verbal IQ of 117, a Performance IQ of 110, and a Full Scale IQ of 115, indicative of overall bright intellectual functioning. He exhibited a superior range of general information (14) and bright comprehension (13) of everyday events and common sense data. He attained a score of 12 on the Similarities subtest, revealing again of bright capacities for abstract thinking and logical reasoning. His vocabulary (12) also was within the bright range. His arithmetical (10) functioning was average. His ability to differentiate essential from unessential environmental details (perceptually and conceptually) was of a good average quality (Picture Completion 11). However, his ability to comprehend and to size up a total interpersonal situation, sometimes referred to as social intelligence, seems to be his weakest point, as he attained but a dull score of 8 on the Picture Arrangement subtest. His visuo-motor performance was interesting insofar as he attained but a good average score on the Block Designs (11) but a very superior score on the Object

Assembly (17) subtest. While both tests involve analytical and synthetic abilities the patient appeared to be less efficient in coping with the neutral and strictly abstract designs than with the recognition and assemblage of natural forms (such as animal or human hand or face.)

The patient gained his second highest score on the Digit Span subtest. He was able to repeat 9 digits forward (which is the highest number tested) and he was able to correctly reverse 7 digits (reversal of 8 digits is the highest number requested by the test). Revealed thereby is not only an excellent recall for numbers, but also a state of mind free of essential anxieties and tensions allowing for total concentration on the task at hand. (Psychopaths and also paranoid individuals often do exceedingly well on this test.)[8]

Briefly summarizing, the patient functioned at a bright level. There were some indications of superior potentials. He worked with calm concentration on the tasks at hand; no overt anxiety being noticeable. Neither did he make any attempts at manipulation, nor was there any evidence of faking.

On the Rorschach inkblot test the patient produced 19 responses; this is somewhat less than the expected average of 25 – 30 but not unusual for the inmates at the prison ward services. All of his associations involved the whole blot. Adults with an IQ above 110 average about ten of such (W) responses. They are basically representative of a person's intellectual capacity and, depending upon their good form and structural integration, they are revealing of tendencies to engage in planned and persistent endeavors of initiative, and the efficient planning and pursuit of external goals. This patient, however, with his unusually high number of this type of response employs overexpansive, overcompensatory means in order to make up for marked passivity and deeply felt inadequacy. This finding is, especially, supported by the fact that the record contains not a single genuine human movement (M) association, suggesting (among other things) a profound lack of ego-strength, self-esteem and will power with which to turn wishful thinking into realistically desirable achievements.

Feelings of emotional deprivation and an unwholesome passivity in conjunction with forced attempts to overcome his passivity by fighting for his needs must have appeared early in life.[9]

Concerning this patient, who felt already broken and fragmented, depressed and isolated as a child, this concept seems to be essentially revealing of a "still-born" self-identity. He feels dead, and he is dead — emotionally.[10]

His psychological test record provides two major routes for understanding of this question. Firstly, his intellect being the only aspect of his personality that functions relatively well, does so exactly because it is almost totally cut off from the rest of his personality. He has no contact with his inner life, no insight into his motivation, no self-understanding. Hence, his intellect, split off from the rest of his personality, is free to function relatively unencumbered by the rigidly dissociated content of his mainly unconscious emotional life. Experiencing his affects and emotions, and the whole range of instinctual urges as alien to himself, he ascribes them, without any insight, to external forces stronger than himself and beyond his own control. According to his Rorschach profile this process most probably started before the age of six (as mentioned above) and according to the patient, he became vaguely aware of "evil and sinister forces" surrounding himself at about the age of seven. (This is incidentally, the age when, according to the patient, his parents told him that he was an adopted child.)[11]

Minnesota Multiphasic Personality Inventory. The patient diligently answered all questions. The validity scales, which provide information as to the level of confidence at which the inventory may be accepted, suggested regarding the L (Lie) scale that the patient made no significant attempts at lying. Furthermore, research results demonstrated that high L scores are associated with psychoneurotic scale elevations, whereas low L scores are associated with psychotic scale elevation, as is the case in this patient's MMPI profile.[12]

The clinical scales indicated pathological elevations regarding the following scales: schizophrenia; paranoia; psychopathic deviation; depression; hypomania; psychasthenia and social introversion. The scales concerning hypochrondriasis; hysteria; and male-female interest patterns remained essentially within the average norm.

Seven out of ten scales are in the deviant range which in combination with the deviant F Scale indicates an extremely high degree of anxiety, in spite of his outwardly calm facade.[13]

Some of the characteristics least descriptive of this patient:

Has "diagnostic" insight; awareness of the descriptive features of his own behavior. Is "normal," healthy, symptom free. Is able to sense other person's feelings; is an intuitive, empathic person. Genotype has psychopathic features. Would be organized and adaptive when under stress or trauma. Is cheerful. Has good verbal-cognitive insight into own personality structure and dynamics. Exhibits good heterosexual adjustment. Is socially extroverted (outgoing). Has the capacity for forming close interpersonal relationships. Presents a favorable prognosis. Has a resilient ego-defense system; has a safe margin of integration. Appears to be poised, self-assured, socially at ease. Genotype has hysteroid features.

Her diagnosis of paranoid schizophrenia seemed to have been based upon her questioning Berkowitz directly and this misled her. Clinically there were no delusions or hallucinations.

In commenting about the psychologist's tests, it is strange that the psychologist found Berkowitz was unspontaneous. Referring to her own remarks, he was rather spontaneous, and he made good eye-contact, which means that he showed ambivalence toward the examination. In other words, Berkowitz was very much aware of the testing and reacted quite well within the normal range of behavior in such a test situation.

He was aware of the charges against him, and admitted to them. Throughout the examinations themselves there was only one indication of the presence of a psychotic sign. But this very sign (the M.M.P.I.) at the same test indicated Berkowitz is overclaiming, exaggerating his symptoms. Thus he gives the impression that he is exhibitionistic, asking for help, but at the same time demanding excessive attention. Only by direct questioning does Berkowitz mention his delusions about Sam Carr, the dog, and even here he is vague. On a clinical basis, however, through testing there do not seem to be any delusions or hallucinations.

Another clinical point is (and this was stressed at the presentation of my paper about Berkowitz at the colloquia of the American College of Psychoanalysts) that Berkowitz never exhibited any fear when he spoke about the demons. As a matter of fact, he talked about this as an insignificant happening, without showing any horror or fear about them. He was rather unconcerned about them emotionally, and this was one of the many factors which made me suspicous that his story about the demons was highly exaggerated.

Berkowitz functioned at a bright level, and his ability to differentiate essential from unessential environmental details was of good average quality. He worked with great concentration on the tests, and free of anxieties, as is one of the earmarks of the psychopath. While his answers were overexpansive and overdone, which would indicate inadequate feelings about himself and reflect lack of self-esteem, this does not indicate lack of ego strength, as the psychologist asserts. Berkowitz has needs to display himself so he can be considered successful, indicating exhibitionism and hysterical traits.

He is not shut off from his emotions. On the instinctual level he is in contact with his inner life. He is not cut off from his inner life. He is a nonparticipant observer. He is an alienated person, but he knows what is going on around him.

Because of his hedonistic tendencies, he is highly egocentric, and self-serving. As seen on Rohrschach's test, card X with parade and circus, he is playful and a joker, has charm and is sneaky. He recognizes what is expected of him. But he is not a card-carrying member of society. He can see his conformity, and can put up a good conventional front. He can put on a good show, saying something like: It is my own scenario I have created. The paranoid ideas he has about people being against him are all restricted to female relationships, to castration fear, not discernibly to homosexual tendencies. But he shows a common-sense orientation. He exposes himself.

When he says he feels, "dead," "drained," "nothing left," a point which was so strongly emphasized by the two psychiatrists, this feeling has to do with his masturbation, losing his sperm. But this is not psychotic. If he had seen sperm on cards VIII, IX, X of the Rohrschach Test, it might indicate a psychotic trend.

Berkowitz is manipulative, seductive. No thought disorder was present. He has double standards, one for others, one for himself, which means his character is distorted. There is no deterioration of his judgment. The sharpness of his perception is very high, and gives the basis for ego strength. His ability to perceive is comparable to that of the general population. Rohrschach tests: F + 85%. When it is lower than 60, it is indicative of impaired reality testing. Berkowitz perceives reality well, and is in pretty good contact with reality. When on Plate II and III the psychologist says he sees blood spots which reflects sadistic and cruel feelings but which are not alien to him, it should be noted that such spots are also seen in hysterical patients, and are not unusual in the records of normals and neurotics on these two cards. She states Berkowitz talks about the blood spots without any feeling about them, he still adheres to the form. He still remains under the aegis of the ego. And while the splatters indicate sadism, they are still under control, still under his volition.

On card V, Berkowitz gives a normal response (bat or moths); it is the reality card.

Card X: He talks about an animal trap, as if he is afraid of being trapped and castrated by the woman. It shows intense fear of sexual intercourse. It is as if he may be saying: I regard the female as dangerous. If enticed by the female, it may be dangerous. It reflects early hostility toward the mother figure. All women are deceitful, because I myself was fooled. He has been victimized. Seeing a circus and a parade is like a play, and is exhibitionistic in the context of spectacular importance. This area can frequently be seen as musicians or magicians, in a quasi-human form.

The range of information was bright normal, and the attention span was quite good. He is able to integrate. He is not apathetic. He has very strong emotions and strong affectionate needs. He is not bland. It shows he has hope of getting by. His emotions are egocentric, and has not developed a moderation between pleasure and pain. The pleasure is for me, the pain is for you. He does not show anxieties in the test situation. He is almost immune to normal anxiety. When other people may react to a matter of somewhat catastrophic nature, he reacts without anxiety. But all the time he knows what is expected of him.

There is no isolation in Berkowitz, no extinction of affectional needs. The lipstick blotches he saw on the Rohrschach test are not psychotic. They rather show a strong infantile oral need for direct oral, tactile affection, a need for response.

The Multiphasic Personality Test showed a highly elevated score on the deviancy scale (F). Extremely low score on the defensive scale (K) is a clear indication of exaggerating, making a desperate effort to exaggerate his symptoms. He is trying to make himself appear more ill than he thinks others perceive him to be. He is making up the story about the demons. It doesn't come from his unconscious mind. He is lying to himself. He believes somewhat in his deception, and which is hysterical in nature. The story about the demons is a fiction he has built up in himself.

My diagnosis was as stated before: Pyschopathic personality with malingering concomitant paranoid and hysterical traits with acting out.

The second competency hearing had been rather drawn out, and I was glad when Jultak had ended his cross-examination of me. This hearing had produced the same result as the first one.

The following week, Judge Joseph Corso, in a substantial report, found Berkowitz able to stand trial, and set the trial date for May 8.

Would Berkowitz plead guilty? His defense attorneys had, with assistance from Dr. Schwartz, consistently and strenuously opposed a guilty plea. They all advocated that he declare himself not guilty because of insanity. There was strong pressure from all sides. His adoptive father Nathan, who believed David was insane, felt for this reason that he should plead not guilty. Nathan Berkowitz's situation was particularly tragic since insanity could explain his son's murders and to a large degree excuse the father. On the other hand, David felt guilty of his homicides, for which he sought punishment.

If a person feels guilty, then he knows what he has done. He is not insane.

On May 8, 1978, before three judges from the Supreme Court — Joseph Corso, Brooklyn; Nicholas Tsoucalas, Queens; and

Milton Kapelman, Bronx — David Berkowitz declared himself guilty of his crimes.

At this point, Bronx District Attorney Mario Merola injected a dramatic note as he read from Berkowitz's notes (mistakenly referred to as "diaries"), in which he claimed to have set 2,000 small fires in the Bronx. Since Berkowitz, however, was going to be sentenced for six murders, whether or not he had set fires to some brush, abandoned cars, and buildings would have little effect on the length of his prison sentence.[14]

An increasing sense of guilt and the realization that the life of a convict was soon to be his, spurred the Son of Sam. With reality closing in on him, he spinned in his fantasy the following scenario of the competency hearing, which he wrote down and sent to me some time later from Attica prison.

Judge. Has the jury reached a verdict?

Jury. We have, your honor.

Judge. Then will the foreman of the jury please read the verdict to the defendant and the court.

Jury. David Berkowitz, we the people of New York City find you not guilty by reason of insanity.

Defendant. Wait! I'm the killer! I killed all those people. I shot them with my gun.

Jury Foreman. No, David, you didn't kill anyone. Your sick mind was the killer and it wasn't your fault. We all lose our marbles once in awhile. Now go in peace and stop tormenting yourself with guilt.

"Yes, at one time in my life this is what I wanted to hear." The letter reflected his manipulative tendencies and his desire to be the center of attention.

"I vividly recall the talks I had with Dr. Daniel Schwartz [one of the Court-appointed psychiatrists who had found Berkowitz to be insane], for they were, to me, ecstasy. They were the talks that produced the feedback I wanted. What a pleasure it was back then to hear this man exonerate me of all blame for my six murders. Oh, the pleasure of hearing this man telling his colleagues how sick I was — how ill — how insane.

"I knew, that all I had to do was slide "Sam Carr" and the "demons into the conversation and I'd have him bending over his chair in my direction. Why he'd practically be wiping the tears from my eyes and comforting me, saying, in a sense, "don't fret, don't cry, you're a sick, sick boy."

"Goodness, what a nice man he was—always telling me what I wanted to hear—always helping to push my rising guilt feelings back down into my mind. And, thank God he listened to it, for it was all I had. Had someone taken it away, then I'd have been standing there stark naked, guilty as ever, with nothing to hide behind, no safe ground, nothing but my own self.

"However, I think that you, Dr. Abrahamsen, would be missing an important clue unless I told you this. That Dr. Schwartz was me! So were the police officers who caught me and so was my defense counsel. They, too, were me.

"All the others were my little puppets. People to be manipulated. They bent forward when I wanted them to, they talked about the subjects that I wanted to speak of, and they told me just what I demanded to hear—that I was not guilty!

"So, in a sense, they were extensions of me, to be picked up and placed back down on the ground when I was finished with them.

"You, however, wouldn't allow youself to be manipulated that way. You did stick to your guns. You refused to yield and, as you know, I fought you like an alley cat would fight an alley cat—two males fighting over a lovely feline.

"You didn't allow me the joy of receiving confirmation that I was not responsible for my crimes. I desperately wanted someone, preferably a doctor like yourself, to clear me of all wrongdoing.

"Unfortunately for me, too, I lived a most lonely life in the year before my capture. I was lonely for I had a deep, deep secret that I wanted to share with friends. It was on the tip of my tongue and I wanted very much to say it: "Hey, I'm Son of Sam."

"There were so many times that the temptation to share my hidden secret became overpowering. I often stared at my telephone, my hands trembling somewhat, as I thought of picking the receiver up, dialing, then saying to the party at the other end: 'Hello, is this the Son of Sam Task Force? Well, guess who this is?'

"I was often tempted to telephone my father saying: 'Dad,

have you got a minute because there's something I want to tell you?' Or, I wanted to sit my two precious neices, one on each lap, and say: 'I know you kids won't believe this but I want to tell you that I'm . . .

Sincerely,
David Berkowitz[14]

Monday morning, May 22, 1978, began early for me, with several telephone calls which delayed my departure for Brooklyn, where I would attend the sentencing of David Berkowitz. To make up for lost time, I bypassed my car in favor of the subway, a means of transportation I rarely use, only to have the express break down halfway to my destination.

Hurrying over to the block-long Kings County Court building, I found a large crowd of newspeople and TV cameramen already there, waiting for the van and the escort of police cars which would bring Berkowitz to the Court. Security was tight. Everyone was carefully screened. I was finally admitted to the Courtroom on the seventh floor, the largest one in the building. I moved to the back of the room crowded with reporters, lawyers, court attendants, and a sprinkle of family members of Berkowitz's victims. No room for the public. Some people were writing, others sketching, some stretching tense limbs. The atmosphere was taut, the talk loud—undoubtedly most of the people trying in their own way to alleviate their own anxiety.

Two weeks before, in the same courtroom, Berkowitz had quietly pleaded guilty to his murders and attempted murders. Today he was going to be sentenced.

It was now 10:05 A.M. The sentencing was set for 10 A.M. I began to have a gut feeling that not everything would proceed according to plan. Suddenly the order for "Quiet!" rang out. The large courtroom fell silent. The walking around stopped. No more loud talking, only whispers. Tension grew. But then, as nothing happened, the audience again became restless.

The clock ticked away. By now it was 10:30, and I knew that Judge Corso was scheduled to preside at another trial at 2 P.M.

The air was tense. I had learned that Berkowitz had said that he would have some surprises at the sentencing. Knowing his irascible mind and that his extraordinary sentencing situation would be presided over in turn by three judges — from Brooklyn, Queens, and the Bronx—nobody could foretell for certain what his reaction to his sentencing would be.

At 11:20 A.M. the door from the anteroom to the courtroom was opened. All stretched their necks to see. Berkowitz, handcuffed and surrounded by five Correction Officers, appeared. He looked panicky, upset, wild-eyed, and was fighting with the officers, who were trying to hold him. On entering the Courtroom, he was chanting loudly in a sarcastic, yet emotion-laden sing-song: "Stacy is a whore, Stacy is a whore. I'll shoot them all."

The room was in an uproar. Mrs. Moskowitz, sitting just in front of me, cried out with anguish, "You're an animal!!"and hurriedly left the room. Robert Violante, sitting in front of me, who had been almost blinded by one of Berkowitz's shots, had to be comforted by his father.

But not many paid attention to them. The audience only wanted to get a better look at the defendant.

"Sit down! Be seated!" someone called out. But no one listened. The officers battled Berkowitz, and he fought them off. He bit one and twisted the hand of another. They carried him back to the anteroom.

An eerie atmosphere hung over the courtroom. It seemed as if what had happened during the two short minutes of Berkowitz's panicky outburst was unreal. Yet everyone had seen it.

As people again took their seats, somebody remarked. "Mad as a hatter!" "Not so," I answered dryly. His carefully orchestrated effort in avoiding the sentencing showed that he was not insane, not psychotic. If he had been insane he would be unconcerned, indifferent, not caring about what happened to him.

After a short while, Justice Corso read from a pre-sentence report that Berkowitz was able to be sentenced. Now the sentencing would be postponed until June 12, depending upon a new pre-sentence psychiatric report.

A new uproar. A young, tall, handsome man in his early

twenties, dressed in a black sweater and jacket, stood up. In a powerful voice he called out, "Berkowitz should be sentenced today!" The audience came alive and applauded loudly. Judge Corso, in a stern voice, admonished the public that he would direct the court proceedings according to the American system of justice. "I will not be led by public clamor!"

The judge had really acted like one. But District Attorney Merola of the Bronx requested that Berkowitz "be sentenced today." Judge Corso had the last word. The court was adjourned at 12 noon. Berkowitz had succeeded in postponing his own sentencing. He had dominated the court proceedings with a sure exhibitionistic hand. It was a spectacle which not even Hollywood could have staged better.

Berkowitz had pleaded guilty because he felt guilty and had to atone for his murders. But why did he refuse so vehemently to be sentenced on May 22, 1978, when so shortly before, on May 8, he had so docilely pleaded guilty to his crimes? The emotional reason is probably that when he pleaded guilty, he was in control of the situation and still the star. But when he returned to the court to be sentenced, the control had passed from him to the judge. Faced with this new situation of which he was not the master, he invented this rebellious scheme to get out of his intolerable situation.

The sentencing date was reset for June 12th, three weeks later. Berkowitz had been instructed to behave and not to make a scene again. It would be of no use if he did, and if worse came to worst, he could be excluded from the courtroom and sentenced in absentia. This was the Court's privilege. He promised to behave.

This time, he was given thorazine prior to sentencing. He was now quiet and docile, not so much because of the tranquilizer, as of the strong authoritarian advice he had been given about controlling his emotions. Knowing that part of his personality yearned for approval, it was my thought that at this second sentencing he would be a "good boy." Even more important, though, was that his feeling of guilt would make him finally accept the sentence.

As Berkowitz was being sentenced to a total of 547 years (his actual sentence was 25 years to life on each count of murder — and he would have to serve 25 years, to the year 2003, before he would be eligible for parole) a young man in back of me leaped over my head and ran to the front of the courtroom to try to grab Berkowitz. Before he could get that far, however, he was caught, wrestled to the floor, and carried out. It was the rage of a wild animal. Berkowitz was immediately led out of the courtroom to the back hallway. Sitting down, he said to the court attendant: "Why didn't you let him get at me so he could tear me to pieces?"

Tuesday morning, June 13, 1978, at 4:30 A.M. Berkowitz was secretly marshaled off to the Ossining Correctional Facility (formerly known as Sing Sing Prison) and from there to Clinton Correctional Facility near Dannemora, New York, where he was to undergo psychiatric and physical tests. On July 7 he was transferred for a short stay of six to eight weeks to Central New York Psychiatric Center, Marcy, New York, for examination, and he was then sent to the Attica Prison to serve his time.

At last the murderer was being allowed to atone for his deeds. Hardly a madman, he was now freed of his "demons" and ready to return to the realities that he, as Son of Sam, had tried to hide from.

8

SEX AS A FORCE
FOR MURDER

Love and hate are so closely intertwined that one does not always know where one emotion ends and the other takes over. It may surprise us to learn that our sexual drive, used most often to express loving feelings, is also intimately associated with hateful and murderous emotions. One may even go so far as to say that the sexual force, in most instances, through jealousy, envy, competition, hate, and revenge is the force that initiates, stimulates, mobilizes, and maintains murderous impulses. We may well say that without this stimulus, there would be few murders, or, for that matter, very little violence of any kind.

Keeping in mind that sexual emotions are practically always involved in homicide, it would be a foregone conclusion that David Berkowitz's sexual feelings played a significant role in his murderous spree. Although it has been very difficult to pinpoint this aspect of his behavior — in all my interviews with him he minimized, even denied, that sexual impulses had anything to do with his murders — persistent probing into his desires, fantasies, day- and night-dreams, and his relationship to women, has revealed the powerful impetus his sexual fantasies and impulses had upon his attitudes and his behavior—specifically, his multiple murders.

Although in my first interview with Berkowitz in the prison ward of Kings County Hospital he had reluctantly conceded that sexual feelings might have had something to do with his murders, in subsequent interviews he defended himself vehemently against any such intimation. At one point, as I questioned him about his relationship to women, he began to talk about the demons who had wanted so much from him.

"What did they want from you?" I asked quietly.

"The demons wanted my penis," he answered abruptly, almost suddenly.

Understanding the implication, the association between murder and sex, I repeated my question, but by then he felt he had already said too much, and absolutely refused to go on. His answer stuck with me. It was one of those moments in an interview where patience is necessary and where probing for further clarification can only damage any relationship that exists. It was one of those moments which separates the expert from the inexperienced psychiatrist. Berkowitz was not ready; he had entered into a minefield of feelings and then had hurriedly retreated to safety behind a wall of defensiveness. Maybe he would be receptive to my question at another time. That time was not to come for almost a whole year. It came during my very first interview with him at Attica.

"Attica Prison to be a Convict's Paradise," *The New York Times* headline read when that institution first opened its doors in 1931.[1] How cruelly ironic that prophecy was in light of the brutal events that, 40 years later would turn Attica into a national tragedy: In the worst riot in the history of American prisons, buildings were burned and ravaged, guards held hostage by desperate prisoners armed with kitchen knives and tools, and a total of 42 guards and inmates killed when state troopers came in with guns blazing. Within its walls, as in all prisons, was a system based on force which engenders violence — to make a prison a brutal nightmare.

Driving from the Buffalo airport, I had taken a wrong turn and it was almost 10 A.M. before I found a parking space for my rented car outside the high stone walls, whose foreboding towers at each corner were manned by armed guards. The gray prison contrasted sharply with the surrounding fertile and benign green fields stretching away to the low mountains ranged against the horizon. Attica was as fortress. Heavily protected, its defensive, hostile facade left no doubt that it was a maximum security prison. The emotional climate inside delivered on the promise of its threatening exterior. No one wanted to serve time there: Attica was hardly a convict's paradise.

If it is difficult to get out of a prison, it is by no means easy to get in—that is, for a visitor. The bureaucratic red tape is as long and knotted at Attica as it was at the other prisons where I have had assignments, among them the old fashioned and often cruel Illinois State Penitentiary in Joliet and at Sing Sing in Ossining, New York. After writing Berkowitz's name and number on a form, I was directed to a large room with four rows of benches, where already a number of couples, some older, some young with small children, were waiting. After a time my name was called. First I was frisked by a prison guard, and then I was directed to walk through an electric scanning device and finally toward an iron door which opened with a click. Through the doorway, I entered a small room with one large glass window. Another click, and another door opened into a courtyard. I was directed across the yard to a small building, where again I waited — this time for an escort to take me to the Reception Building where Berkowitz was housed. There I was taken into the Conference Room just off the entrance hall, where I was seated at a wide table to await the prisoner.

It was May 17, 1979, and a gentle breeze flowed through the barred windows behind me. It had been several months since I had last seen the prisoner. Preoccupied with my own thoughts, I hardly noticed that Berkowitz had come in. He had entered just as quietly as he had the first time I examined him at the prison ward of Kings County Hospital.

Wearing a light blue tee shirt and green trousers, his thick black hair, sprinkled with gray, had been closely cropped. Berkowitz seemed pleased with himself. He greeted me quite warmly, while his blue eyes scrutinized me. His tone was more familiar, more open, than before. He was feeling good and given the circumstances, liked being at Attica. When I remarked that he had gained weight, he tilted his head, smiled, and said, "The food is starchy here," but then hurriedly added, "I can't complain." Ever compliant.

He sat down opposite me and drummed his fingers nervously against his chair. Eager to talk, he asked about my trip. I admitted that I had taken a wrong turn, and he laughed with me, glad to know that I too was fallible.

My previous contacts with the Son of Sam had been in an official capacity as a forensic psychiatrist. I had been specifically requested to determine his fitness to stand trial, and his state of mind when he committed the final murder. Now I was intent on getting behind the categorization of his personality in order to put together a meaningful portrait of a tortured human being who violently and repeatedly had broken the law of the sacredness of human life. Now I wanted an answer to the bedevilling question: Why did he kill?

The central theme of our Attica interview, both in his words and in my thoughts, was the force that had driven Berkowitz to commit murder. Our focus was on those specific feelings whose peculiar nature has an affinity to violence and death.

I had always suspected that Berkowitz had not had a "normal" or active sex life, and, the information he supplied then, and in our subsequent interviews and correspondence, pointed clearly to his distorted sexual development. Berkowitz, however, was unaware that what he was telling me was relevant, and actually resisted my suggestions of a connection with his crimes.

Some of what follows may seem a bit farfetched to those unacquainted with the work of psychiatrists and psychoanalysts and the basic ideas that underlie their profession. Although Sigmund Freud's theories have undergone some slight modification over the past eighty years, clinical practice has confirmed the validity of his basic theory—that feelings, dreams, attitudes, thoughts, and actions of adults are influenced by the extent to which they have successfully passed through the psychosexual stages of childhood, thereby being able to free themselves to a high degree from the inordinate binding and dependency upon their parents or parent substitutes. The clearing up of the child's relationship to his parents — the Oedipal situation — is the main requisite for reaching emotional maturity. While the sexuality of the adult human being is by no means the only determinant of behavior, it is certainly one of the strongest ones and, acting alone or in combination with other emotions, it affects our behavior throughout our lives.

Although there were several topics which Berkowitz and I touched upon for the first time that day in Attica, one remark in particular surprised me. "I joined the Army," he declared, "in order to lose my virginity."[2] (I thought, there must be an easier way to lose one's virginity than to go to Korea!) I remembered how at Kings County he had bragged to me that he had "lost his virginity" at 16, when he had oral sex with a girl. At the time his claim had sounded hollow.

He had made similar boasts to his first lawyer, Mark Heller: "I told Heller that I had sex with girls many times. This wasn't true. I was just showing off, bragging." And a few days later he wrote to me, "When my former lawyer, Mark Heller, mentally manipulated me to write for him, I told of all my conquests of American girls since the age of 16. My pride and ego got the best of me. I never had those girls that I wrote I did. I made that up to impress Heller because he wasn't much older then me."[3]

Later he admitted to me: "I never had oral sex with [name withheld] from Co-op City. I only said it . . . in order to make myself look big and experienced in the way of love."[4]

Now Berkowitz claimed that his first sexual experience was in Korea at about 19, an age considered late if compared with most young men, who start having sex at 13 or 14. At Attica he said that in Korea, if you wanted "to have oral sex [it sounded as if this was his preference], you went to one town, and if you had to have sex naturally then you went to a different town. I was most satisfied when I did it to them, when I sucked them. However, they had to be clean."[5]

The way he said "if you had to have sex naturally" suggests that he himself wasn't interested in actual sexual intercourse. His preoccupation with oral sexuality to the exclusion of genital intercourse (both in fantasy and in reality), suggests his immature sexual development—he preferred petting and fondling. At 19, 20, and older, he exhibited the sexual behavior of a five or six-year-old child (the infantile period). An age at which children fondle and examine their own and each other's genitals and display themselves. His ever-burning desire, as an adult, to call attention to himself, to be in the limelight, was another expression of this sexual exhibitionism and voyeurism.

His use of masturbation as a substitute for sexual intercourse was another sign of Berkowitz's undeveloped sexuality. Berkowitz had begun to masturbate when he was nine years old, and by the time he went into the Army he masturbated several times every day. Even when he raged against sex as a sin and was actively enrolled in every available church program, he "couldn't wait to go back to my room in the barracks and masturbate." It was more than habitual, it was compulsive. Whenever he masturbated, he fantasized he was with a girl. As he says, "When I did it, most often my fantasy involved oral sex between heterosexual couples."[6] ". . . I always fantasized about girls. Now I cannot go to sleep unless I masturbate first."[7]

Used occasionally to relieve sexual tension, masturbation is normal. But when an adult prefers it to sexual intercourse, it indicates an impaired capacity for sexual satisfaction. His incessant masturbation was in character a neurotic symptom. More and more, his sexual fantasizing had become his reality. Because his neurotic shyness induced him to masturbate rather than actually approaching a woman, he never learned that she was capable of giving him better and greater pleasure.

He was a loner. "I didn't have a date. I met some girls. I wanted to. They were shy. . . . The first time I had sex . . . was in Korea . . . a month before I left Korea I didn't have any sex because I didn't want to get sick. . . ."[8] In fact, he was afraid. Afraid of being impotent, he blamed women for his own shyness, painful shyness that was, in fact, a fear of impotence. Fantasy became his escape from fear. In his daydreams he always had a girlfriend. Finally, there was little incentive to leave the security of the controlled fantasy for the uncertain world of real women, where rejection was always such a frightful specter.

And what happened when he got out of the Army? "When I returned home from the Army, I tried to go out with some of the girls in Co-op City. They didn't find me attractive. They had no sexual interest in me even though they were sexually experienced."

"How did you feel about that?"

"I began to hate girls, I always hated them. All the time I have had sexual fantasies with girls. . . . his is as true today as it was when I was younger."[9]

"Almost every waking moment," he once told me, "I find myself fantasizing. . . . But I'm greatly troubled by my fantasies. They are almost all either sexual in nature or violent. I'm really quite perverted," he confessed. "I do believe however, that others fantasize the same things as me. If I could be absolutely sure they do, I'd be greatly relieved."[10]

Berkowitz was unaware that all people daydream or fantasize in varying degrees. Every child starts, between the age of three and five, to fantasize. A boy might daydream that he is big, drives a car, carries out heroic deeds, has girlfriends. As he grows older, he fantasizes about having sex with those girlfriends.

Fantasy is defined as thinking which is not followed by action. We distinguish between two types of fantasy: *creative fantasies,* which prepare for some later action; and *daydreaming fantasies,* which are the respository for wishes that cannot be fulfilled. While creative fantasy can be a stimulus for action, daydreaming fantasy can become a substitute for action. We are faced with the question of whether the fantasy stimulates the wish, so that the inclination to realize fantasized ideas increases, or whether the fantasy channels the wish so that a fantasy of winning which might otherwise be satisfied by actually playing sports, for instance, no longer needs to be truly realized.

So far as sex is concerned, if a person fantasizes about sexual intercourse, his longing for sex increases. But, should his fantasies stimulate him to masturbation, the longing may be sufficiently satisfied so that desire fades. This is what happened with Berkowitz. Masturbation was the "fantasy activity" which kept him not only from entering into a healthy sexual relationship, but into any real relationship at all. The fact that he did not have a girlfriend when he reached adulthood was in great part rooted in the ease with which he substituted fantasy for reality. His reaction—in part fear, in part rationalization—was always that "I didn't think I could satisfy them."

Berkowitz's sexual shyness did not grow out of thin air; it was rooted in the circumstances of his childhood. Because he knew from a very early age that he was an adopted child, he lived in the fear and danger of being deprived of basic physical and emotional gratification. Having already lost one mother, he might well lose a second. When Pearl died of cancer when David was fourteen, this in fact is exactly what happened. His loss caused him so much anxiety and grief that it overwhelmed his feelings of love, inhibiting their natural expression.

To complicate matters further, his relationship with his adoptive mother, the most important woman in his early years, was always characterized by ambivalence. "I never liked to kiss," he recalled. "In those days you had to be masculine, a strong guy, like James Dean. I kept away from girls because to stay with them was 'sissy stuff.' I remember Mom when she kissed me, but it wasn't affectionately. My grandmother Helen also wanted to kiss me, but I didn't want to. As to father, I wouldn't let him kiss me. I always resented him quite a bit because he wanted to be with my mother. I resented my father because he had my mother."[11]

Immobilized by a lack of mother love, he had become too shy to approach a girl. Instead, he began, in early childhood, to fantasize about being close to the young girls to whom he was attracted. In reality he stayed far away from them.

Embarrassed to kiss or be kissed, he told me that his mother had kissed him without affection, perhaps giving him the impression that kissing was wrong. This notion could also have been fostered by the "secret relationship" he suspected between Pearl and Nat, from which he was excluded.

There is, however, reason to believe otherwise. I believe that David's enormous need for affection overwhelmed Pearl to such an extent that she could not satisfy him; thus he felt she was cool to him. Demanding as he was, he was certainly not shy about demanding affection from her. That, as a child and adolescent, he stayed away from girls was probably also because of his own ambivalence. On the one hand he wanted affection, and years later still criticized his mother for not "delivering." On the other hand he himself felt a dislike for kissing. It was a bind, for him and particularly for her. No matter what she did, it was bound to be wrong.

When, at the beginning of adolescence, he lost Pearl, whatever feelings of love he could still muster were further inhibited. Love and affection became feelings intimately bound up with loss and separation — a poor preparation for adult relationships.

Berkowitz also associated physical affection with competition and antagonism. He recalled the sleeping arrangements in his parents' apartment and their need for privacy:

"He made me leave the room when they wanted to be alone. I resented it. When they talked, they made me leave the room. I felt deprived. It was my father who took me out of the room. I asked him 'What are you going to do, kiss?' My father would answer:

"'David, your mommy and I have something important to talk about.' I wanted to be in their bedroom, that was the only place the TV was. 'So what are you going to do,' I asked, 'kiss or something?'"[12]

He laughed.

Left in the uneasy position of wanting affection from his mother, but stymied in his feelings by his father, Berkowitz was upset, particularly during the Oedipal stages of his life (between 2.5 and 5 years of age) with its romantic pull toward mother and its resentment of father.

This is the classical psychological confrontation of childhood, in which the young boy competes with the father for the affection of the mother. The child's way of coming to terms with this struggle is the beginning of self-determination, the opening of

successful growth into adolescence. But Berkowitz was not secure enough to assimilate and transcend this experience. Thus,
he turned toward fantasies to find an outlet for his sexual desires.

One consequence of Oedipal conflict is that the boy often
becomes afraid of losing his manhood — a fear recognized as
castration anxiety. As a very little boy, David bathed with his
mother in the shower room at the beach club: "I saw her naked
often. In fact, I saw hundreds of naked women,"[13] but when he
got to be five years old, at the end of the infantile period, he was
taken to bathe with his father. This, then, is the situation. At the
age of five, when his Oedipal stage is peaking, David is nude in
the shower room with his father and other male adults. He has
already seen that his mother has no penis, and he sees not only
that his father and the other men have penises, but also that they
are larger than his. Characteristically, he is proud that he has a
penis. But its smallness is a blow, which he resents and which
makes him feel inferior — particularly to his father, his rival.

During this phallic phase the boy identifies with his penis, so
to speak. He values it highly, because just at this period he feels
rich sensations with his penis and has the desire to penetrate
with it. But David never successfully achieved this stage. He
feared the consequences of his possessiveness toward his mother.
Because of his desire for exclusive access to her, he anticipated
the wrath of an avenging father. His aggressive, extroverted
sexual feelings were blocked by fear of the powerful father, who
might, the child fantisized, cut off the young boy's sexual organ.

This castration anxiety was deeply rooted in David's relationship with Pearl. Until the age of five, these active phallic impulses
go hand in hand with passive ones, the latter being increased
when the small child's penis is fondled. Naturally Berkowitz
does not remember such a thing happening. When I asked him
about it, it upset him and he told me, bluntly, he had "No
memory of it."

Pearl was very taken with her beautiful boy, overwhelmed by
the intensity of the mother-son tie. There is ample reason to
believe she fondled the little boy while bathing him (not unusual),
thereby increasing his interest in his penis and his passive incli-

nations. That David knew at an early age that women are shaped differently from men, and that he felt satisfying sensations in his penis, brought out his fear that something dreadful might happen to his sensitive and prized organ. We know that Berkowitz was highly egocentric; his castration anxiety was enhanced by this high evaluation of himself — as if he were the only one who had such a precious organ.

From all this he learned an important — and negative way — to behave. Rather than gaining the confidence and security to form mature relationships, to reach out to others for the affection and sexual gratification his adoptive parents got from each other, his sexual drive — through fear and anxiety about what could happen to him if he did direct it outwardly — became directed inwardly.

If Berkowitz's sexuality was conditioned by this unresolved Oedipal conflict, so also was his attitude toward authority. During our initial conversation at Attica, having just discussed sexual matters, he moved almost instantly into a diatribe on religion.

"I hate God, and I don't like him because of all the things he did. I blame him for taking my mother. I hate him for taking both my grandmothers. They both died. I hate him for making me, my life. I was always dissatisfied with life, and I wanted to die. I always felt that if God had any sense he would have taken my miserable life a long time ago. I never asked God to let me live — I never wanted to live. I believe God is everywhere. I believe that God exists, but I think he is a liar. He has disappointed me.

"I almost believe in God, in his existence, in his power and in heaven and hell, but not in his powers of justice, love and mercy as it is quoted in the Bible. It is hard to express it."[14]

Emotional and upset, but still in control of himself, he continued:

"I fear God, his power, his ability to kill, hell, a personal terror. God has a grip on me and many others via fear."

"Fear?" I asked.

"Fear of hell, fire, eternal agony. Can't love anyone I fear. I can't love anyone who holds me in check with fear. The Bible talks about fear and hell and eternal damnation; it has caused me untold mental pain and misery."[15]

By now he was exhausted and perspiring. He had produced emotions of which he had been aware, but had not heretofore verbalized. He had said he couldn't love anyone he was afraid of. His fear of God was the same fear as that of his father, when he challenged him for his mother's attention. He *had* to be his mother's favorite. This narcissism was manifest in other areas of his life; again, his religious feelings are but one dramatic example.

As with everything else in his life, Berkowitz had ambivalent feelings about religion. If he lived in fear of an angry god, he also felt that he was "one of the 'elected' and 'chosen.' I always hope to be the first one to go to heaven, one of the first fruits. I do feel more important to God than other people. This is probably why I am alive today because, despite my anger towards God, he still loves me the most."[16] That God could be so two-faced seems to have bothered David Berkowitz not at all.

As this outburst came to a close, I wondered, did he feel relieved? Was he more confident of himself? He became quiet and seemed to be waiting for me to speak. I was thinking about what he had told me at Kings County—that the demons wanted his penis. This expressed his fear of his father, his castration fear. But at the time I had thought it was also something more, and now, I felt, was the time to ask him about it.

"Some time ago," I said "you told me that demons wanted your penis." Berkowitz nodded, remembering.

I ventured again, "Was it really the demons who wanted your penis?"

He did not seem startled by my question. He thought for a while, then said without much emotion: "No, it wasn't the demons, it was women."

I told him that in Greek and other mythologies there are no male demons, only female. He looked at me, his blue eyes seductive, and smiled. And I looked at him. While he didn't comment directly on the fact that he had chosen male demons, he understood that his demon story was not according to accepted concepts.

Berkowitz changed the subject.

"One of my greatest weaknesses or faults," he said, "is blushing when talking in public. This is why I hated public speaking in the classroom or in social events. No matter how confident I felt, no matter how well I knew the subject I was to talk about, when I began to speak the blushing started. I cannot, however, seem to consciously control it."[17]

I explained that people who are shy may blush. The blushing may be a disguise, one way to cope with and cover up aggressive and hostile feelings or other feelings such as shame.

It should come as no surprise that Berkowitz was shy. His shyness was the mask for the hostile, aggressive, violent behavior he had shown so many times.

Just as one kind of emotion can be a mask for another, seemingly unrelated emotions can sometimes be linked together in surprising connections. For instance, unable to cope with his anger at his neighbor, Craig Glassman, Berkowitz had sent him threatening letters and set a fire outside his apartment because, his said, "This man had his TV on too loud. He drove me crazy."

"Why didn't you go downstairs [Berkowitz lived on the seventh floor, just above Glassman] and tell him so?" I asked.

"I was afraid to approach him. I was afraid to approach people. I didn't dare talk with Glassman."[18] He had covered his aggressive hostile feelings toward Glassman by fearing him. Incapable of any normal give and take, he then overcompensated for his fear by becoming violent. His response to the event was out of all proportion to the event itself. His reaction had been exaggerated in a similar way when he claimed Glassman was a demon — which claim he subsequently denounced and admitted that Glassman was a mere human being. This exaggerated reaction was connected to his repressed sexual feelings. They were an integral part of the sexual immaturity that also lead to his fear of women. His shyness expressed his sexual repression and suppression. There was one specific cause and effect of this disastrous immaturity.

"I don't," he said, "have the capacity to love. When I did have the capacity, I did. But after mother died, I didn't have the feeling."[19]

But even when Pearl was alive, he had been extremely destructive and hateful, so he couldn't blame his hatefulness and destructiveness on her death. And when at the competency hearings it was brought out that he had declared himself "emotionally dead," this had not been the case either. The eagerness and alertness with which he followed the court proceedings revealed that he was emotionally active. To top it all off, he had once declared, "I don't have any emotions." And then added reflectively: "The truth is good to know." When he says he felt dead, drained, "nothing left," he may have been unwittingly referring to his excessive masturbation and losing his sperm.

Berkowitz had mentioned to me that all his fantasies were either sexual or violent in nature, and that he felt himself to be quite perverted, implying that it disturbed him. Although unconsciously he had made the connection, consciously, it did not seem to occur to him that sexual feelings and violent deeds lie close to each other. As mentioned earlier, sexual feelings, beside expressing love, are also intimately connected with violent emotions.

Within our sexual fantasies themselves, violence often plays a part. In the disturbed (though not necessarily psychotic) mind, however, these feelings — sex and violence — fuse together. Divergent or dissimilar emotions become associated with, connected to, or merged with each other. Such was the case with Berkowitz. Violence took over sexual aggression. He confessed to me that he "had fantasized about shooting women for a long time." Although he had nobody particular in mind, he "knew it was going to be pretty women:

"I do fantasize about women and my fantasies are not violent. That is, when I'm making love to them in these daydreams. I envision myself as a lover who is passionate, well endowed, and is able to please my mate by giving her a multitude of orgasms. I picture myself as one who has no qualms about performing oral sex with the female genitals. In fact, I know I would enjoy it very much. I would also be able to prolong (delay) my ejaculation for hours* until my partner has numerous orgasms and is begging for mercy.

"When I fantasize myself having sex with a woman, it's never violent. But in my mind, sometimes I have the desire to cause bodily harm but not while having sex. My violent fantasies are miles apart from my heterosexual fantasies.[20]

Despite his assertion that his "violent fantasies are miles apart from [his] heterosexual fantasies," it is clear from his linking the two that his sexual and murderous fantasies were much closer to each other than he wished me to believe. The sexual drive in men is at times related to aggression, leading sometimes to cruelty, which may motivate and which is often carried out violently. Berkowitz seemed inclined to express his sexual urge violently. His killing of women really expressed his sadistic feelings.

It is almost certain that, as a child, he had seen his adoptive parents making love. He had repressed all conscious memory of that primal scene, but his sexual fantasies were almost certainly rooted there. Now he was to be a witness to another sexual scene: Stacy Moskowitz and Robert Violante. As he explained, he had observed a couple sitting in a car for an hour. He was sitting in the shadows in the playground; their car was under a street light so he could clearly see whatever they did.

"They made out," he recounted, "kissed and embraced." He sat there watching them and became aroused himself; he had an erection. They got out of the car in the playground.

"I watched Stacy on the swing and then they stopped swinging. Her and her date then started to kiss passionately for several

* That Berkowitz not only sought to prolong his forepleasure, but really prolonged and delayed his end pleasure for hours, shows that he, like an anal erotic person, enjoyed the delay.

minutes. At this time, I too, was sexually aroused. I had an erection.

"Shortly after their deep kissing, they went back to the car, but a little more to the rear. I had my gun out, aimed at the middle of Stacy's head and fired. One bullet struck her head and another nicked her. I didn't even know she was shot because she didn't say anything nor did she moan.

"Then I got in my car and drove off."

In observing the young couples having sex, he both participated in it, and was also to an intense degree a voyeur, a situation which he greatly enjoyed and was used to. When he too wanted to partake in the act, he shot his victims. He was transfixed, continuing to pull the trigger; he was both emotionally and sexually engaged.

Why, I pondered, had Berkowitz chosen as his victims women in parked cars? Was it a matter only of convenience? Hardly. As I became more and more knowledgeable about the case, his use of the car as part of the murder strategy grew in significance.

In one of my early letters to him, I had asked him if any one of the couples he had shot at were making love at the time.

"I'm trying to remember if Esau and Suriani were having sex. I know they were embracing," he replied," but I can't remember if they had their clothes off or not. If they did have their clothing off, and were engaged in sex, then I would be somewhat justified in killing them. Sex, outside of marriage, is a heinous sin."[22]

I kept returning to the subject, finally suggesting to him that since he had been so upset with the idea of Betty Falco, his real mother, "sitting in those parked cars with Klineman," he may have felt that somehow there was a connection. He later wrote me:

"Betty never told me that she ever sat in a car or that she was impregnated in a car. But it is true that many unwanted children are brought into this world as a result of careless sexual encounters in automobiles. As for these parked cars, I cannot say what drew me to them. Maybe you could take an educated professional guess. I'm at a loss to explain the hidden motivations for cars. Maybe it was just a question of opportunity — a chance to catch them off guard and with their pants down — to catch them unawares so to speak."[23]

My "educated guess" is that he was literally trying to "catch them off guard with their pants down." His "reunion" with Betty Falco was enough to make him want to catch a woman with her "pants down" and to punish her — he was that furious and that disappointed with his newfound mother. The style of he killings was also, in all probability, related to his feelings about her. In his mind there was a connection between her and the young girls. He may have been associating his young victims with his own mother at the time she became pregnant with him. It was as if he wanted to "relive" a situation he had fantasized about, a situation associated both with sexual pleasure and with the "sinfulness" of his his natural mother.

From the beginning he denied any sexual element to his shootings; but from the outset he also contradicted himself. He had told me at Kings County Hospital that he had no feelings about shooting his first victim, Donna Lauria. Asked further about it, he confessed: "My feelings were that I was extremely relieved. I didn't want to tell it to anyone that time." Wanting to hide it indicates his guilt.

He went on: "I was literally singing to myself on my way home, after the killing. The tension, the desire to kill a woman had built up in me to such explosive proportions that when I finally pulled the trigger, all the pressures, all the tensions, hatred, had just vanished, dissipated, but only for a short time. I had no sexual feelings. It was only hostile aggression. I knew when I did it it was wrong to do it. I wanted to destroy her because of what she represented."

"What?" I asked.

He answered, "A pretty girl, a threat to me, to my masculinity, and she was a child of God, God's creation. I couldn't handle her sexually."

The contradiction: "I had no sexual feelings," yet " I couldn't handle her sexually. . . . A threat to my masculinity."

In a letter he elaborated:

"While shooting these people, I actually became transfixed with the event. The report of the gun, the screams, the shattering of glass and windshields, the blaring horn, it all just possessed my mind so that I'd take no notice of anything else. During the first incident, I had become so transfixed that I could not move until that car horn started blasting in the quiet night. That horn brought me back to reality in a way. I got back my senses and realized what I had done and just took off running to my car.

"I don't mean that I departed reality. I knew what I was doing. I knew right from wrong, and I knew that my gun could snuff out someone's life. However, I developed such an obsession to do what I did, all the laws or promises of the gas chamber couldn't get me to stop or turn back.

"I was transfixed, true, but I wasn't sexually aroused. First, because violence doesn't turn me on. Second, even if it did, I'd have been too nervous to get an erection. To get one, I have to be relaxed and at ease. There was no way that I could relax knowing that I was about to commit a felony crime and take some lives.

"These weren't 'sex crimes.' Passion may have been involved but it wasn't directly sexual. The victims were pretty. But I had no desire to have sex with them at the time. I have looked at their pictures often, though. I have had fantasies about them that were sexual. But I'm no rapist—I'm not capable of that."[24]

If there is little doubt that his main motivation was revenge against women, there is also little doubt that Berkowitz was sexually involved with his killings.

He had previously said that he continued to pull the trigger without realizing he was doing it. Describing himself as "transfixed" is a strong indiction of how emotionally and sexually absorbed he was in the act.[25] That he says he didn't have an erection does not mean that he didn't have one (as he says did occur when he was shooting Stacy Moskowitz). Although he admits, "Passion may have been involved, but not directly sexual," he denies adamantly that these were "sex crimes." But, he also concedes he has often looked at pictures of his victims and "has had fantasies about them that were sexual." But, "I'm no rapist," he is quick to add. "I'm not capable of that." Finally, one must infer that could he have had a real sexual encounter with a woman, he would in all probability not have killed. He himself said it: "if I were to have a good, mature sexual relationship with a woman, I wouldn't have killed."[26]

It was the battle between his sexual impulses and his inconsistent control over them that produced his murderous behavior, and we shall now see the same play as it was acted out between his distorted sexual feelings and his compulsive arson. The petty arson that was a constant activity in Berkowitz's childhood reemerged after his release from the army. In children and in sexually immature adults, the sight of fire is sexually arousing. Starting a fire gives both sexual enjoyment and pleasure in the power to destroy. Where the desire for destruction—the sadistic element—is locked in with the perpetrator's sexual urge, pyromania is a substitute for sex.

Although embarrassed, Berkowitz confessed to having set "many, many fires between 1974 and 1977." Several notepads (described by the newspapers as "diaries") found by the police, showed that his first reported arson took place on May 13, 1974. It was a "rubbish fire set just before midnight on 13 May 1974, at Pinkney and Tillitson," just above Co-op City in the Bronx. This was around the time he had returned from the army to live with his adoptive father and stepmother at 170 – 17 Dreiser Loop. Berkowitz had written the dates in his so-called diary in a military style, with they day preceding the month, apparently a carryover from three years as a clerk in the army. He gave detailed information of 1,411 fires for the years 1974, 1975, and 1977, including the date and time of the fire, street, borough, weather, number of the firebox, and the fire department code indicating the type of responding apparatus and building and/or property burned.[27] In comparing his post office work schedule from March through July 1977, with the list of fires he supposedly set, however, and considering the distances he had to travel in heavy traffic, it was impossible for him to have set all the fires —old cars, rubbish heaps, brush, empty buildings—he claimed. In keeping with his inherent tendency to dramatize himself ("I loved to cause the excitement," he told me once), he clearly exaggerated these activities, which also included calling in many false alarms.

In contrast to these hectic activities, (his notepads show that during 1974 he set hundreds of fires — in one day, December 13, he set ten fires!) there is no recorded firesetting activity between December 25, 1974 and June 6, 1975. This is exactly the time during which Berkowitz was "hunting" for Betty Falco. While he might have found the time to continue his pyromaniac behavior, his libido, his emotional and sexual energies, were absorbed and directed in what was a quest, a sexual search, a hunt as if for an animal. This gave him sufficient sexual satisfaction to refrain from pyromania.

Was there a relationship between fire and murder? On December 24, 1975, two days before he attempted the first murder, he set a fire at Bogard and Paulding Avenues. On April 16, 1977, he set a fire at Adee and Edison. The following night, April 17, he shot a young couple to death. On June 16, 1977, he set a fire on Ferry Point Park, and ten days later shot and wounded a young couple. His last fire was on July 23, 1977, on Avenue S and E. 155th Street. One week later he shot his last victim to death. The fires, just preceding his murders, were apparently insufficient to satisfy him.

For a while arson had afforded Berkowitz an outlet for both sexual and hostile feelings. But it did not, in the end, satisfy him; he had to branch out to killing. He himself had told me that his firesettings gave him "some sort of emotional satisfaction, comparing it with the satisfaction an artist gets just after completion of a picture." In comparing himself to an artist, Berkowitz unwittingly stumbled on the true nature of artistic creativity — it is sexually rooted. That he believed it was only his destructive inclinations (as he says, he "was angry with the world") which were satisfied, shows that he had no idea how deeply his sexual desires were also involved. The act of arson gave him sexual enjoyment plus a feeling of destructive power — both emotions rooted in the intensity of his sadistic urges and anchored to his sexual drive. He went about his strange and bizarre activities without ever wondering about them, or having a notion of what they really meant.

On the basis of Berkowitz's inflamed sexual drive, I always wondered what he felt deep within himself about his victims. My way of finding out was to ask him about his dreams. As I expected, he became mum, reluctant even to acknowledge my question. (In response to my frequent earlier inquiries as to whether or not his dreams were sexual, he had either denied or minimized it.) Finally he admitted to several sexual dreams. "They are restless dreams, when I wake up the cover is off. In my dreams I see a couple of my victims. The girl looks very attractive," he kisses her and has sex with her passionately, but these are not wet dreams. After having had sex with her, "I feel alright afterwards." He wakes up. He confessed also to daydreams of sexual intercouse with some of his victims.[28]

These daydreams reflect the intense sexual desires he had felt at the time of the shootings — the close and definite connection between his desire and murder. It also helps up to understand his wild outburst in the courtroom at his first sentencing, when he chanted, "Stacy is a whore, Stacy is a whore!" I could not help but think the words were meant for his own mother, Betty. Berkowitz killed young women to prevent them from having illegitimate children who would have to go through all the misery, unhappiness and pain he himself had experienced.

Further, by hating women he could keep them away from him. At the bottom of our hate is fear. Or to put it bluntly, we hate what we fear. Berkowitz feared his own sexual feelings; they had to be pushed out of his mind. These very fears were also unconsciously stimulated by his own illegitimacy.

Because of his fear of women, Berkowitz was unable to establish a sexual relationship. Unaware that aggression is a normal part of sexual feelings, his aggressive feelings, present in his love emotions, turned into hate. Resorting to murder was, in the last analysis, his attempt, consciously or unconsciously, to enhance his self-esteem by achieving power over women. While this search for power played a large role in launching the career of Son of Sam, it depended finally upon to what extent he sexually felt a man.

Everyone possesses both feminine and masculine traits. Berkowitz inclined heavily toward characteristics usually considered to be feminine: he was shy, dependent, submissive, intuitive, passive, flirtatious, and seductive. His movements were gracious and swift, his voice light. In order to cover up his own passivity, he often felt the need to act and speak in a "manly" fashion; no "sissy stuff" for him. These female tendencies, which he seemed to sense in himself, unstabilized his sexual identity as a man and was another reason he hated women. Hating the female feelings in himself, he exaggerated his masculinity in order to overcome his femininity — and, as we shall later see, his homosexual yearnings.

Berkowitz's thwarted sexuality fused with his vengefulness at being abandoned to produce a volatile and deadly mixture. In shooting women, penetrating them in a symbolic and impersonal way, he did not need sexual intercouse. Thus, he also refrained from making them pregnant, a danger which must have loomed large in his mind.

Berkowitz's failure to pass through the normal stages of psychological growth left him emotionally stunted — an emotional and sexual child in a man's body. Symbolically, the closest he could come to adult genital sexuality was with knife and gun.

9

DAVID BERKOWITZ

VS. SON OF SAM

"When they arrested me, everybody said, 'I can't believe it! He's the killer?!' Well, if they could have read my mind and seen my thoughts, then they would have known without a doubt that I was the Son of Sam!"[1]

Berkowitz was pleased with himself for having hidden his identity so well that nobody believed he was the murderer. In his words lie a hidden pride that nobody had discovered his ignominious deeds, but also a revelation of self-hate. At the same time that he enjoyed his secret life, he also believed that had the world really known him, it would have known he *was* a murderer.

He wrote to me:

"It is interesting to note my changes in behavior and actions during the daylight hours and at sunset. They were two opposites. At night I hunted. In the day, I helped. I became vicious and lethal at night to people I never even knew before and whom I just met by chance. On the other hand, during the day, I was kind, friendly and courteous to other motorists and pedestrians, also, neighbors and strangers. However, these two extremes I cannot explain. This is where you, Dr. Abrahamsen, come in. Maybe you can say WHY."[2]

In David the child was the psychological key to David the man; his contradictory, divided behavior was already evident in his early years. The child's compliant, helpful attitude contradicted his destructive narcissistic and sadistic activities, giving the impression that he was two different people. A passive submissive, ingratiating manner existed side by side with a willful cruelty — the nature of which David himself sensed early in life.

As a child his life had already begun to take on a dual meaning. He had a double: the kind who knows everything about you — even the things you never tell. The German word *Doppelgänger* is more expressive. It describes a person whose characteristics are opposite to, and contrast strongly with, those traits everyone sees. The English word "double," in contrast, connotes similarity. That *Doppelgänger* was not to leave him. Berkowitz told me that he knew he was a "wicked, evil" child, and he felt guilty. This wicked, evil part was following him; later it would call him "Son of Sam."

In the history of crime, this is the first time, I believe, that two such contradictory sides of a personality have been documented in the childhood of a mass murderer. In Berkowitz, one side was agreeable, submissive, conforming, and law-abiding. The other was truant, calculating, thieving, manipulative and hostile-aggressive — the traits that later led to murder. As a child, he wanted to be on the side of his parents and their community, so he hid his misbehavior. But, unable to identify with them, he actually chose to be on the outside, against them. Basically antisocial, he behaved as if he were playing a game with himself and others. When we recall that his first memory from childhood was playing,[3] it should come as no surprise that this game-playing was deeply, almost instinctively embedded in him. This enabled him to take risks, whenever it was opportune, and according to his feelings of the moment — either passive or cruelly aggressive. He could be either law-abiding and constructive, or criminal and destructive.

In talking to me about his murderous nocturnal activites and his good behavior during the day, he said, "I ventured very carefully.[4] To which I responded: "As if you were perhaps two different people. A murderous hunter at night, a law-abiding Milquetoast during the day."

"No," he answered. "Even if I behaved during the day, I still had evil thoughts." His remark made sense. He was bothered by his destructive and hateful feelings. I commented: "You were able to behave reasonably during the day, which showed you had some constructive thoughts." I went on, "Do you seem to have possessed two different types of feelings and attitudes — two aspects of your behavior? You have, for instance, told me you paid all parking tickets — four in all — you received for parking illegally outside your building on Pine Street. You felt you had to be law-abiding to the external world, and yet, when nobody saw — at night — you already had shot several people. When you got the ticket for parking by a fire hydrant the night you shot Stacy Moskowitz, you paid that one, too."[5]

Had he heard of Robert Louis Stevenson's *Dr. Jekyll and Mr. Hyde*? Yes he had, he answered eagerly. Aware of Berkowitz's avid interest in the mysteries of the criminal mind, I was not surprised. What did he know about it? "An adventure story — written a long time ago, [1886] about two different people, good man and criminal, in one person."

"Dr. Jekyll and Mr. Hyde was a fantasy," I answered.

"Yes, but interesting."

Berkowitz was waiting for me to say more. Through my mind flashed Stevenson's famous story of Dr. Jekyll, a noble and charitable physician, who, by swallowing a concoction of his own invention, transformed himself into the nocturnal murderer, Mr. Hyde. Then, by taking another drink, he could change himself back to Dr. Jekyll. As had millions of others, I had been impressed, if not enchanted, with this simplistic yet powerful fantasy of a potion that could, in an instant, change a person from good to evil and back again.*

---

* It might also be that the case was in some way connected to the ancient and medieval fantasies of being able to turn a human being into a bird, or a dog, or a horse.

The magic of the mind is its power. The story appeals immensely to our magical wish to become, for a short while, evil beings who can perform violent deeds, and then, undiscovered, return to our normal, good selves without ever having to take responsibility for the evil we have done. This fantasy wish is to a large extent promoted by our conscious or unconscious desire, through some magic, to enable us to step outside ourselves and outside of civilized and lawful behavior. The beast lives in the breast of every man. It has manifested itself in Frankenstein's monster, the fixated opium visions of De Quincey, Ibsen's trolls, and the Son of Sam's "demons."

While Stevenson's story was, of course, a fantasy, the case of Berkowitz was terrifyingly real, with all the differences and nuances that separate fantasy from reality. A few days after our session, Berkowitz, having had time to reflect, wrote me:

"It's been said that I have a split personality like Jekyll and Hyde. Everybody has these two personalities in them. It's a dual personality, but not schizophrenia.

"There are two sides to my behavior. I go to both extremes. There isn't need to mention my evil sadistic and homicidal side. It's been fully publicized. However, much to people's surprise, I do have a "good" side. I often gave to charity an amount much larger than what others would give. When the ladies would come around my apartment in the Bronx, I would often give five or ten dollars to their polio crusade while others only gave a dollar the most. Doing this made me feel very good. When I gave I felt very humane and nice. I actually felt this.

"I did favors for several of the elderly tenants in my old Bronx building, such as carrying out their garbage or go to the store for them.

"In Yonkers I gave the newsboy nice tips for my weekly deliveries of the local paper and a nice tip on Christmas. His name was Frank and he lived in the apartment next door with his sisters and mother. They were wonderful people. A rare breed.

"I can't remember all the better things I did with my life, but they were an acceptable number. Likewise I cannot remember all my evil doings. There is good and evil in all of us. We all have the potential to murder. We all have 'evil' and sadistic fantasies. We, too, have homicidal fantasies at times. But, due to a series of circumstances, our negative thoughts become actions and we turn to anti-social behavior as a result."[6]

Berkowitz thought he could make up for his sadistic behavior by being charitable and helpful to others. This apparent helpfulness could also have been a way to manipulate others to believe he was good. Interesting in this respect was when, in the Army, he raged against the "sinful" behavior he saw around him —and then returned to the dormitory to masturbate. Berkowitz's ready comment speaks for itself.

"What I expressed verbally against the girls, they were whores and it was sinful to have sex, it wasn't what I felt. Strange, I felt hypocritical, but I couldn't help it. It was a need, to do it." He added: "I was anxious that people should have a good impression of me."[7]

In the same interview he told me that, "In the Army they called me Wolf. I was not offended by it." He smiled. "It was said as if it were a joke." It was because he was so hairy. Berkowitz was unaware that his pals may have seen the way he looked at women. He kept his yearning for women to himself.

Eager to make a good impression, he let out his real feelings only anonymously. Typical of this were the following incidents I unearthed during my visit to the Bronx apartment house where Berkowitz had lived for a year.

A woman I spoke to there, Mrs. S., knew him because she used to visit her mother, who lived on the same floor as Berkowitz. Beneath Berkowitz lived another woman in her eighties, who was deaf and played the television loudly. Mrs. S. told me that "One night the elderly woman showed my mother a note she had received. It said words to the effect: 'What is the matter you? Are you deaf or something? Why do you play your TV so loud? It is disgusting to me. I hope you die!'"

The old woman was frightened. Having nothing to do, she watched soap operas all day. She had no way of knowing that the letter writer worked at night and slept during the day. The mother of the woman I interviewed recognized from the handwriting that the letter came from David. She showed it to her husband, who was unwilling to go to the police. The mother confronted David. "Did you write these letters?" He lowered his head. Did not say yes or no; he smiled. She went on: "A nice boy like you shouldn't write such threatening letters. If someone bothers you, tell them." He didn't apologize, he did nothing. The woman received no more letters. Everybody else continued to think of him as friendly—the superintendent, the people next door, everybody.[8]

Berkowitz's response when he was discovered as the letter writer was the same as when he had been caught misbehaving in school — being late or truant, or not having his homework done. He stood with bowed head and said nothing. But even though he did not, as a rule, express anger when he was scolded, he was angry nonetheless; and he acted out that anger violently and in secret. He could control himself until the opportunity arose to set a fire — or commit a murder. But during this time of "control," his anger increased enormously, until it was out of all proportion to its original source, or cause. His strange behavior—the secret, anti-social behavior on the one hand, and his innocent demeanor on the other—effectively served to protect his local reputation.

He followed the same behavior pattern when he shot his victims. He never aroused any suspicion. At the Post Office, for instance, where his co-workers often discussed Son of Sam and whether or not he was insane, Berkowitz never told them Son of Sam was insane. "I was only a casual listener. Sometimes I asked 'What do you think of the guy? Is he crazy or what?'" With a triumphant voice he added, "Nobody really figured out that I was Son of Sam."[9]

He played his double role with incredible coolness: "I would walk into work at the Post Office one day after a shooting. I would see the faces of confusion and fear. Then I would say 'What happened? Gee, that's too bad. I hope they catch the bastard.'"[10]

Berkowitz's greatest enjoyment in all this was that *nobody* guessed the truth. His total anonymity made him feel superior, omnipotent.* His double role came to encompass almost all his activities.

His description of his double role vis à vis his real mother, Betty, is a case in point and must be reiterated: "Behind my mask (Richie the nice guy) I was filled with anger and rage toward her. With absolute control, I managed never to show or verbalize this."[11]

His secretive behavior became a ritual: "I never could go to the refrigerator at home when somebody was around. When there was nobody I would put food on the plate and sneak into the room and eat it." He was a phantom. No wonder that "my father used to call me a sneak and spy." It was true. "I used to spy on my father. I used to look in his face. Did he look clever or not?" Apparently he had realized that his father not very clever, because he hadn't as yet discovered his son's true nature!

It came as hardly a surprise to me when David asked me how his own face looked. Did it look honest or dishonest? I turned the question back to him. "I think," he answered, " I look honest," but then he smilingly added, "not always" — and laughed.[12]

His religious proselytizing while in the Army, his attempt to get away from his "sinful" life, was restricted to men. "I made it my purpose never to witness for women."[13] On them he turned his hate: "Women — I blame them for everything. Everything evil that's happened in this world — somehow it goes back to them. I hate them for messing up everything in this world. They've really screwed my life up good."[14] He didn't understand that he had screwed up his own life by himself.

While religion seems to have made a deep impression upon Berkowitz, he confessed that he exaggerated its effect:

"I did exaggerate my religious behavior while I was at Kings County Hospital. I never really believed from my heart that I

---

* The principle of anonymity equaling omnipotence can be seen in the fairy tale "Rumpelstiltskin." As long as the miller's daughter, now princess, cannot guess his name, he has a claim on first-born child. But as soon as she does guess his name, he loses his hold on her and vanishes in a temper tantrum, never to be seen again.

had been converted to a pious gospel preacher and evangelist. My thoughts were just as evil as ever despite my Bible reading and praying.

"I did try to impress my outward religious piety onto others — the guards, the public, the courts, the judge, the doctors, etc. Secretly, I loathed Ollie Smith [with whom he had studied the Bible] for the praise she was getting for supposedly 'converting' me. It's hard to convert a convict. Sure as hell, I haven't been converted. I had the urge to blaspheme the name of God to Smith's face rather than praise him in front of her.

"The last thing I wanted to do was to preach the gospel to inmates. Who the hell wants to do that? And furthermore, what preaching I did in Kings County was only at the urgings of Ollie Smith."[15]

On an earlier occasion, he had emphatically exclaimed: "I really think I used this religious 'kick' to escape reality and loneliness. It was really a crutch. But boy, did I get hooked with it. I became a fanatic."[16] But he does admit that "My involvement with Christianity while stationed at Fort Knox has had a tremendous impact on my life and thoughts. More than most people realize. There isn't a waking moment that goes by that I'm not thinking of God and the devil, good and evil, heaven and hell, and my usual sex fantasies." He knew no moderation. One way or another, his behavior was always extreme.

Inwardly, he felt ambivalent, dominated by the load of hateful feelings against himself and others that he carried around. Despite his utter self-centeredness — which one would think would enhance his self-love — he loathed himself. "I always felt guilty, but after reading my Bible and listening to endless sermons, I feel more guilty than ever. Now, I know just how wicked I am, how morally filthy.

"The music I listen to, my intimate thoughts, my past thievery, they'll lead me straight to hell."[16]

This hatred of himself, the source of his hatred of others, was central to his double behavior. It started when he was a child, during which time he had developed a poor image of himself and of all four of his parents. Unable to stand on both feet simultaneously, he shifted first to one, and then the other. Always a role player, he wanted everyone to see that he was on the side of the angels, and then secretly to switch to the side of the devil. Berkowitz needed no concoction to accomplish this change. He was able, simply, to talk himself into criminal behavior.

"Do you like yourself?"

"Sometimes I tolerate myself. Other times I hate myself."[17]

A child hates himself because he doesn't feel liked by others. He therefore thinks there is something wrong with him. Such was the case with Berkowitz. Described by school authorities as "moody . . . very easily upset," his gradually increasing self-hate was instrumental in his becoming preoccupied with himself and self-analytical. Why? Because "self-hatred," as Otto Weininger has written, "is the best foundation for self-examination."[18] Berkowitz, being a self-hater, apparently, felt the need for self-examination.

We cannot know exactly how Berkowitz was thinking in this respect, but we can be pretty sure that more than once he wondered about his destructive feelings and angry thoughts. With his expansive imagination, he once speculated that if the evil side of his nature could be isolated from the rest of him, he could find tranquility. But this, of course, was never to happen.

Every child needs a loving influence, understanding and regard, and a feeling of acceptance. Unless these constructive emotions are present in his life, he feels he is a failure, develops feelings of guilt, and begins to hate himself. Teased as a child because of his chubbiness, his Jewishness, and his self-centeredness, feeling unwanted by viture of his adoption, feeling that he had lost Pearl to Nat, he wanted desperately to get some positive attention. Because he needed it so badly, he wanted a great deal of it from somewhere! Nothing less than the limelight would do. He secretly wanted to be a star!

His self-hatred expressed itself most dramatically when, in the Army, he had himself baptized. His conversion to Christianity was a denigration of both his adoptive and birth parents. It dramatized his hatred for his Jewish ancestry. Indeed, the hatred of Judaism symbolized his hatred for both his mothers. Feeling weak and powerless, he feared he was castrated and impotent; this feeling was expressed in his attitude toward the Jewish people. A feeling of castration is, generally speaking, the deepest unconscious root of anti-Semitism.[19] Berkowitz's personal psychology fits this description.

Possibly the strongest self-hate in any ethnic group is found among the Jews.[20] Through centuries of persecution, they have internalized other people's hatred of them. While non-Jews may be anti-Semitic, they may also hate other groups. In contrast the Jews' need for hatred is more exclusively directed first against themselves, and second against other Jews. Their weakness and powerlessness is so intricately connected with their self-directed bigotry, that they apparently receive gratification from anti-Semites.[21] They do no need to turn their hatred anywhere else.

As we have seen, Berkowitz's self-hate was also related to his female traits. We cannot say that a person has a "male" or "female" character. Rather, since every person has masculine and feminine elements, we have to speak in terms of balance, or proportion. Berkowitz despised his own strong feminine inclinations. It is noteworthy that many men feel more masculine, stronger, at night. Perhaps this is because, their day's work done, they feel freer to assert their independent selves. Masculinity and freedom reinforce each other. It would seem then that Berkowitz killed at night, not only to hide himself in darkness, but also because at that time of day he felt more masculine, more daring.

Despite his deep fascination with all that was feminine, he feared women, undoubtedly because he felt himself not enough of a man. The psychological tests (not previously published) administered during the first month of his stay at Kings County by the hospital psychologist and by me[22] show this fear of women expressed as: "I regard the female as dangerous. If enticed by the female, it may be dangerous. All women are deceitful because I myself was fooled."

Since he confessed that he had intended to kill only women, one may wonder about his feelings for men. He always liked men, he said, and had several male friends whom he used to meet "on the block." As to homosexual experiences, he flatly denied having any. When I asked whether he had been propositioned in the army he said:

"You asked about my "homosexual experiences," But I have nothing to say here because I never had any. Neither do I desire any.

". . . you asked about this type of sexual activity occurring in the Army. I myself never witnessed any of this. But it has been the brunt of many jokes, all of which were invented. I might add, too, that this type of sexual activity is frowned upon in the Army, and is punishable by court martial. So none of this, if it does occur, is done in an overt manner.

"As for being 'attacked,' no, I have never been sexually attacked by another man."[23]

His own female traits plus his hatred of women would indicate some deeply repressed homosexual feelings. A psychological test (Minnesota Multiphasic Personality Scale), indicates deeply buried homosexual leanings which threatened his weak masculine ego. Remembering that Berkowitz's vivid fantasy life and his passive yearnings are rooted in female inclinations, it is not out of line to speculate that he may have imagined passive anal intercourse without experiencing it. Vacillating between the masculine and feminine, Berkowitz could find no way to deal with his strong sexual drive.

Nor does it seem far-fetched to venture a symbolic association between his hatred of women and his short-lived devotion to Christianity. Having possible homosexual leanings, he secretly denounced women in order to show that he was just "one of the guys." (When he was nine years old he had tried to start, among the boys, a "hate group" against the girls.) Along the same lines, he thought his anti-Semitism would bring him closer to his male friends, most of whom were gentile.

His self-hate made it particularly hard for him to endure his loneliness — who among self-haters desires his own company? He sought love from others but couldn't find it. Finally, he adopted the only role that could give him any satisfaction or relief. Berkowitz became a man who showed off, posed, exhibited himself. Hysterical and dramatic, he was all the while suffering from displaced and painful sexual feelings.

He had often told me he liked excitement. "I only like it," he said, "when I cause it myself."

"Why?"

"Well, because it attracted attention to myself," he finally answered.[24]

As he was later to write me: "I knew . . . I wanted to be the center of attention. I love the limelight. The Army, auxilliary police, and fire departments; I wanted to make a dramatic rescue, to be a hero."[25]

His whole life became a drama. His existence, filled with traumatic situations and combined with sexual impulses, had given rise to hysterical symptoms.

Wishing as desperately to impress himself as he wished to impress others, he tried to be more than he was by showing off his feelings, ideas, and activities — murderous as they finally became. His intense desire—his craving—to expose and display himself, which consciously or unconsciously had become a *raison d'être* for him, stimulated his tendency to exaggerate which, already present in childhood, became a significant part of his young life, and gradually took an aggressive and violent form. It drove him from truancy, pilfering, lying, and fire-setting to game-playing with demons, the Son of Sam, and murder. He had to be noticed, attract attention, create a sensation, at any and all costs. His attempt as a boy to start a club of "girl haters," his firesettings, the lies about his sexual experience prior to Korea, his supposed use of large quantities of drugs (as reported to the other psychiatrists) in his religious "conversion," his crowning of himself as Son of Sam with the demons as his court, and finally, despite the unspeakable tragedy of his murders, his cat and mouse game with police and public—all had a grotesque character. In particular, his so-called "manly" behavior (the "girl-haters club," the sexual braggadocio) was a caricature. His life had become a performance, his very being a stage for his theatrical experiences. These hysterical, role-playing traits — law-abiding vs. criminal, compliant vs. sadistic—were the stamp of his personality.

On various occasions he had claimed some form of demonic possession — that an outside force had entered his mind and commanded his murderous behavior. All of this nurtured the popular notion that he had a multiple personality. This, however, is not the case.

In order to understand the much misunderstood concept of multiple personality, we must first state that it is a matter of controversy whether or not the person with a double or multiple personality exists. Because Berkowitz's psychology might easily be confused with the psychological mechanism of true double personality, it is worthwhile to look into the structure of this much acclaimed phenomenon.[26] Popular interest in the mental illness known as multiple personality arose around 1870, at a time when mental illnesses were inadequately understood, and imprecisely formulated.

There are certain people who have two or more sides or facets to their character or behavior. All of these aspects exist side by side, often without being in touch with or aware of each other. Each of these personality states shows different character traits, attitudes, and behavior; and each claims lack of memory and/or ignorance of the other. While the sub-personalities may differ from each other in such matters as age, sex, and general behavior, in each personality one may encounter symptoms like hysteria, paresis, or paralysis; visual disturbances; suicidal, and homicidal attempts; violent outbursts and attacks; traumas; even a psychosis (insanity) of short or extended duration.

The existence of multiple personality is open to question. In the whole literature, only 20 persons in the last 25 years have been identified as multiple personalities,[27] and even some cases have been considered doubtful because many were borderline personality disorders that exhibited role playing rather than showing true double or multiple personalities.[28] A case in point was that of Dr. Cornelia B. Wilbur's patient Sybil (a pseudonym), who claimed 17 personalities. Dr. Herbert Spiegel, who participated in the investigation of Sybil, was skeptical of her claim. He believed that Sybil was role playing, and he was therefore not listed among the authors of the book that bears her name.

The number of multiple personalities varies from case to case. In the case by Hervey M. Cleckley, "Eve" claimed to have had

22 personalities. A movie, *The Three Faces of Eve*, was made about her, with Joanne Woodward playing all three principal parts.

Sometimes an imaginary playmate, a common childhood phenomenon, may become an unconscious sub- or secondary personality. This can lead to what may appear to be double personality, but only where the playmate — or other dissociated feelings, values, and behavior—*displace* normal consciousness[29] can it be diagnosed as such. In this case, part of the mind would be separated (dissociated) from the total personality, with the rest of the mind unable to exert control over the split-off portion.

As mentioned earlier, Berkowitz had imaginary conversations and games with female "playmates" who existed in reality. These imaginary relationships helped him overcome his loneliness. His games with them, while strictly fantasized, were, however, not dissociated, not shut out from his consciousness.

When Berkowitz wrote his notorious Son of Sam notes, he sometimes wrote in script and at other times he printed. There was such a marked difference in the notes that it was as if there were two different personalities penning his words. One might be tempted to regard this as evidence of a dissociated personality. However, dissociation may also be present in the automatic writing of hysteria.[30] Furthermore, Berkowitz's elusiveness throughout the Son of Sam period suggests that he used the two contrasting styles of writing to avoid detection and also, very probably, to give the impression that he was mentally ill, that he indeed had two different personalities.

The single most important indication of the presence of a true double or multiple personality is loss of memory (amnesia or no memory at all of one's other personalities). For this reason I often asked Berkowitz whether he remembered his multiple fires and his many murders. His memory of all these events was excellent. His total recall of them, his ability to describe where and when every crime had taken place, were clear illustrations that he had no amnesia of his deadly attacks. His memory of his childhood and adolescent experiences was equally vivid. Every detail had been engraved on his memory.

The nature of these events could, in and of themselves, have made him defensive, made him desire to suppress them. He was too alert, too aware of his own activities, to even imagine that "Son of Sam thoughts" could have displaced his normal consciousness or commandeered his behavior. Since he never showed any evidence of a thought disorder (personality disorganization) always present in a psychotic condition such as schizophrenia (and the Rohrschach test showed no psychosis), nor was there any amnesia, I concluded that Berkowitz *consciously* played a role that contrasted with his compliant daytime role, when he went out at night. His behavior had the superficial markings of a double personality, but at its core it was role playing, the performance shaped by his hysterical personality. Each side of his character had its own feelings, fantasies, and points of view. One was compliant, representing the more-or-less practical person who adhered to the rules of his community and was in steady contact with his environment. The other was his *doppelgänger,* the personification of which was "Son of Sam." He had these two moods, two phases — the apparently nice, gentle, fearful and tender mood, and the hostile, murderous one — both consciously nurtured and in touch with each other. A kind of co-consciousness existed.[31]

Berkowitz had grown up with two sets of parents, one real, one fantasized. He lived simultaneously in two different worlds, moved on two separate tracks, trying in vain to make reality conform to his fantasy, and creating in himself a divided identity and a divided loyalty. This ambivalence, within him since childhood, characterized his entire life. His ambivalence was sharpened when he later discovered the strange lifestyle of his birth parents.

Joseph Klineman was married, but had maintained, since about 1946, an extramarital alliance with Berkowitz's birth mother, Betty. This alliance lasted until he died 29 years later. Betty was his sexual partner, and gave birth to their child David, but Klineman spent only his days with her. At night he returned to his legal wife (who had refused divorce), slept at her domicile, and then in the morning came back to Betty's apartment where he remained until nightfall. Betty Falco was his real family.

Betty Falco for her part, was never legally divorced from her husband, Tony, although he had left her for another woman in 1940, after about four years of marriage. She was married officially to Falco, but shared her life with Klineman. Betty and Klineman each played two roles: Klineman married and apparently separated, Betty apparently married and in actuality separated, each was involved with the other in a long-term liaison. Although their alliance was overt—his three children spent much of their time in her apartment; when Klineman died they sat shiva there, she came to his funeral — he left her nothing in his will. He had given her nothing permanent and lasting, except for one thing—their issue, Richard, who was put up for adoption and became David Berkowitz.

Whatever way we turn in the story of Berkowitz's birthparents, double feelings and double attitudes characterize their behavior. Strangest of all is the fact that without knowing anything about his true parents' (his real father—"wild-tempered, greedy, impatient") duplicitous behavior, he instinctively was to follow the strange pattern of their life together. By the time he first met his real mother and learned about her "double" life, he had already been walking that path, following in her footsteps, playing his own double role since earliest childhood.

One could say it was not a coincidence. He was his parents' son. It was David Berkowitz vs. Son of Sam.

10

HIS OWN

EXECUTIONER

Human behavior is famous for its failure to comply with our theories about it. Except in the case of hired killers, the majority of murder cases have fundamental conflicts and emotional forces that instigate the homicide. Every murderer has his own psycho-social characteristics that depend upon his family and emotional background, environment, and his personality reactions to his experiences. A murderer may kill for a particular reason, such as jealousy, fear, frustration, depression, some of which go back to his past, but the causes may not suffice to explain *why* the murderer has killed.

We must go a step further than merely stating what happened with Berkowitz in his past. We must ask why did it happen? Why did he become a murderer? To answer that question, we must discover the *meaning* of his behavior. To find out Berkowitz's intentions, his purposes in his psyche are as significant, if not more so, than the one line of casuality, the one line of determination. What were his leitmotifs and what was their meaning?

Berkowitz's death wish was one reason which gave meaning to his murders. His death wish, being partly a product of his self-hate, he satisfied consciously or unconsciously in his fantasy, by turning it directly against others, but at the same time indirectly against himself by finally bringing about his own punishment and imprisonment. The circumstances of his birth and childhood were such that they, so to say, led to self-hatred. As a child he had been told by his adoptive parents that his real mother had died when he was born, and this circumstance made him feel guilty. Fantasizing that he was the cause of her death — and therefore could not be thought of as a good boy — he deserved to be punished, and this intensified his desire to die. However, when he later, as a young adult, discovered that his natural mother was still alive, it was a shock from which he could not free himself. She had forsaken him, and his adoptive mother and father had lied to him.

The child David carried in him as a result of the burden of being adopted, his feeling of guilt over having caused his mother's death, and his indulgent adoptive parents, who gratified him in his every whim: all these circumstances were obstacles to the development of his sense of self. It was the relationship with Pearl that was the critical one for him. During his infancy and early childhood she was the one directly responsible for him. Anxious to have a child, she overmothered and overindulged him, and satisfied his every demand in such measure that he hardly understood the word no. He became a little tyrant, and Pearl, for the sake of peace, frequently gave in. Thus, partly because of his defiant dominance of her, she was in effect dominated by him and so she failed him in certain basic but vital ways during the first years of his life.

His knowledge of his birth parents had been cut off, and as with other children in this situation, his emotional relationship with his adoptive family had become blocked. Neither Pearl nor Nat was aware of David's destructive behavior outside the home. Says David: "It frightens me to look back and see what I was and what I became. It also angers me, for I ask out loud, "Why didn't someone see all the signs?"[1]

A few more lines may round out the picture of his disruptive and anti-social behavior:

"I was a disruptive, uncontrollable terror in school. . . .

". . . I never got caught — never. I left behind me, even when I was only about 12 years old, a trail of burned trash bins and burned automobiles. There were the dead fish, all of which I killed. The dead, poisoned bird (Pudgy). The torture chamber I created for ants, flies, roaches and any other hapless insects who may have been unfortunate enough to enter my room. The vandalized apartment building with the yanked out elevator plates, the floods in the basement . . . the broken windows and the can of paint all over the hallway.[2]

He continued, he was "not trying to brag or boast about these destructive acts, or how I managed to evade capture, much less punishment. I only want you to know what occurred — see the signs — learn something."[3]

He then remarks: "I have often noticed just how unobservant people are. It's been said that parents are the last to know. This may be true in my case, for I wonder how I, at ages nine, eleven, thirteen, etc., managed to do so very many negative things and go unnoticed. It is puzzling, indeed. And I think you will agree it is sad."[4]

If Pearl did discover him, he may have listened to her scoldings without bothering much about her. Showing her concern for him, she visited his school, and sent him to a psychologist for help. Her interest in him can also be seen in the way she dressed him in fine clothes and displayed photographs of him in the living room — all done to show off this beautiful boy. But how deep did her concern go? Did she perhaps want to see only the good side of him? When he behaved badly in school, and when she was told by neighbors about his wild conduct, she certainly should have taken him to task.

Pearl seems to have had little understanding or empathy for David, possibly because he wasn't her own flesh and blood, but more likely because she was afraid of him. Parents frequently are afraid of their children, not daring to criticize or discipline them. Then, too, Nat seems to have been a shadowy father figure, with whom David did not identify. Nor did he serve David as a male role model.

This situation was considerably worsened when Pearl developed cancer. She died when her son was fourteen years old.

That she was somewhat unempathetic may be inferred from the extraordinarily egocentric, narcissistic character of David's behavior; it has been shown that lack of empathy is often a characteristic of parents with narcissistic children. Telling in this respect is his naming himself "Son of Sam," and his grandiose and omnipotent-like behavior after his arrest. His grandiosity was a compensation for: an inadequate sense of self, and lack of self esteem.

Crucial to turning David Berkowitz into a murderer was that he was adopted. His search for his birth mother after he had returned from the Army in Korea was a search to reestablish his feelings of self-worth and his being preoccupied with death, and finding a meaning with his existence.

His real mother embodied his fantasy of "family romance," and this fantasy persisted up to and beyond the time he completed his actual search for her. But when he finally met his real mother, Betty Falco, in the flesh, the discrepancy between his "family romance" mother and the real woman was shocking, overwhelming. His disillusionment produced a narcissistic rage against her and his half-sister, who had been kept while he had been "thrown away." His rage against them meant that they were as worthless as he felt himself to be.

In most cases, the reunion of adoptees with their birthparents has not been salutary. This in itself should not discourage an adoptee from looking for his true parents if he feels it to be a life-necessity. The adoptee's opportunity to learn about his or her birth parents can fortify his relationship to his adoptive family. There has been, and there still is, a taboo against knowing the natural parents. When this knowledge is cut off it may frequently lead the adoptee to block his emotional relationship to his adoptive family. To Berkowitz, it was essential that he find his birthparents.

His relationship — or rather, lack of it — to his birth mother played a direct causative role in his murders. His first homicidal attempt occurred six months after he had met her. Feeling worthless and, in the face of her rejection and abandonment, lacking a sense of self-esteem, gave meaning to his killings. He had to show that he was *not insignificant*. Wishing to be united with and simultaneously afraid of being overwhelmed by his birth mother because of his fear of women, made him afraid that he would be abandoned and rejected by women. He had the imperative need, unconscious though it was, to proclaim that he was not a helpless little boy, that he was capable of acting on his own, even killing in his own way. He was no longer afraid of his mother's power to throw him away; he had the power to strike back. He could take revenge on her for rejecting him. He knew what he was doing.

"I did know why I pulled the trigger. I did know why I deliberately killed. I knew who the person was whom I wanted to hurt — on whom I wanted revenge.

"These shootings were planned long before they took place. Nobody knows the reason but me and perhaps one day, you.[5]

When asked whether he felt powerful as he was sneaking up on people and killing, he not only agreed, but was in a hurry to elaborate. "The desires," he answered, "to do it, to kill, had filled me up to such explosive proportions, it caused me such turmoil inside, that when it released itself, it was like a volcano erupting itself, and the pressure was over, for a while anyhow."[6] In obtaining power thus, he was trying to boost his narcissistic, masculine self-esteem which was rooted in his impaired sexual identity.

These feelings, for the most part unconscious, were also directed against his half sister. He himself did not understand why he chose only victims who lived in Queens, but it was nothing short of an obsession. When the urge to kill struck him, he compulsively turned toward Queens. It was there that his sister and her family lived. But he was not consciously aware this was the reason he selected that borough.

Berkowitz's victims (and this is true of every killer) were

substitutes — in his case, of his mother and/or sister, and of himself. Both the fantasies of murder and the actual killings mobilized in him both conscious and unconscious. Homicidal and suicidal impulses became intertwined, so that the murders were an unconscious killing of self. Every suicide, in a sense, is a psychological homicide.

His hatred developed thus: first of all against himself, then against his birth mother and half sister. And then, in his fantasy, he created other objects (women), for his rage, defensively reworking and recharging his raging emotions. Selecting his victims at random, he then invested them with his fantasies. He killed girls he didn't know, he told me, because then nobody would suspect him. This, however, was his rational explanation. His real reason was rooted in his fantasies about killing his mother and half sister.

Why did he shoot at the women's heads? "My goal," he says, "in all these murders and attempted murders was only to kill my victims as quickly and painlessly as possible. I didn't want to wound them. Aiming for the head was the surest way."[7]

Clinical, yes — and cynical, too! What he didn't know was that he was shooting at their heads because he wanted to destroy them instantly — he wanted to render immediate death. He performed instant castration, acting out his own castration fear and illustrating the stunting of his own emotional development. He was doing to them what he felt had been done to him.

Another motivation which gave meaning to his murders, unconscious though it may have been, was to prevent young women from becoming pregnant and giving birth to another David Berkowitz who would have to go through the same painful childhood and adolescence he had suffered.

While emotionally tense during the shooting itself, after the discharge of the gun he felt a great deal of pleasure and enormous gratification and intense power and mastery. He alone knew who the killer was, and this secret made him feel even more omnipotent. After each murder had been accomplished, he had a release of tension and feeling of exhilaration, a sense of great well-being. In the execution of acts of violence, we know that extreme tension is followed by gratification and exhilaration, as is so well depicted in the Electra myth where Electra is so gratified when her brother Orestes murders their mother and her new husband Aegisthus (who had killed their father) that she became exalted.

Berkowitz's shootings took place over the course of a single year. He carried them out in intervals from one to three months in a pattern resembling a repetition compulsion. The way the shootings developed can in some way be compared to the way a person gets hooked on a drug. The first time he or she may be somewhat afraid to try it, but then the next time it gets easier. With each subsequent experience, the fear lessens, the gratification grows, until finally the person is fully addicted. The same mechanism may have operated in Berkowitz's murders. Each homicide was carried out more readily and with greater ease than the one before it. His reaction to his murders became less intense. Then, as the tension built up again, the urge to kill struck him in an almost regular, cyclical one- to three-month pattern, accompanied by the release of his emotional tension.

Was Berkowitz, in the act of murder, discharging his hatred for the mother objects whom he resented so much? His birth mother, adoptive mother, and stepmother? Or were his homicides less symbolic than "I hate my mother; I therefore will kill a representative, or symbol, of her"? Were they more directly an expression of a more essential hate, a hate residing deep within him?

"It took me 24 years to erupt, to explode like a volcano. It took me 24 years before I reached the ultimate destiny — MURDER [sic]. This is the ultimate climax — MURDER. I reached this point, Hillside and Ted did too.* I reached the point where I just couldn't keep it in — I wanted to, but I couldn't. So I gave up resisting."[8]

Frustrated and vengeful, he was like a volcano under pressure, until finally it came to explosions and explosions and explosions. What did he release? His violent fantasies.

---

* Berkowitz is referring to the Hillside Strangler and to Ted Bundy.

The murders were directly related to his instinctual sexual perversion and to a discharging of his aggressive hatred. That he had, all his young life, directed his fantasies and feelings toward death show that the idea of death was deeply ingrained in him. It was an all meaning part of his psyche. Obsessed with his own death wishes, which he always kept a secret, his homicidal desires and impulses finally surfaced. How strange, then, that engulfed and absorbed in such consumingly threatening thoughts and fantasies, he could on the surface appear to be a law-abiding citizen, going about his business as a post office worker.

We should not assume that because he was obsessed with death, Berkowitz merely wanted to die. Co-existing with his fascination with death was his enormous fear of it. His suicidal feelings were ambivalent. Because fear originates from situations in which we feel helpless, we use various defense mechanisms to cope with it. Fear feeds on our fear of the unknown, on our mortality. Confronting one's fear in a controlled atmosphere is one way to deal with threats and terrors in the deepest recesses of our minds, and it is something that most of us do. Our fascination and consumption of murder mysteries and horror films testifies to this. As a child, Berkowitz was partly able to deal with his inner terrors through horror films. But when he grew up and became more sexually aware, the ante kept being raised: his thwarted energies and impulses could no longer find an outlet. Finally, it was through murder that he found a way to exert some control over his own world. And it gave meaning to him.

The most evil acts are done out of fear. Berkowitz's fear, an all-pervading element in his life, which began with the mystery of his origins, grew as he developed into young manhood. He partially coped with it by obsessively displacing it onto another area of his existence. Finding it easier and more acceptable to be obsessed with something mundane and concrete rather than confront something as ineffable, amorphous, and threatening as fear, he developed a hypersensitivity to noise. It became an intrusion upon his very existence.

He writes: "It was just too much. I never felt so hopeless, so powerless against those noisy forces in my neighborhood. I felt like worthless shit—never would there be peace and quiet. Never would I have a real girlfriend and intimate companionship to share my life with. I wanted these things so much but they seemed unattainable. I couldn't please a woman or make her love me. These women are insatiable anyhow. It was all hopeless."[9]

And:

"Loud, excessive or annoying noises have always been my weakpoint. I cannot bear these sounds, a chorus of barks, yelps and howls, which continued throughout the day. I couldn't read, relax, sleep or even watch television with these intrusions. This in how bad it was."[10]

Asked why he shot some of the neighborhood dogs, he replied:

"If you could hear what horrid sounds these 'bad' dogs were making, then you could very well understand my motives — a last resort — for shooting them. It was an act of desperation. You can disagree all you want, but it's true. I had tried phone calls, letters, everything including calls to the police. NOTHING BUT NOTHING WAS DONE! I was then forced to use more extreme measures, Molitove [sic] cocktails, shootings, etc. I had no choice. . . ."[11]

"As far as noise is concerned, I can't tolerate loud playing of television sets either. Alas, Craig Glassman enters into the picture. This creature was one of the most inconsiderate of the whole animal kingdom. At 2:00 A.M. his t.v. was playing at a volume that sent chills through my spine and vibrated my bed as if I was sleeping on a subway car.

"If you understand all this then you could understand why Glassman came under my attack. Truly, people like this shouldn't be allowed to live with others, and they should have some type of penal institution for the "cruel" of this world.

"I just acted out of desperation and because violence was all that they would understand. This was the last straw. Yet, all I sought was peace and quiet."[12]

At the time he writes about, he was feeling great stress and strain. He complained and "raised the roof," but nobody seemed to listen—a state of affairs to which he had been subjected since Pearl died, but which he never could accept. Once again he felt ignored and rejected.

He eventually made creative use of his noise obsession when he spun out the story of the barking dog-demons.

The commands to kill which he said he received from the demons were actually signals from his own sexual impulses. Exhibiting sadomasochistic traits and aggressive, violent emotions, he had developed a double standard: one for himself, one for others. There was no thought disorder, no insanity, no deterioration of judgment; he did, however, manifest a character disorder (literally, a disturbance of his character — a psychopathic personality).

We were fascinated. Fascinated with the demons and fascinated with the killer's mystery. Our own hostile, frustrated, and aggressive feelings, hidden or dormant, are often mobilized and activated by any violent act, be it murder or execution. Through conscious or unconscious feelings we participate; without really knowing it, we become, in a strange way, partners to the crime. Thus some people came to identify with "Son of Sam." Some secretly admired him, even came to root for him as he continued to elude capture for such a long time. One may venture to say that some came to regard the homicides as entertainment. Many of those who lead lives of "quiet desperation" identify, in their fantasies, with the *Sturm und Drang* of others' lives of noisy desperation. Dr. Karl Menninger once said, "We do not only tolerate violence, we love it."[13]

If one observes the interplay between the criminal, the public and the victim a triangular relationship emerges, a relationship which heretofore has been largely neglected. When one examines it one sees a closer connection between these three than one might ever suspect.

Such a relationship was operative in the murderous career of Son of Sam and the public's reaction to his acts. In addition to those he killed and wounded, the people of New York were also the victims with Berkowitz the victimizer.

But it was Berkowitz himself who ended the triangle, It was

his own guilt that finally forced him to abandon the game, relinquish the relationship and give himself away:

"Yes, I remember the Court Hearing [October] very well. Obviously you were believed over those other doctors and this is good. Now, you ask how I felt inwardly. I can say that I went to great lengths to suppress my guilt. So I did feel guilty. But I managed to mask it in such a way as to not be bothered by it— at least not bothered by it on a conscious level. But obviously it was eating away at me on the inside. However, I did succeed in suppressing it all to a large degree. So I didn't feel so bad. Besides, you mustn't forget how angry and frustrated I was at the time. I explained this to you before. The constant noise, my social failures, my built up and unfulfilled sexual urges, etc., all amounted to an explosive situation so that I felt justified at the time. My guilt was consciously suppressed and justification took over. However, slowly, but surely, my guilt surfaced in my mind. I couldn't mask it for long."[14]

Guilt, most often unconscious, is a major driving force in homicide. It is guilt that compels criminals to return to the scene of the crime (Berkowitz did). In another famous murder, the 1924 case in which Nathan Leopold and Richard Loeb killed little Robert Frank, it was guilt that caused Nathan Leopold to leave his (very distinctive) eyeglasses at the scene of the murder. Confronted with the glasses, he had no choice but to confess. Thus he received what he unconsciously wanted — his punishment. Guilt caused Berkowitz to park his car by a fire hydrant —thus getting a parking ticket—on the night he shot Moskowitz and Violante. By now he needed to be caught; he needed to be punished. Sometimes unconscious guilt is itself the motivation for murder. The murderer kills *in order* to be caught — and punished. A pervasive sense of guilt is exquisitely described in Dostoyevsky's *Crime and Punishment*.

That Berkowitz felt guilt proves that he was not insane. At the outset he played insane, constructed a delusion system, and devised auditory hallucinations to avoid justice. His later admission of malingering—pretending psychotic symptoms—was clear evidence that his guilt feelings were too strong to allow his ego to keep up the show. He pleaded guilty in order to get some internal peace. But such peace did not come cheaply. He told me: "Just before I pleaded guilty I was very apprehensive. I knew that I would be going to prison and that it would be for a long time. I didn't know what it would be like and I was being my usual pessimistic self. So to me it seemed as if only terrible horrors awaited me in prison. As it turned out, Attica Prison isn't too bad."[15]

But neither was it too good. The day the newspaper headlines read: "'Son of Sam' Killer Slashed in the Neck at Attica,"[16] I was hardly surprised. He had it in his blood to create a situation which people had to notice.

All prisons engender brutalities. Attica, with its huge inmate population, about 2,000, is more brutal than most. The rigid discipline and harsh routine of prison life, added to the cruelty of its occupants, do nothing to mitigate the violent atmosphere.

Despite the lawlessness of their lives, the convict population of most prisons conforms to a definite social hierarchy and rigidly enforced code of behavior. Highest in social acceptability among inmates are cop killers and bank robbers — lowest are child molesters. Only one rung above the child molesters are the rapists and killers of young girls. Prison morality is simple: you don't kill young girls. This is what Berkowitz had done and it made him a virtual outcast among his fellow inmates.

He had been at Attica a year and a half when somebody tried to kill him. When I wrote to him asking for details, he replied:

"I am confined to my cell for disciplinary action as a result of that incident. I have allegedly violated Attica Behavioral Code — 5:20:12 "lying and giving false statements or incomplete information."

"The attempt on my life, which I will only tell you about in person, is one of the best and most positive events of my recent past/present. It didn't upset me in the least, but, as a result, I have a more positive outlook on life. We all learn from our mistakes and misjudgments. It was for the better"[17]

Later he added: "everyone here seems to agree that I've taken this trivial incident very well. The wound has healed, the stitches are out and I feel fit as a fiddle."[18]

A week after the assault I went to see him in Attica. He looked surprisingly well, having lost 5 or 10 pounds. He greeted me warmly. As he sat down facing me, I noticed the long red scar on his neck, which he had tried to cover with his shirt collar.

The scar was seven inches long and a half inch wide. It stretched from below his left jaw, under his chin, around his neck to the mid line at the back of the neck. The surgeon had had to take between 50 and 60 stitches, Berkowitz said.

He had been delivering hot water to the inmates in protective custody at the prison's reception building. These prisoners are considered to be more dangerous than the others, and for that reason are issued razor blades for shaving only one at a time.

"How did the attack happen?"

"I was bringing the men hot water for shaving, and while pouring water into a cup, I bent foreward and was cut on the neck."

"Did you see the razor blade?"

"I think I saw it, but before I knew it, I was cut."

"What did you do then?"

"I walked over to the guards. They were drinking coffee a few feet away. I told them I had been cut. They noticed the cut was open and they gasped (dramatic!) when they saw that the edges of the wound were split. It didn't bleed much. I was taken to the Medical Unit and the surgeon told me the wound was superficial except for two inches in the back of the neck where it was deep." Some muscles in back of his neck had been cut. Whether or not any nerves had been involved, he didn't know. "The doctor checked my muscle strength in my arms and fingers. The strength was all right. I myself tested the strength in my arm and it was good."

He refused to name his attacker. "A corrections sergeant demanded that I tell him who did it. I told him that all I could say about the guy was that he's a big pain in the neck. Everybody laughed, and I felt good, secure and calm.

"I had expected to be attacked," he told me, "so it wasn't terribly surprising. A little while ago I talked with an inmate and I told him I expected to be attacked. Among other things, I said to him, 'I am close to the angel's death.'" (He meant the angel of death.)

"Were you afraid of being attacked?"

"No, not afraid. I sort of willed it."

"Were you conscious that you willed it?"

"I'm not sure." (His uncertainty showed that there had been an element of wish.)

I continued: "When you say that you willed the attack and you expected it, did you feel that you deserved it?"

"Maybe, I don't know."

He was later to tell me that "the slashing I got was metaphysical in nature. "It was I who brought it on . . . who unconsciously willed this for myself. I was the one who dropped these little hints about someone trying to 'ice' me."

Was he trying to retain some measure of control over what had happened to him by announcing that he himself had "willed" it? Was he trying to minimize the other inmates' hostility toward him? or was he really his own executioner?

A few days after our interview, he wrote me:

"It was quite an experience — a positive one in the long run. Plus, this scar gives character to my face. It shows other inmates that I've been around. They see I've been through the ropes and also, that I'm not a 'stool pigeon.'"

"But most important of all, I now feel secure and that there is a sense of justice in the world. There is really a law of cause and effect. I've always wanted punishment, the punishment that I deserve—I love being punished. So, this was it. I've been trying to expiate my sins for so long. This just felt so good (mentally). It felt almost as if I was miraculously cleansed for a time being."[19]

Berkowitz had been tested. He probably knew who his attacker was, but he never told me or anyone else. He felt "miraculously cleansed" (almost the same words he used at Kings County when he admitted his guilt), not only because he had shown himself *not* to be a stool pigeon, but also because he had quietly accepted his punishment.

I reminded Berkowitz that at his sentencing on June 12, 1978, one of the spectators had leaped up, trying to get at him. "You told the corrections officer that he should have let him tear you to pieces." In this case, at Attica, he appears to have been literally asking for it:

"There is something that no one knows. This seven inch slash on my neck — I did it . . . I 'set myself up.' I willed it and unconsciously wanted it. I needed it. Does this sound strange.

"Believe it or not, and I didn't realize this myself until several days after the assault . . . I unknowingly but not quite unwittingly transmitted messages to my assailant that I would be better off dead. I hinted often that one day I was going to die in the 'joint' because I had my enemies. I actually implanted in this ruffian's mind the idea that I should and must die. I must have also hinted that I had no fear of death and I now have no doubt that he literally picked up my death wish vibes.

"If it wasn't for my frequent talks about death and someone 'knocking me off,' I don't think this would of [sic] happened. This was a clear case of 'victimology.' You may not be aware of it,* but victimology is the belief that a victim in some ways causes his or her own homicide, unconsciously. The F.B.I. men who visited me several months ago talked quite extensively on this subject. This is quite a radical theory but they were enthralled by it and so am I. Plus, now I see how it works."[20]

For the rest of his life, I thought, he would have to carry the red scar on his neck like the mark of Cain.

Had he had any dreams since he had been at Attica?

"A few days following the attack, I woke up in a sweat. My pajamas were wet."

Did he remember anything of the dream?

"No, there was no dream."

Not only a dream, I thought, but clearly a nightmare. Despite his strongly repressed feelings, the nightmare had broken through to his conscious mind and was undoubtedly related to the attack. It expressed his fear that he would be attacked again.

Berkowitz remained preoccupied with the attempt on his life for some time afterward. The other inmates were closing in on him. Like a fog, they were engulfing him. They were many, he was alone. His terror of being killed had at last surfaced. And

---

* Berkowitz had apparently forgotten that he had read about victimology in my book, *The Murdering Mind*.

yet, he had set himself up for this attack just as he had set himself up to being caught when he parked his car by a hydrant on the night he killed Stacy Moskowitz. A week after the arrest he said: "I consciously set myself up."[21]

Despite his bravado, the courageous façade, in his inner soul he was terrified. Again, we meet another situation — this time a life-and-death one that is loaded with contradictory feelings. He wanted to die, to atone for his behavior; but he wanted to live to tell about it, and to enjoy his now-clear conscience.

"I really do want to be punished. Yet, I also don't want to be. I want to live. Yet, I want to die. Sometimes I feel guilty for what I've done. Other times I feel good about it and I want to live a little longer so I could gloat over my sins."[22]

In our early interviews at Kings County, he had often mentioned that he thought of committing suicide — for instance, throwing himself off the fire escape. Or when he had so many guns, shooting himself. But none of this did he do, because "how would my parents feel?" He played with the idea of suicide, but he never attempted it.

Still, he was more in rhythm, more in pitch, with death than with life.

"Death is a friend of mine," he had once told me. In all my years as a psychiatrist, I never had heard anyone describe death as a friend. His death wishes, instinctual more than intellectual, dominated his life, and from them originated his all-encompassing destructive activities. It was these very death wishes, coupled with his theatrical, hysterical traits that, to the eyes of the world, made him look awesome, strange and dangerous.

He had shown a cold-blooded indifference to the fate of the five young women and one young man he had killed. He had an urge to kill. But when the time was ripe he had an urge to confess. The crimes and their punishment were contained in the same man.

Berkowitz, victimizer and victim, was his own detective, his own betrayer, and his own jailer. In the end he was his own judge and executioner.

AFTERWORD

Berkowitz's behavior was rooted in his deviant, anti-social and criminal character. In his grossly egocentric, apparently fearless, secretive and manipulative conduct (one sentencing judge described him as "sly and cunning") was ingrained hysterical exhibitionism and a histrionic self-dramatization bringing about a character disorder with hysterical features.

This exhibitionistic self-dramatization may also have been at work in him when in 1979 it was reported that the Queens District Attorney has reportedly "assigned at least two assistants and a number of detectives to look into the possibility that David R. Berkowitz, the so-called Son of Sam murderer, might have had an accomplice when he killed some of his victims."[1]

On and off there had been reports in the news media — words to the effect that such an accomplice existed. The notion was first brought out by the Gannett Westchester Papers, by Maury Tarry and Tomy Bartley. Their story appeared in the Westchester Rockland Newspapers, March 1, 1979, under the headlines, "QUESTIONS: DID DAVID BERKOWITZ ACT ALONE?"[2]

The story went on to speculate how Berkowitz claimed that "others could go to jail if he tells all he knows about the .44 caliber case,"[3] As reported in *The New York Times*, Berkowitz's claim of having accomplices in his murders received further impetus when it was reported that John Carr, a son of Sam Carr, who allegedly knew Berkowitz, had died in February 1979 in North Dakota — "either by suicide or murder."[4]

In January 1982, the .44 caliber killer revealed (in an interview with a lawyer, Harry Lipsig) "that there were at least three or four members of the cult with him each of the nights he murdered."[5] Berkowitz also claimed that the members of the cult planned his murders.[6] In March 1981 it was reported on television that Berkowitz's "conspiracy confessions" had been backed by allegedly new evidence, "such as Son of Sam's letters, which were purportedly written by different persons."[7]

Bringing into Berkowitz's story the notion that there had been several murderers who had killed Berkowitz's victims reminded me of Lee Harvey Oswald's murder of President Kennedy, who allegedly had been killed by several people. Whenever a mystery is involved in a murder or in any other crime, vigorous attempts are made to change the story in order to satisfy people's fantasies. The story of Oswald was strange, because who could believe that one single man could kill our President? Inexhaustible research seems to have shown that Oswald was the sole killer.[8]

Berkowitz's story — without comparing it to that of President Kennedy — about his demons being responsible for his crimes was weird and almost unbelievable until he himself admitted he had invented the story. But as happens, one weird story leads to another tale. Since the demon story fell through, some people fell victims to the belief that Berkowitz's killings were carried out by members of a cult group to which Son of Sam was thought to belong. One mystery begets another one.

I had in my hands Berkowitz's many letters and notes of the personal interviews where he had described in detail every murder he had committed. His minute description of the way he found his victims and shot them were not fantasy, since he had given the times and places of his killings, and they were in accordance with those in the police reports. In all this information to me there was no mention of RITUAL GROUP BEING RESPONSIBLE for Berkowitz's homicides. This whole idea might well have been an afterthought, stimulated by his ambivalent feelings and the circumstances that around that time some action was being taken to institute a lawsuit against Berkowitz for millions of dollars for his crimes against his victims.

Resorting to this lame excuse was an attempt to dilute his own responsibility. He never answered my questions about the group killings.

Berkowitz had not only taken part in, but he had also carried out, the murders—which he could not lie about. Although some persons, particularly in the news media, have tried to link Berkowitz's homicides to some ritual group, Berkowitz himself could not have lied about his killings every time. He was the sole killer. I have previously mentioned his dream where he asked for forgiveness for his murders. If he hadn't committed the murders, he wouldn't have had a need to seek forgiveness from the foremost authority in New York City, Mayor Abraham Beame. The conscious mind cannot constantly stand guard over the unconscious. Sometimes the conscious goes to sleep and the unconscious, with its dreams, pops up, breaks through, asserts itself, and tells that the event — here the murders — took place and who did it.

The whole commotion about Berkowitz's "ritual group" must be seen in the light of the mystery which surrounded Son of Sam from the first minute he made himself know to the world.

He was never psychotic to the extent that any mental illness was directly responsible for his crimes. When a murderer declares that a voice told him to kill, we must ask whether he had a choice as to how to behave. While some people kill because they are insane, there are many, many others who do so because they are momentarily overcome by malicious, evil emotions. But they are not insane. In fact, most killers are not insane.

Between normal and psychotic behavior, there are several transitional stages. Normal behavior is not a single line of conduct, it is rather an *area* of conduct when both feelings and behavior may deviate quite widely from "normality" without being categorized as psychotic. Only when a person's leanings toward assaultive, violent action is repetitive can we say that he or she shows abnormal behavior. But even abnormal behavior is not always psychotic. Abnormal actions are often carried out by neurotic or psychopathic people.

How can we delineate those criminals who are truly insane from those who claim to be so? What is the role of the law and how can society and the defendant be protected? Even though the problem of insanity has been with us probably as long as man has committed crimes, the development of the concept of legal insanity as a defense has been slow. In the thirteenth century the jurist Bracton[9] asserted that punishment should depend upon moral guilt, and that therefore the requirement of criminal intent —*mens rea*—was an essential element of crime. The very essence of moral guilt is a mental element in his mind. Those unable to form criminal intent, the infant or the insane, should not be held responsible for their deeds. These ideas were, however, not formulated into law. Instead a criminal convicted of a felony and imprisoned could be pardoned by the King.

In a somewhat similar way, "Insanity became not a bar to criminal conviction, but a recognized ground for granting of royal pardon."[10] It then became a practice to acquit insane criminals. But it was not before the seventeenth century that Sir William Blackstone[11] formulated the concept of legal insanity as a defense in criminal trials. The impetus for scrutinizing this heavily emotionally loaded problem arose in 1843, through the case of Daniel McNaghten, a murderer who had been acquitted on grounds of insanity, a principle which to a large extent determined British and American jurisprudence and which led to a substantial change in the law to determine insanity. This law — the right and wrong test — paved the way for the psychiatrist as an expert witness in the defense of legal insanity for nearly one hundred years. Criticized, however, for its narrowness, and that it did not recognize volitional impairment due to mental illness as an exculpatory factor apart from cognitive deficiencies commanded by hallucinations or delusions, the law was modified.

In 1960, the McNaghten Law was replaced with another law: A person is not responsible for his criminal conduct, if as a result of mental disease or defect he lacks substantial capacity to appreciate the wrongfulness of his behavior or to act within the requirements of the law. The new law substituted knowledge for emotional appreciation, and this change often made it possible to acquit a defendant if he knew right from wrong, but did not emotionally appreciate this difference.

About the same time (the early 1960s), this principle was adopted by the American Law Institute, and it also took the place of the old Durham rule (Durham was the name of the defendant), which was introduced by Judge David Bazelon in the Federal Circuit for the District of Columbia. It stated: "The accused was not criminally responsible if his unlawful act was the product of mental disease or defect." Although I was in sympathy with the Durham rule, many including myself felt the law was too wide in scope and difficult to administer, particularly since how much a product of mental illness was the criminal act? In other words, how diseased does one have to be before the criminal act, in order for that act to have been determined is caused by the mental condition? In practice, the defense attorney had only to show that the defendant was mentally bizarre, and he could then be acquitted, which happened too often. To pinpoint the causation of a crime is in any event difficult, controversial, if not impossible — all of which made the law difficult to handle and which led to its abolishment in 1972. The Rule was taken off the books and substituted with the Law of the American Law Institute.[12]

This new law is clear, in that, in cases involving strange conduct or bizarre behavior, extreme viciousness may not rule out legal sanity. When the person knows and appreciates the wrongfulness of his misdeed and is able to obey the law, he is legally sane. The law asks only if a person has the ability to be morally responsible for his crime. But this has been a crucially difficult problem to decide and has led to excessive battles between lawyers and psychiatrists, sometimes leading to doubtful acquittals. It has pushed some authorities in law and society in the direction of abolishing the legal defense altogether, as was proposed by President Nixon in 1973.[13] It always was my opinion that abolishing the concept of legal insanity from the law would be equal to depriving the person, including the insane one, his right to be a human being. Criminal justice and social justice must be bound.

In order to maintain the law of legal insanity, other suggestions were made. The first one, which went into effect in the State of New York, June 12, 1984, was that a defendant who wants to use the insanity defense has to prove himself that he was insane when he committed the crime.[14] This is in contrast to the previous law, where the burden was on the prosecution to prove that the defendant was sane. That he has to prove his insanity makes the law more fair in that the defendant has less opportunity to hide behind his defense. What, for instance, made it so difficult to prove Berkowitz was not insane and able to stand trial was the fact that the burden of proof was on the prosecution to prove he was not insane. An additional element was that we were dealing with a cunning, sophisticated, and seductive criminal who at one time had everything going for him — including the media's strong impression that he was insane — all of which put obstacles for a clear view of Berkowitz's true nature.

If in the case of John Hinckley, who attempted to murder President Reagan, the Law in Washington D.C. had put the burden of insanity on the defendant, the jury might very well have found him guilty, and not guilty by reason of insanity. The uproar which followed upon the jury's acquittal, became an opener for reviewing the law of legal defense. To many people the law and its application seemed unjust, and the verdict, so thought many, had been a mistake. I myself thought it would be a hung jury. Later we learned it was quite close to that: two jurors had held out for conviction but finally gave in.

In order to avoid the abuse of the insanity as a defense, the Michigan legislature in 1975 passed a law, "Guilty but mentally ill," or an alternative, "Guilty but insane." Such a law, which also was passed in other states, but then repealed, as happened in Connecticut, is a contradiction in terms. One cannot feel guilt and at the same time be mentally ill to the point of being insane. If a person is insane in the legal sense, he is beyond guilt. The concept "guilty but insane" is contradictory. Insanity and guilt are mutually exclusive.

Another attempt at dealing with the insanity defense is the earlier mentioned *mens rea* test (criminal intent), which against the strong advice of both the American Bar Association and the American Psychiatric Association called for acquittal only when a criminal defendant as a result of disease or defect lacked in his state of mind the criminal intent required as the essential element of the crime charged. While such a test would limit the use of the insanity test,[15] it would also limit the abuse of the test. A conviction of a murderer rests on the fact that a defendant not only killed someone, but actually intended to do so. Under this proposal a defendant could be acquitted because he was insane if, for example, in killing a person he thought he was really shooting a ghost or a cabbage, but not if he knew and intended to kill a person, however delusional he might be.[16]

As matters now stand, it would seem that the *mens rea* test is a step in the right direction. This is also shown by the fact that two states, Montana and Idaho, respectively in 1979 and 1982, introduced the *mens rea* test but permitted consideration of mental disease or defect as a factor in mitigation of punishment at the sentencing stage of the trial. All together, approximately 25 states and federal courts have adopted a narrow *mens rea* concept in cases of mental disease falling short of legal insanity."[17]

The U.S. Fifth Circuit Court of Appeals has become the first major court to adopt standards for the insanity defense that holds that the inability to avoid performing illegal action is not grounds for a plea of insanity. This is consistent with the American Psychiatric Association's position on the insanity defense.[18]

Whatever way we look at psychiatry and the law, it clearly shows that while their relationship is complex, they have to live together in an uneasy, if not unhappy, partnership or marriage. We cannot live with it, and we cannot exist without it. This situation lends more weight to the idea that release of acquittees charged with violent crimes can only be conditioned on having a treatment supervision at hand. If the *mens rea* test had been in effect that the time of David Berkowitz's trial, he would not have gone free even if he had proved that he was delusional. He intended to kill all those people. For his sake he pleaded guilty after two competency hearings which found him mentally fit to stand trial, and he was accordingly sentenced.

Will Berkowitz be able to change? He writes:

"I read with interest your article which appeared in *The New York Times Magazine* section [July 1, 1979, pp. 20–24]. I guess you see me as I really am—an animal and unhuman. Your low opinion of me is also consistent with the way I feel about myself. Truly, I must be a very evil and unrepentant man. But in your opinion, do you think there will ever be any hope of me becoming a productive citizen, even in prison? If not, then I will just continue to exist, until . . ."[19]

In a candid letter, he writes:

"I will always fantasize those evil things which are a part of my life. I will always remain a mental pervert by thinking sexual things, etc. However, almost everyone else is like me for we commit numerous perverted sexual acts in our minds day after day.

"I will always think of violence, for only a monk, perhaps, could ever succeed in eliminating these desires and thoughts. But what I hope to do is mature to such a point in which I develop a deeper respect for human life and an increased respect and appreciation for humanity."[20]

He continues on this hopeful note:

"Through understanding myself and for learning of my motives for my crimes, which I've always consciously known, but which I deliberately suppressed behind a story of demons rather than openly admitting it — by doing this I hope to be able to better myself to a point in which I don't need to act out, in reality, my hostilities and frustrations — I won't have take out my personal revenge on others who have done me no wrong. Hopefully, and with much effort, I will no longer feel the need to act out my childish impulses onto the rest of the human race.

"Perhaps this all sounds idealistic. It isn't. And only time will tell. I have plenty of time, and by refusing my rights to appeal, I have all but sealed my fate for life. This, I see, had to be done. If I am to be successful in my own emotional battles, then I must make sacrifices and try to begin somehow. So far, I seem to be managing."[21]

During the time I have known David Berkowitz, he has developed a relationship of a great deal of confidence in me. It would be easy to be taken in by him. As one would expect, he would try to please me by telling me about matters that he, with his intuitive sense, felt I would like to hear. In view of his manner, alternately hostile and ingratiating, one would often have to sail between Scylla and Charybdis, between the monster and the whirlpool.

After two years of confinement he had had some problems in adjusting to the regimented life of prison. But he has said, in fact, "I am doing quite well." He then goes on to say:

"I've also done quite a bit of self-analysis and I am now mentally aware as to the reasons why I committed most of these crimes. I've known the 'true' motives for quite some time, but I deliberately kept them below the surface because of my fear in hurting certain persons."[22]

He had begun to figure out the motives for his crimes. Very early, he wrote me:

"I believe it is vitally important for workers in the mental field, and the public at large to understand what was on my mind and what really motivated me to commit my crimes. No doubt another 'Son of Sam' (multiple murderer) will follow in my path — the path that has previously been cleared before me."[23]

Although my sessions with him have not always been easy going, he has come to recognize both the evil and the good thoughts and fantasies in himself, as well as in all human beings.

His blatant shootings of women showed his shameless degradation of them. And this degradation was a powerful defense against his unconscious fear of the all-overwhelming woman, a matter so predominantly debated in the literature. This degradation, a long time ago perceived by Freud, reduced the female to a sexual object and made sex into a disgusting, repugnant act.

In a nutshell, we must say that what had kept Berkowitz from living through his nightmarish life was what kept him from dying. Overwhelmed by his complex situation, he withdrew into himself when he tried to account for his behavior, but without luck.

What he had done said a great deal for our time and less for him. While we may say that the most sorrowful life was behind him, an equally sorrowful life was in front of him.

In his own mind he wanted to be a hero, but instead turned out to be a villain. But he was not an ordinary villain. He was interesting, dangerous, clever, and seductive.

Berkowitz's story is in a way tragic, since he himself became a victim of his own destructive character. This case has not been only about murder. It came to be a secretive and enigmatic one, where mystical forces played a magic role in the minds of so many people. No more can be said about it.

New York Mills Public Library
New York Mills, N.Y. 13417.

LETTERS QUOTED
IN THIS WORK

Letters from David Berkowitz to Dr. David Abrahamsen

1979			1979 (contd.)	
Number	Date		Number	Date
1	March 20		27	July 4
3	May 16		28	July 17
4B	May 17 (handwritten interview)		35	August 1
5	May 19		37	August 2
6	May 20		39	August 8
7	May 22		42	August 8
9	May 26		43	August 13
12	June 5		53	August 28
13	June 5		56	October 10
14	June 12		64	November 3
15	June 15 (handwritten)		68	November 15
16	June 16		70	November 18
17	June 18		71	November 24
22	June 29		72	November 30
23	June 30		74	December 22
24	July 2		77	December 27
25	July 3			

	1980
Number	*Date*
106	March 2
112	March 27
122	May 29
126	June 20
128	June 28
143	October 18

	1981
Number	*Date*
155	January 10

NOTES

PREFACE

1. Letter 1.
2. Letter 3.
3. Letter 15.

1. ENCOUNTERING A KILLER

1. Special information from *The New York Times*. Nationally, out of 19,555 muders committed in 1976, 76% of the murderers were arrested. In 1977 the figure was 75%, while those convicted of rape, robbery, aggravated assault and automobile thefts were respectively 50%, 26%, 62%, and 15%. *Crime in the United States,1978,* FBI Uniform Crime Reports (released October 24, 1979), pp. 13, 15, 16, 20, 33.
2. I was to learn later that the baseball player Lyman Bostock of the California Angels was shot through a car window. There is, however, no implication that Bostock was involved in gangland activities.
3. *The New York Times,* April 18, 1977.
4. Interview with Mrs. Cassara, September 27, 1977.
5. Interviews with Craig Glassman, September, October 1977, January 1978, April 1980.
6. Report of Detective Charles Higgins, September 6, 1977.
7. Report of Detective John Falotico, September 6, 1977.
8. Report of Detective William Gardella, September 15, 1977.
9. Letter 64, pt. 14, p. 4.
10. Higgins report.

11. Falotico report.
12. Ibid.
13. Report from Captain Harold Coleman, September 16, 1977.
14. Report from Dectective James Fox to the Major Case Squad.
15. Ibid.
16. Interview with Nathan Berkowitz, September 15, 1977.

2. THE TERRORIZED MIND

1. Interview with David Berkowitz September 1977 at Kings County Hospital Prison Ward.
2. Ibid.
3. Interview August 1977 at Kings County Hospital Prison Ward.
4. Ibid.
5. Letter 4B.
6. Letter 5.
7. Interview May 17, 1979 at Attica Prison, p. 6.
8. Ibid.
9. Ibid.
10. Letter 64.
11. Interview May 17, 1979, p. 5.
12. Letter 5.
13. Interview May 17, 1979, p. 12.
14. Letter 7.
15. Letter 9.
16. Letter 14.
17. Interview May 17, 1979, p.
18. Letter 6, p. 6.
19. Letter 16.
20. Board of Education, New York City — records.
21. Interview May 17, 1979.
22. Board of Education, New York City — records (remarks of teacher, A. Torres, Significant Interviews, 1962 – 63).
23. Ibid.
24. Information from Board of Education August 24, 1977.
25. Ibid., also interview with Nathan Berkowitz September 15, 1977.
26. Ibid.
27. Letter 17, p. 1.
28. Letter 22, p. 6.
29. Letter 4B, p. 1.
30. Ibid.
31. Ibid., p. 8.
32. Letter 37, p. 3.
33. Letter 39, p. 2.
34. Letter 17, p. 3.

35. Letter 122, p. 1.
36. Letter 122, pp. 1, 2.
37. Letter 35, p. 2.
38. Letter 22, p. 5.

3. ALWAYS ALONE

1. Interview with Ruth and Charles (pseudonyms), December 11, 1979, p. 8.
2. Interview with Nathan Berkowitz, Septmeber 15, 1977.
3. Letter 77, p. 1.
4. Interview with David Berkowitz, Attica Prison, May 17, 1979.
5. Letter 77, p. 1.
6. Letter 23, pp. 2, 3, 4.
7. Letter 39, p. 2.
8. Ibid., p. 2.
9. Ibid.
10. Interview with Nathan Berkowitz, September 15, 1977.
11. Letter 64, p. 4.
12. Letter 39, p. 2.
13. Interview with Ruth and Charles, December 11, 1979.
14. Ibid., pp. 1, 2, 3, 4.
15. Letter 74, p. 2.
16. Interview May 17, 1979.
17. Ibid.
18. Ibid.
19. Letter 25, p. 2.
20. Ibid.
21. Ibid.
22. Interview May 17, 1979.
23. Letter 106, p. 1.
24. Ibid.
25. Ibid.
26. Ibid.
27. Letter 112.
28. Letter 106, p. 2.
29. Letter 77, p. 1.
30. Interview with Ruth and Charles, December 11, 1979, p. 9.
31. Ibid.
32. Ibid.
33. Interview May 17, 1979.
34. Letter 17, p. 1.
35. Letter 71, p. 2.
36. Ibid.
37. Letter 22, p. 4.

38. Interview, August 31, 1977.
39. Letter 24, p. 2.
40, Letter 70, p. 1.
41. Letter 72, p. 1.
42. Letter 128, p. 2.
43. Interview May 17, 1979; p.p. report.
44. Ibid.
45. Interview with Nathan Berkowitz, September 17, 1977.
46. Interview with Ruth and Charles, September 11, 1977.
47. Interview with David Berkowitz, September 28, 1977.
48. Interview with Ruth and Charles, December 11, 1979.
49. Ibid.
50. Interview May 17, 1979.
51. Interview with Nathan Berkowitz, September 15, 1977.
52. Report from U.S. Army.
53. Letter 12.
54. Ibid., p. 3.
55. Ibid.
56. Ibid.
57. Ibid.
58. Letter from Korea to Nathan Berkowitz.
59. Letter 22, p. 4.
60. Interview with Mr. D., January 18, 1980.
61. Interview with Mr. T., January 18, 1980.
62. Ibid.

4. PROLOGUE TO MURDER

1. Herbert Wider, "The Family Romance Fantasies of Adopted Children," *The Psychoanalytic Quarterly* (1977) 46(2):188–200.
2. M. Mahler, *On Human Symbiosis and the Vicissitudes of Individuation.* (New York: International Universities Press, 1968). Bernard L. Pacella and Marvin S. Hurvich, "The Significance of Symbiosis and Separation-Individuation for Psychiatric Theory and Practice." In D. V. Siva Sankar, ed., *Mental Health in Children,* vol 1. (Westbury, N.Y., PJD Publications). David Abrahamsen, *The Emotional Care of Your Child* (New York: Trident Press, 1969).
3. David Abrahamsen, *The Psychology of Crime,* 2d ed. (New York: Columbia University Press, 1967), p. 115.
4. Interview with David Berkowitz, May 17, 1979.
5. Letter 7, p. 1.
6. Ibid.
7. Interview with David Berkowitz, September 1977.
8. Letter 17, p. 2.
9. Ibid., and Interviews, August 1977 and May 1980.
10. Letter 64, pp. 4, 5.

11. Ibid.
12. Ibid.
13. Interview with Betty Falco July 1980.
14. Interview with David Berkowitz September 1977.
15. Letter 143.
16. Interview with David Berkowitz September 1977.
17. Letter 68, p. 2.
18. Letter 64, p. 2.
19. Interview with Betty Falco, July 1980.
20. Letter 68, p. 2.
21. Interview with Betty Falco, July 1980.
22. Ibid.
23. Ibid.
   24. Attica interview with David Berkowitz, April 1980.
25. Interview with Betty Falco July 1980.
26. Ibid.
27. Letter 22, p. 3.
28, Letter 22, p. 3.
29. Letter 7, pp. 2, 3.
30. Letter 22, p. 3.
31. Letter 22, pp. 2, 3.
32. Letter 6F.
33. Letter 7, p. 2.
34. Letter 64, p. 2.
35. Letter 7, p. 2.
36. Letter 7, p. 2.
37. Interview with David Berkowitz, September 1977.
38. Interview with Betty Falco, July 1980.
39. Letter 7, p. 1.

5. STALKING THE VICTIMS

1. Notes 1, p. 5.
2. Interview with David Berkowitz, Kings County Hospital Prison Ward, September 1977.
3. Ibid.
4. Letter 128.
5. Letter 24, pp. 1, 2.
6. Letter 53.
7. Letter 35, p. 3.
8. Letter 13.
9. Interview with David Berkowitz, Kings County Hospital Prison Ward, August and September 1977.
10. Interview with Charles and Ruth (pseudonyms), December 11, 1979.
11. Ibid.

12. Letter 12.
13. Letter 126, p. 2.
14. Notes 1, p. 6, June 1979.
15. Letter 35, p. 3.
16. Letter 43, p. 1.
17. Confession in Queens County, August 11, 1977, 4:30 A.M.
18. Letter 70, p. 2.
19. Ibid.
20. Letter 53, p. 1.
21. Letter 43, pp. 1, 2.
22. Letter 70, p. 2.
23. Letter 53.
24. Letter 43, p. 2.
25. Letter 70, p. 3.
26. Letter 42, p. 2.
27. Letter 70, p. 3.
28. Letter 43, p. 2.
29. Letter 70, p. 2.
30. Interview with David Berkowitz September 8, 1977.
31. Letter 14.
32. Letter 64, p. 3.
33. Letter 70, p. 2, re: first murder.
34. Letter 70, p. 3.
35. Interview, September 1977.

6. MADMAN OR MALINGERER?

1. Psychiatric report, August 26, 1977, by Dr. Daniel W. Schwartz and Dr. Richard H. Weidenbacher.
2. Interviews at Bronx Post Office, September 1977.
3. Psychiatric psychological report to District Attorney Eugene Gold, October 6, 1977.
4. Interview with Sheldon Greenberg, October 6, 1977.

7. THE BATTLE OF THE PSYCHIATRISTS

1. October 20, 1977.
2. This and the following part of the other Competency Hearing took place on October 20, 1977.
3. Court record, October 20, 1977.
4. Court record, October 21, 1977.
5. Ibid.
6. Psychological tests, September 1977, p. 1.
7. Ibid., pp. 1,2.

8. Ibid., p. 3.
9. Ibid., p. 4.
10. Ibid., pp. 5,6.
11. Ibid.
12. Ibid., p. 15.
13. Ibid., p. 16.
14. Court record, May 8, 1978.
15. Letter 126.

8. SEX AS A FORCE FOR MURDER

1. *New York Times,* August 22, 1931.
2. Interview with David Berkowitz, Attica Prison, May 17, 1979.
3. Letter 5.
4. Letter 14.
5. Interview May 17, 1979.
6. Letter 12, p. 5.
7. Interview May 17, 1979.
8. Interview May 17, 1979.
9. Interview May 17, 1979.
10. Letter 17.
11. Interview May 17, 1979.
12. Interview May 17, 1979.
13. Letter 39.
14. Letter 12, p. 2.
15. Interview May 17, 1979.
16. Letter 12, p. 3.
17. Letter 22, p. 1.
18. Interview May 17, 1979.
19. Interview May 17, 1979.
20. Letter 39.
21. Letter 14.
22. Letter 4, p. 4.
23. Letter 64, p. 1, pt. 2.
24. Letter 35, p. 3.
25. Interview June 12, 1979.
26. Letter 12, p. 2.
27. *FBI Enforcement Bulletin* (July 1980) 49(7):8.
28. Interview April 1980.

9. DAVID BERKOWITZ VS. SON OF SAM

1. Letter 35, p. 2.
2. Letter 35, p. 2.

3. Interview, August 31, 1977.
4. Ibid.
5. Ibid.
6. Letter 35, p. 2.
7. Interview, June 26, 1979.
8. Interview, September 1977.
9. Interview June 26, 1979.
10. Letter 6, p. 8.
11. Letter 7, p. 2.
12. Interview June 26, 1979.
13. Letter 12, p. 6.
14. Letter 12, p. 5.
15. Letter 17.
16. Letter 12, pp. 2, 3.
17. Interview, August 31, 1977.
18. David Abrahamsen: *Mind and Death of a Genius — Otto Weininger,* Columbia University Press, 1946, p. 65.
19. Sigmund Freud, *Collected Papers,* (London, 1975) 3:179 See also Abrahamsen: *Mind and Death of a Genius,* p. 184.
20. Mortimer Ostow: "The Psychologic Determinants of Semitic Identity," *The Israel Annals of Psychiatry and Related Disciplines,* vol. 15, no. 4, December 1977. See also Jonathan D. Sarna, "Anti-Semitism and American History," *Commentary,* vol. 70, no. 3, March 1981.
21. Nathan W. Ackerman and Marie Jahoda: *Anti-Semitism and Emotional Disorder, A Psychoanalystic Interpretation.* (New York: Harper 1950), pp. 79-80.
22. Reports — September 1977, March 1978.
23. Letter 55.
24. Interview June 26, 1979.
25. Letter 12, p. 4.
26. Philip M. Coons, "Multiple Personality: Diagnostic Considerations; Journal of Clinical Psychiatry 41:120 — October 1980, p. 330–336.
27. A. M. Ludwig, et al., "The Objective Story of a Multiple Personality," *Archives of General Psychiatry* (1972) 25:298–310.
28. See also Herbert Spiegel, "Trance and Treatment," *Clinical Uses of Hypnosis* (New York: Basic Books, 1981), pp. 322ff. Richard P. Horevitz, "Are Multiple Personalities Borderline?" *Psychiatr. Clin. North Am.* (March 1984) 7(69):87.
29. D. K. Henderson and R. D. Gillespie, *A Textbook of Psychiatry* 4th ed. (London: Oxford University Press, 1930).
30. E. A. Strecker and F. G. Ebaugh, *Practical Clinical Psychiatry* (Philadelphia: Blakiston, 1935).
31. Morton Prince, *The Unconscious* (New York: Macmillan, 1914), p. 176.

10. HIS OWN EXECUTIONER

1. Letter 155, p. 5.
2. Letter 155, p. 6.
3. Letter 155, p. 7.
4. Ibid., p. 7.
5. Letter 3, p. 1.
6. Interview, June 26, 1979.
7. Letter 43, p. 2.
8. Letter 42, p. 1.
9. Letter 24, p. 1.
10. Letter 35, p. 1.
11. Ibid.
12. Ibid., pp. 1, 2.
13. Fred Powledge, Rankin Reports 'Many Oswalds,' *The New York Times,* December 13, 1964.
14. Letter 57.
15. Letter 155.
16. *The New York Times,* July 11, 1979.
17. Letter 28.
18. Letter 23.
19. Letter 37.
20. Ibid., p. 2.
21. Letter 43, p. 2.
22. Ibid., p. 1.

AFTERWORD

1. *The New York Times,* October 19, 1979.
2. Westchester Rockland Newspapers, March 1, 1979.
3. Ibid.
4. *The New York Times,* October 19, 1979.
5. *New York Post,* January 20, 1982.
6. Ibid.
7. *Daily News,* March 18, 1981.
8. David Abrahamsen, *Our Violent Society,* pp. 129 – 160.
9. Bracton, *De Legibus et consuetudinibus Anglia* (ca. 1250).
10. AMA Committee on Medicolegal Problems, Report of Conclusion and Recommendations regarding the Insanity Defense, *Journal of the AMA* (June 8, 1984), 251(2):2967 – 81.
11. *The American Student's Blackstone* 4:24.

12. For further details: See David Abrahamsen, *The Psychiatry of Crime,* 24th ed. (New York: Columbia University Press, 1967).

13. David Abrahamsen, *Insanity in Criminal Behavior. The New York Times,* Op-Ed page, July 8, 1973.

14. *The New York Times,* June 13, 1984.

15. *Psychiatric News,* American Psychiatric Association, January 6, 1984.

16. Ibid.

17. Letter 27.

18. *Psychiatric News,* September 21, 1984, vol. 19, no. 18.

19. Letter 27.

20. Ibid.

21. Letter 3.

22. Letter 15.

23. Ibid.

INDEX

Information about David Berkowitz is placed under subject followed by DB in parentheses, wherever possible.

Abandonment (DB), 62, 65, 86, 183, 204
Abrahamsen, David: *Murdering Mind, The,* 2, 14, 136, 214*n*
Acquittal: in insanity defense, 220, 221, 222
Acting out (DB), 155, 223
Adopted children, 67, 68, 77
Adoptee's Liberty Movement Association (ALMA), 17, 70–71
Adoption (DB), 17–18, 44, 53, 57, 67–72, 78, 169, 192–93, 201; factor in his becoming a murderer, 203
Affection, need for (DB), 169–70
Aloneness (DB), 44–66
Ambivalence (DB), 48, 191; characterized his life, 38, 59, 198–99; about his killings, 98, 129*n;* in his relationship with adoptive mother, 18, 19, 60, 136, 169–70; toward religion, 173; shown in one-handed shooting, 92, 93; sources of, 55, 70, 85; about his suicidal feelings, 207; in temptation to identify himself as Son of Sam, 74
American Bar Association, 222
American College of Psychoanalysts, 118*n*, 152

American Law Institute, 220
American Psychiatric Association, 222
Amnesia, 197
Anal stage, 56
Anger, rage (DB), 87
Anti-Semitism, 193, 194
Anti-social behavior (DB), 39–42, 185, 201–2, 216
Anxiety (DB), 69–70, 151, 154; about food, 54–56
Appalachian Mountain Club, 50
Army service (DB), 23, 61–65, 166, 167–68, 188, 190, 192, 194
Arson (pyromania) (DB), 7, 8, 39, 142, 180–83, 195; notes about, 156, 181
Attention, need for (DB), 36, 38–39, 53, 152, 156, 192, 195
Attica prison, viii, x,13, 161, 163–65, 211
Authority, attitude toward (DB), 172–73

Bartley, Tomy, 216
Bazelon, David, 220
Beame, Abraham, 3, 11–12, 119–20, 218

Behavior: abnormal, 218−19; normal, 218

Behavior (DB), 216. *See also* Anti-social behavior (DB)

Berkowitz, Carol (pseud.: step-daughter of Nathan Berkowitz), 60, 65, 86

Berkowitz, David: arraignment, 11; arrest of, vii−viii, 7−12, 109; aversion to being hemmed in, 19, 22, 37; athletic prowess, 48−49; attacked in prison, 211−15; Bar Mitzvah, 57, 58−59; conflicted state of mind in killings, 93 (*see also* Ambivalance [DB]); in control of murderous impulses, 108, 116, 138 −39; conversion to Christianity, 62− 63, 192−93, 195 (*see also* Religiosity [DB]); defeat, disappointment in life of; 88; desire for limelight 31, 57, 167 (*see also* Exhibitionism [DB]); disap- pointment in natural mother, 17, 75, 77−78, 177−78; double role/secret life, 43, 70, 74, 184−99, 207; dual parents, 198−99; early attacks on women, 88−89, 114; education, schooling, 19−20, 36−37, 52−53, 65 −66; fear for his safety, 126; fear of dark, 33; feelings toward natural mother, 177−78, 190; fitness to stand trial, 15; "good" side, 43, 186, 187− 88; grandparents of, 83−84; hatred for both mothers, 192; interest in murder, 14−15; interest in sex life of parents, 32−33, 45−47; justification of crimes, 93, 103; killing animals, 40 −41; knowledge of his guilt, viii−ix, 100 (*see also* Guilt feelings [DB]); lawsuit against, 218; mental state; 14− 16, 24−25, 111; mental workings of, 27−43; and/on natural father, 76−77, 78, 81; physical description of, 12, 22, 28; pleasure in his secret, 184, 189 −190; possibility of change in, 223− 25; post-trial admissions of, viii; psychic purposes in, and murders, 200 −15; psychological care as child, 37; reaction to death of adoptive mother, 59−60, 61, 70, 170, 175; reaction to finding natural mother, 88, 177− 78; reaction to second marriage of adoptive father, 60−61, 64−65; reali- zation that he was unwanted, 72;

relationship with adoptive father, 32− 33, 44−45, 49, 55, 60−61, 63−64, 170, 173; relationship with adoptive mother, 45−46, 49, 53−54, 55, 69− 70, 136, 169−72, 173, 201−3; rela- tionship with adoptive parents, 17− 18, 21, 28, 44−46, 72; relationship with girls, 34−35, 60, 143 (*see also* Women); relationship with natural mother in his becoming a murderer, 203−5; resistance to murderous im- pulses, 107−122; resistance to reunion with natural mother, 177−78, 203; role of innocent, 41, 43; search for natural mother, xi, 17, 67−68, 181, 203; search for something to hold onto, 63; self-analysis, 224; self- destructive drive, xii; self-dramatiza- tion, 180−81; shock at discovering natural mother alive, 201; temptation to tell he was Son of Sam, 157−58; upbringing, xii (*see also* Childhood [DB]); victim of his own destructive character, 200−15, 225; wanted to be caught, 24, 104, 107, 119

Berkowitz, Mary (pseud.; second wife of Nathan Berkowitz), 60−61, 65, 86

Berkowitz, Nathan, ix−x, 16, 17−18, 19, 32−33, 38, 50, 58, 61−62, 67 −68, 69, 71, 190, 201; believed David insane, 155; David's relationship with, 21, 44−46, 49, 55, 60−61, 63−64; move to Florida, 62, 70, 86; as parent, 202−3; second marriage, 60−61

Berkowitz, Pearl, 16, 34, 38−39, 40− 41, 51−54, 67−68, 175; David's relationship with, 44−45, 49, 53−54, 69, 201−3; illness, death of, 18−19, 31, 59−60, 70, 86, 137−38, 169, 170, 203, 209; mastectomy, 47; obser- vant Jew, 58

Blackstone, William, 219

Bracton (jurist), 219

Broder family, 83−85

Bronx Community College, 65

Brook, Belman, 126

Bundy, Ted, 206n

Carr, John, 217

Carr, Sam, viii, 6−7, 12, 114−17, 142, 149, 152, 156, 217

Carr, Wheat, 6, 7
Cassara, Jack, 140
Cassara family, 6, 7
Castration anxiety, 171–72
Castration anxiety (DB), 127, 153, 173, 193, 205
Central New York Psychiatric Center (Marcy, NY), 161
Character disorder (DB), 185, 200–15, 216, 225
Character traits (DB): compliance, 56, 65; compulsiveness, 42; cruelty, 70; running, 25, 100; duplicity, 100; furtiveness, 54–55; insensitivity, 70; jealousy, 162; manipulativeness, 4, 26, 70, 122, 153, 156, 157, 188, secretiveness, 21, 56, 68, 190; seductiveness, 4, 70, 122, 153, 221, 224, 225; self-centeredness, 191, 192
Childhood (DB), 16–21, 26, 27–28, 31–32, 34–43, 48–51, 53–54, 57, 126, 131, 136, 195; and his becoming a murderer, 201–4; key to divided behavior, 185; poor self-image in, 191–92; sexual shyness rooted in, 169–73
Cleckley, Harvey M., 196–97
Clinton Correctional Facility (Dannemora, NY), 161
Codd, Michael J., 3
Coleman, Captain, 8
Competency hearings, 110, 123–24, 125–61, 175, 223
Confessions (DB), 2, 12
Connecticut: insanity defense, 221
Contradictory statements (DB): about adoptive mother, 47, 105; about the murders, 178
Control, emotional (DB), 85
Co-op City, 60, 99
Corso, Joseph, 155–56, 158–60
Countertransference, xi
Creative fantasies, 168, *See also* Fantasies
Creativity: is sexually rooted, 181
Crime and Punishment (Dostoyevsky), 210
Criminal behavior, 39
Criminal intent (*mens rea*), 219, 222
Criminal Justice Agency, Inc., 12

Davis, Cecilia, 5–6
Daydreams (DB), 29, 35, 168, 182. *See also* Fantasies (DB)

Death, 21; (DB) preoccupation with, 15, 21, 22, 29–30, 88, 203, 207, 215
Death wish (DB), 15, 31, 61, 201, 207, 215
Delusional thinking (DB), 111–12, 122–23, 130, 136, 137, 139–42, 148, 152, 210. *See also* "Demon stories"
"Demon stories," viii, 12, 23, 24, 55, 105–6, 111, 113, 122–23, 156–57, 173–74, 195–96, 209, 217, 223; DB began to doubt, 145–46; as evidence of insanity, 109–10; lack of fear in, 152–53; sexual implications of, 163; in testimony at competency hearing, 128–30, 131–32, 135, 138, 139, 140–41; truth/falsehood of, 85–86, 108, 121–22, 142, 155
DeNaro, Carl, 3, 100–1
Dependency (DB), 69
Depression (DB), 131
Diehl, John, 3, 102
DiMasi, Donna, 3, 101
Dissociation, 197
Dr. Jekyll and Mr. Hyde (Stevenson), 186–87
Dogs, viii, 6, 23, 115–18, 138–42, 152, 208
Doppelgänger, 185, 198
Dostoyevsky, Feodor: *Crime and Punishment,* 210
Dowd, Timothy J., 4, 10
Dreams, 121
Dreams (DB), 32–33, 119–21, 162–63, 214, 218; sexual, 182
Durham rule, 220
Dusky Rule, 110

Eating habits (DB), 54–56
Ego Strength (DB), 101, 123, 146, 148, 150, 153–54
Egocentricity (DB), 153, 154, 172, 203, 216
Emotional control (DB), 85, 108, 189; surface, 28
Emotional deadness issue (DB), 112, 128, 131, 134–35, 151, 153, 175
Emotional deprivation (DB), 150
Emotional state (DB), 111–12, 122
Emotions (DB), 121, 151, 153, 154, 173, 174, 189
Employment (DB), 24, 66, 94–95, 117, 118

Esau, Alexander, 4, 104–5, 177
Eve (multiple personality patient), 196–97
Exhibitionism (DB), 16, 20–21, 31, 152, 160, 167, 194–95, 216

Falco, Betty (née Rebecca Broder), 17, 72, 73–87, 88, 90, 177, 181, 182, 190, 198–99, 203–4
Falco, Richard David (birth name of DB), viii, 44, 73, 80
Falco, Tony, 73, 76, 79, 84–85, 199
Falotico, John, 7–11
Family life, 44
Fantasies, 167–68; of adopted children, 67; sexual, 168–69
Fantasies (DB), 55, 70, 194; about death, 88; about girls, 35–36; about natural mother, 71, 74, 77, 78, 86, 88; about perfect family, 203; about punishment, 62; of self-aggrandizement, 50 (*see also* Exhibitionism, [DB]): sexual, 162–63, 167–69, 175–76, 179, 223; about his victims, 179–80; of violence, 175–76, 205, 206–7. *See also* Hero wish (DB)
Fear, 207
Fear(s) (DB), 207; of dark, 33; of death, 207, 214–15; lack of, 85
Feelings (DB): antisocial and destructive, 39–42; after/about his killings, 24, 95–98, 100, 102–3, 178–79, 205–6; toward natural mother, 76–78, 85–87, 177–78, 190. *See also* Emotions (DB); Guilt feelings; Sexual feelings (DB)
Feminine traits (DB), 183, 193–94
Fighting (DB), 57
Fires (DB). *See* Arson (pyromania) (DB)
Food, 54–56
Forensic phychiatrist, 13
".44 caliber killer," 4. *See also* Son of Sam murders
Fox, Detective, 11
Frank, Robert, 210
Freud, Sigmund, 165–66, 224
Freund, Christine, 3, 102
Friends, friendships (DB), 21, 35, 65–66; male, 193–94

Galante, Carmine, 5
Gannett Westchester Papers, 216

Gardella, Sargeant, 8, 9–10
Glassman, Craig, 7, 8–10, 12, 113, 174, 208
Gold, Eugene, 12–13, 15, 79, 114, 121, 142–43; at competency hearing, 126, 129, 130–35, 136
Gratification, 68
Gratification (DB), 37, 169; fantasy life as compensation for lack of, 36; from killing, 205–6; need for immediate, 56, 136–37
Greenberg, Sheldon, 124, 126, 147
Greenman, Leon, 50
Guilt: and homicide, 210; insanity and, 221; moral, 219
Guilt feelings (DB), 24, 119, 121, 122; at being immoral person, 191; over conversion to Christianity, 63; over excessive eating, 41; over homicides, 98, 131*n*, 146, 155, 157, 160, 178, 210–11, 215; over sexual desire for adoptive mother, 55; over supposed death of natural mother, 71, 78, 201
Guilty plea (DB), x, 147–48, 155, 158, 160, 223
Gurra, Detective, 89*n*

Hallucinations, 113, 118
Halluncinations (DB), 116, 118, 123, 134, 139–42, 152, 210. *See also* "Demon stories"
Hamptons, 107–8, 138–39
Hate, 162; in Son of Sam murders, 206–7
Held, Gerald, 113–14
Heller, Mark, 13, 123, 166
Hero wish (DB), 20–21, 31, 61, 102, 195, 225
Higgins, Charles, 7–8, 9
Hillside Strangler, 206*n*
Hinckley, John, 221
Homicide: guilt and, 210
Homicide Task Force, 4–5
Homosexual tendencies (DB), 153, 183, 193–94
Horevitz, Richard P., 236*n*
Hysterical traits (DB), 153, 155, 194–95, 198, 215, 216
Hysteria, 196, 197

Idaho: insanity defense, 222
Illegitimacy (DB), 36, 76–77, 80, 83, 86, 182

Illinois State Penitentiary (Joliet), 164
Illusions, loss of (DB), 86
Imaginary playmate, 197
Imagination, 33–34
Importance, sense of (DB), 120
Inadequacy, sense of (DB), 150
Insanity defense, 219–23; potential of, for DB, 133–34, 135–36, 142, 147, 155. *See also* Sanity/insanity issue (DB)
Intelligence level (DB), 25, 37, 112, 122, 149–50, 153; social, 149
Izvestia, 12

James Monroe High School (New York City), 38*n*
Jewishness, rejection of (DB), 57–59, 192–93
Jews, 193
Johnson, Doris, x
Jultak, Ira, 13, 127, 129–30, 136–43, 148–49, 155
Justus, James, 7

Keating, Robert, 126
Keenan, Redmond, 3, 10
Keenan, Rosemary, 3, 100–1
Kennedy, John F., 217
Kensico Dam, 49
Kings County Hospital, Brooklyn, xii, 1, 14
Klausner, Lawrence, 90
Klineman, Joseph, 76, 79, 80, 81–83, 177, 198–99
Kopelman, Milton, 156

Laudato, Dominic, x
Lauria, Donna, 2–3, 178
Laws: insanity defense, 219–23
Leopold, Nathan, 14, 210
Leventhal, Mr., 47
Lipsig, Harry, 217
Loeb, Richard, 210
Lomino, Joanne, 3, 101
Longo, Detective, 8, 9
Loss in life of DB, 36, 86, 169, 170; of love, 56
Love, 162
Love (DB): impaired capacity for, 69, 169, 170, 175
Love/fear contradiction (DB), 117
Lubin, Martin, 145, 147
Lupo, Salvatore, 5, 105

Maariv (newspaper), 12
McNaghten, Daniel, 219
McNaghten Law, 219
McRann, Inspector, 8
Magical thinking, 187
Mahler, Margaret, 68
Masculinity (DB), 194, 195
Mass murderers, 3; psychoanalysis of, xii–xiv, 13
Masturbation (DB), 63, 153, 167, 168–69, 175, 188
Media, vii, ix, 3, 103, 104; "accomplice" story in, 216–17; at competency hearing, 127; demon story in, 109; at sentencing, 158
Menninger, Karl, 209
Merola, Mario, 156, 60
Metesky, George, 13*n*
Michigan: insanity defense, 221
Minnesota Multiphasic Personality Inventory, 151–52, 155, 194
Montana: insanity defense, 222
Moskowitz, Mrs. (mother of Stacy), 117, 126, 127, 210
Moskowitz, Stacy, 5, 6, 10, 24, 105–6, 176–77, 186
Mother-infant symbiosis, 68
"Mother of Satan" (poem, DB), 87
Motivation: in homicide, 4, 200, 218. *See also* Son of Sam murders, motivation in
Mountain climbing (DB), 48, 50–51
Multiple personality, xi, 196–97
Murder: motive in, 4, 200, 218; sex as force for, 162–83
Murderers, 3, 13, 200
Murdering Mind, The (Abrahamsen), 2, 14, 136, 214*n*

Narcissism, 136
Narcissism (DB), 70, 93, 102, 173, 185, 203, 204
Neto, Mara, 117
Neurotic symptoms (DB), 167
New York City: murders in, 2
New York City Police Department, 6–7
New York State: insanity defense, 221
New York Times, 216–17
New York Times Magazine, 223
Nicknames (DB), 54
Nightmares (DB), 27, 32–34
Nixon, R.M., 220

Noise sensitivity (DB), 118, 139, 140, 207–8, 210
Nudity, 46–48

Oedipal conflict (DB), 69, 166, 170–72
Omnipotence, sense of (DB), 42–43, 56; through anonymity, 189–90; from killing, 205–6
Oral needs (DB), 155. *See also* Food
Oral sex (DB), 57, 166, 167
Oral stage, 55
Osservatore Romano, L', 12
Ossining Correctional Facility, 161
Oswald, Lee Harvey, 13*n*, 217

Paralysis, 196
Paranoia, 24–25, 113, 143, 150; diagnosis of DB, 111, 112–13, 145
Paranoid psychosis (diagnosis), 135
Paranoid schizophrenia, 113, 147, 148; diagnosis of DB, 152
Paresis, 196
Passivity (DB), 150, 171–72, 183, 185, 194
Peltz, Philip, 11
Personal traits (DB), 56–57; caution, 99; charisma, 54; charm, 70. *See also* Character traits (DB)
Personality (DB): disorganized, 25, 160; dual, 43, 70, 74, 184–99, 207; hysterical, 198; psychopathic, 136–37, 155, 209
Phallic phase, 171
Placido, Judy, 5, 105
Playing, 16, 26, 27, 35–36, 185
Police: in Son of Sam murders, 4–12
Power, sense of (DB), 46, 100; destructive, 181; in killing, 108, 109–10, 204; over women, 182. *See also* Omnipotence, sense of (DB)
Powerlessness (DB), 109–10, 208
Psychiatrist as expert witness, 219, 220
Psychiatrists, court-appointed, viii, 13–14, 23, 116, 121, 122, 136–37, 141–43, 144–45; diagnosis of insanity, 110–14
Psychiatry: and the law, 222–23
Psychoanalysis: of a mass murderer, x–xi, 13
Psychological testing (DB), 148–55, 193
Psychopath(s), 136–37, 150, 153
Psychopathic personality (DB), 136–37, 155, 209

Psychosexual development, 166, 183. *See also* Sexual development (DB)
Psychosis, 114, 121, 123, 148, 196
Public (the): relation with Son of Sam, 4, 5, 12, 14, 103, 104, 126, 209
Punishment, 219, 222; fantasies about (DB), 62; need for (DB), 24, 155, 201, 210, 212–215
Punishment fears (DB), 63

Queens, 92, 101, 103, 105, 204

Reagan, Ronald, 221
Reality orientation (DB), 113, 153
Recall (DB), 31
Rejection (DB), 39, 50, 65, 76–77, 204, 209
Religiosity (DB), 111, 145–46, 147, 167, 172–73, 190–91, 194, 195
Remorse (DB), 119
Repetition compulsion, 206
Repression (DB), 47
Revenge, 162; as motive in Son of Sam murders, 92–93, 107, 179–80, 204–5
Rivalry, incestuous, 45
Role playing (DB), 195, 198
Rorschach test (DB), 150–51, 153, 154–55, 198
Rubinstein, Seth, xii
Rye Beach, 50

Sadism (DB), 56, 90, 122, 153, 176, 185
Sanity/insanity issue (DB), viii, 13–14, 24–26, 98, 109–24, 155, 156–57, 210–11, 221
Schizophrenia, 25, 112, 123, 187, 198
Schwartz, Daniel W., 110–13, 127–36, 137, 141–42, 144–45, 147–48, 155, 156–57
Self-delusion (DB), 93
Self-esteem (DB), 150, 153, 182, 203, 204
Self-hatred (DB), 184, 191–93, 201, 205
Sense of self (DB), 49, 70, 201, 203
Sentencing (DB), viii, 158–61, 213; outburst at, 159–60, 182
Separation anxiety (DB), 69
Separation-individuation, 68–69
Sex: as force for murder, 162–83; in Son of Sam murders, 175–80
Sexual development (DB), 165–75, 183; and the homicides, 179–80

Sexual feelings (DB), 46–47, 121, 194; fear of, 182; in his arson, 181; in his homicides, 100, 106, 162–63, 176–77, 178–80, 182–83, 207, 209; in relationship with adoptive mother, 45–46, 55, 181; repressed, 174–75, 176
Sexual identity (DB), 183, 204
Sexual intercourse (DB), 166–67
Sexuality, 166
Shilensky, Detective, 10
Shoplifting (DB), 20
Shorehaven Beach Club, 34, 46
Shyness, neurotic (DB), 167, 169, 174
Sing Sing prison, 164
Smith, Ollie, 191
Solitary activities (DB), 49–50
Son of Sam murders, vii–viii, x, 2–12, 24, 195; accomplice theory, 216–18; guns, weapons in, 90–91; locations of, 92, 94, 98–99, 101, 102, 103, 104, 105, 204; meaning for DB in, 204, 207; motivation in, xii, 12, 29, 143, 165, 175–80, 182, 204–9, 224; notes in about, 105, 135, 197; obstacles in, 107; parking ticket in, 5–6, 9, 105, 186, 210; significance of car in strategy of, 5, 177–78; tips in, 4, 7; victim selection in, 92–108; victim stalking in, 88–108. *See also* Sexual feelings (DB)
Speck, Richard, 14
Spiegel, Herbert, 196
Starkey, John R., 127, 129, 144–45
Stealing (DB), 41
Stern, Leon, 13, 127, 129, 134, 143, 144, 147
Stevenson, Robert Louis: *Dr. Jekyll and Mr. Hyde*, 186–87
Stick, Fay, 66
Suicide, 205; DB's contemplation of, 31, 215
Suriani, Valentina, 4, 104–5, 177
Sybil (multiple personality patient), 196

Tarry, Maury, 216

Thought disorder, 25, 113, 123, 198; lack of, in DB, 153–54
Threatening letters (DB), 6, 7, 8, 188–89
Three Faces of Eve, The (film), 197
Transference, xi, 28
Truancy (DB), 37–39, 42
Tsoucalas, Nicholas, 155–56

U.S. Fifth Circuit Court of Appeals, 222

Valente, Jody, 2–3
Vandalism (DB), 39–40, 42
Victimology, 214
Victims in Son of Sam murders, 92–108, 204–5; search for, 66–80, 88–108
Violante, Robert, 5, 105–6, 159, 176–77, 210
Violence, 218; sexual feelings and, 162, 175–76
Violent criminals, xii
Virility, xii
Voskerichian, Virginia, 3, 103–4
Voyeurism (DB), 167, 177

Wax, Stephen, 126
Wechsler Adult Intelligence Scale, 149–51
Weidenbachker, Richard L., Jr., 110–13, 132, 135, 136, 137, 141–42, 144–45
Weininger, Otto, 192
Weiz, Moishe Florenz, 79
Wilbur, Cornelia B., 196
Women: attacks on, by DB, 88–89, 114; DB's rage against, hatred toward, 5, 63, 86–87, 88, 154, 183, 190; DB's relationship with, 162–63, 166–67, 173–74, 182, 188, 193, 204–5, 208, 224; in life of DB, 86–87; revenge against, as motive in Son of Sam murders, 92–93, 179–80; as threat, 65
Woodward, Joanne, 197
Wyman, Bea, 46

Yonkers Police Department, 7, 8, 11

Zigo, Detective, 8